ETHNOGRAPHIC CHIASMUS

Für Roman
mit Wünschen für eine
fruchtbare Zusammenarbeit
zu Themen die wir beide
verfolgen. Ivo
Mai 2012

D1618206

The Hamar of Southern Ethiopia

edited by

Ivo Strecker and Jean Lydall

Volume V

LIT

Michigan State University Press

Ivo Strecker

ETHNOGRAPHIC CHIASMUS

Essays on Culture, Conflict and Rhetoric

LIT

Michigan State University Press

Cover photograph: Ivo Strecker, *Hamar spokesman*, 1973

Text Design: Axel Brandstetter, Mainz (D)

Gedruckt auf alterungsbeständigem Werkdruckpapier entsprechend
ANSI Z3948   DIN ISO 9706

First published in Europe by LIT Verlag
(World Rights except North America)
Fresnostr. 2   D-48159 Münster
Tel. +49 (0) 2 51-620 320   Fax +49 (0) 2 51-922 60 99
e-Mail: lit@lit-verlag.de   –   http://www.lit-verlag.de

First published in North America by Michigan State University Press
(North American Rigths only)
1405 S. Harrison Rd., Ste. 25
East Lansing, MI 48823-5245 USA
e-Mail: msupress@msu.edu   –   www.msupress.msu.edu

Bibliographic information published by the Deutsche Nationalbibliothek
The Deutsche Nationalbibliothek lists this publication in the Deutsche
Nationalbibliografie; detailed bibliographic data are available in the Internet at
http://dnb.d-nb.de.

ISBN 978-3-8258-7858-0 (LIT Verlag)
ISBN 978-0-87013-990-1 (Michigan State University Press)

A catalogue record for this book is available from the Library of Congress
A catalogue record for this book is available from the British Library

©LIT VERLAG Dr. W. Hopf Berlin 2010

Distribution:
In Germany: LIT Verlag Fresnostr. 2, D-48159 Münster
Tel. +49 (0) 2 51-620 32 22, Fax +49 (0) 2 51-922 60 99, e-mail: vertrieb@lit-verlag.de

In Austria: Medienlogistik Pichler-ÖBZ, e-mail: mlo@medien-logistik.at

In Switzerland: B + M Buch- und Medienvertrieb, e-mail: order@buch-medien.ch
In the UK: Global Book Marketing, e-mail: mo@centralbooks.com
In North America: Michigan State University Press, 1405 S. Harrison Rd., Ste. 25
East Lansing, MI 48823-5245 USA
Tel (517) 355-9543, Fax (517) 432-2611; (800) 678-2120
secure fax for orders only (517) 432-7484
email: msupress@msu.edu   www.msupress.msu.edu

CONTENTS

ACKNOWLEDGEMENTS

Many thanks go first of all to the *Sonderforschungsbereich* (295) of Johannes Gutenberg-University, Mainz, which from the year 2000 up to the present has enabled not only myself but also a host of students to do fieldwork in southern Ethiopia. We have jointly engaged in empirical research, have tried to rethink our methods and theories for the study of culture, and have further developed the *South Omo Research Center* to serve both as a field-base and a local forum for transcultural debate and understanding (see *www.southethiopiaresearch.org*). The present collection of essays is meant to express my appreciation of the strong support received from the *SFB* and its devoted spokesman, Walter Bisang.

Also, I am grateful to my Ethiopian colleagues and friends who for so many years now have made me feel at home at Addis Ababa University and have let me share their intellectual climate! In particular I want to thank my two *misso* ("hunting friends") Alula Pankhurst and Baye Yimam, as well as Gebre Yntiso and Tadesse Berisso.

Jean Lydall—my wife and co-researcher—has discussed with me all the topics addressed in the present book, and she has carefully read and edited both the earlier and the present versions of the essays. A thousand thanks to you, *Kadweshem*!

Finally I thank Axel Brandstetter for formatting and preparing the essays for publication.

I am indebted to several publishers for those essays, which were previously published elsewhere. Some were first written in German, and while I translated them into English, I occasionally changed them to fit the present volume. The original publications have also been revised and at times considerably changed, including their titles. They are listed chronologically.

2009 "Anmerkungen zu mantischem und magischem Vertrauen in Hamar, Südäthiopien." In *Zwischen Aneignung und Verfremdung: Ethnologische Gradwanderungen; Festschrift für Karl-Heinz Kohl*, edited by Volker Gottowick, Holger Jebens, Edita Platte. Frankfurt/M.: Campus. Pp. 423 – 432.

2008 "Lomotor's talk or the imperial gerund." In *Genauigkeit: Schöne Wissenschaft*, edited by Wolfgang Marschall, Paola von Wyss-Giacosa, & Andreas Isler. Bern: Benteli. Pp. 99-109.

2007 "What caused Baldambe's death? " In *Writing in the Field; Festschrift for Stephen Tyler*, edited by Ivo Strecker and Shauna LaTosky. www.rhetoricculture.org

2006 "Don Quijote: icono de la teoria de la cultura de la retorica. Una contribucion a James Fernandez; La tropologia y la figuracion del pensamiento y de la accion social." In *Revista de Anthropologia Social*, 15: 21-42.

2006 "'Face' as a metaphor of respect and self-esteem." In *The Perils of Face: Essays on Cultural Contact, Respect and Self-Esteem in Southern Ethiopia*, edited by Ivo Strecker and Jean Lydall. Münster · Berlin: Lit. Pp. 83-103.

2005 "Was sagen die Sterne? Zur Rhetorik lokalen Wissens in Hamar (Südäthiopien)." In *Lokales Wissen–sozialwissenschaftliche Perspektiven*, edited by Nicolaus Schareika and Thomas Bierschenk. Münster · Berlin: Lit. Pp. 59-91.

2005 "To share or not to share: Notes about authority and anarchy among the Hamar of Southern Ethiopia." In *Property and Equality. Volume: Ritualisation, Sharing, Egalitarianism*, edited by Thomas Widlock and Wolde Gossa Tadesse. Oxford · New York: Berghahn. Pp. 175–189.

2003 "Die Magie des Rituals." In *Rituelle Welten*, edited by Christoph Wulf and Jörg Zirfas. *Paragrana: Internationale Zeitschrift für Historische Anthropologie*, 12: xx-xxx.

2002 "The *genius loci* of Hamar." In *Cultural Variation in Southern Ethiopia Regional Comparative Studies*, edited by Jon Abbink. *Northeast African Studies* [Special Issue] 7: 2-3.

2000 "Hamar rhetoric in the context of war." In *Proceedings of the XIVth International Conference of Ethiopian Studies*, edited by Baye Yimam. Addis Ababa: Institute of Ethiopian Studies. Pp. 1004-1025.

1999 "The temptations of war and the struggle for peace among the Hamar of Southern Ethiopia" In *Dynamics of Violence: Processes of Escalation and De-Escalation in Violent Group Conflicts*, edited by Georg Elwert, Stephan Feuchtwang and Dieter Neubert. *Sociologus* [Special Issue]: 219-52.

1998 "Our good fortune brought us together. Obituary for Baldambe." In *Paideuma*, 44: 59-68.

1996 "Do the Hamar have a concept of honor?" In *Proceedings of the Xth Conference of Ethiopian Studies*, edited by Eric Godet. Paris. Pp. 419-29.

1994 "The predicaments of war and peace in South Omo." In *Proceedings of the XIth Conference of Ethiopian Studies*, Vol. II, edited by Bahru Zewde, Richard Pankhurst and Tadesse Beyene. Addis Abeba: Institute of Ethiopian Studies. Pp. 299-308.

1990 "Political discourse among the Hamar of Southern Ethiopia." In *Proceedings of the First National Conference of Ethiopian Studies, Addis Ababa*, edited by Richard Pankhurst, Ahmad Zekaria and Tadesse Beyene. Addis Ababa: Institute of Ethiopian Studies. Pp. 39-47.

1990 "*Micere*: Zur Bedeutung der Rute bei den Hamar
     Südäthiopiens." In *Völkerkunde Museen 1990: Festschrift für
     Helga Rammow*, edited by Volker Harms. Lübeck: Baruth.
     Pp. 147-60.

1988 "Some notes on the uses of '*barjo*' in Hamar." In
     *Proceedings of the First International Symposium on Cushitic
     and Omotic Languages, edited by* Fritz Serzisko and
     Marianne Bechhaus-Gest. Hamburg: Helmut Buske. Pp.
     61-74.

1976 Hamar speech situations." In *The Non-Semitic Languages of
     Ethiopia*, edited by M. Lionel Bender. East Lansing:
     African Studies Center. Pp. 583-96.

INTRODUCTION

The ethnographic chiasmus

Already as a student, but especially when doing fieldwork in Hamar, I liked to open *Tristes Tropiques* and read this extremely evocative book. On the 12th of December 1973 I made the following entry in my diary:

Before going to sleep last night I read a little. Shakespeare: too many words. Joyce: too many words. Lévi-Strauss's *Tristes Tropiques*: that I again liked very much. It conveys what it says in a meandering linearity that is akin to my way of thinking. Of course there is more to it. I also share the author's dreams and have undergone some similar real-life experiences. This brings the book very close to me... But then there is a passage in the introduction to which my fieldwork is going to be an answer. He writes that, "ethnographies are necessarily always false because the ethnographer, however honest he may be, cannot—not anymore—relate to us other ways of life in their authentic form. In order to make them acceptable for us, the ethnographer has to sort and sieve his memories—a process that the most honest of us will at best do unconsciously—and use stereotypes as substitutes for the original experience". He is right! Much of our ethnographic literature has become sterile in this way. Yet despite this, I hope to catch something of the authenticity of Hamar life by putting my analysis behind and not in front of my data. I am talking, of course, of Baldambe's model (account of Hamar culture) and my long and continuing effort to record live conversations, the drama of which will later be visible in its authentic form, even if it has gone through the transformation from pure sound and gesture to script (Lydall and Strecker 1979a: 210-211).

I only slowly learnt the art of recording when in the field, and the way I progressed was closely related to my emergent competence as researcher. Here are some excerpts from my work journal that demonstrate what happened. The first shows how Jean Lydall (my wife and co-researcher) and I began by using the tape recorder as a tool for linguistic studies:

> 17.11.1970; At noon we have coffee in Surrambe's house and his wife Ginonda is serving. I bring the tape recorder along and ask Ginonda to say for us a number of words, the pronunciation of which is crucial for an understanding of Hamar phonetics. Not only has Ginonda a very clear pronunciation, but she is also very lively and intelligent, she does not simply repeat words; she puts them into phrases and invents little stories to illustrate the use of a word. The recording is a beautiful bit of cooperation and convinces us that it will be worthwhile to come back to work in Dambaiti again (Lydall and Strecker 1979a: 36).

As one can see, Ginonda quickly realised the potential of the tape recorder and surprised us by making use of it with ingenuity. Our experience of Ginonda's expressiveness was similar to what Jean Rouch found when he filmed among the Dogon (and elsewhere): Rather than closing up and freezing in front of the camera, people would open up and become more vivacious and expressive. Rouch called this phenomenon "ciné trance". However, not only the camera but also the tape recorder may induce a kind of "trance" as the subsequent example shows. Again our interlocutor is Ginonda:

> 28.4.1973; In the evening I record Ginonda's description of Dube's ritual. She talks in a gentle manner and yet she is forceful and articulate at the same time. The longer I watch and listen, the more I like her. This is a mad, delicious and intimate 'interview-theatre', a form of entertainment and an art of which I have never dreamt before. It is as if the tape recorder, the microphones, the

wiring, my earphones amplify the Hamar's ability to speak (Lydall and Strecker 1979a: 102).

In other words, rather than separating us, the recording process brought us closer together. Furthermore, the recordings allowed us to understand each other better. Once the Hamar knew what I knew and what not, and when they knew what I wanted to know better, they could help me in my efforts more easily, like in the following example:

> 1.6.1973; At night I record a group of young men singing and dancing at 'our' cattle camp. When they have finished singing to their dance oxen and dance goats, an intelligent and comical boy starts to lead a series of dances in which he satirizes the dances and songs of his fathers and forefathers. As he leads the singing he improvises joke after joke that reduce his mates to tears of laughter.

> 2.6.1973; Everyone comes to listen to the music which I recorded last night. While we listen I ask questions about different singers, the songs and their meanings and so on and everybody is extremely gentle and co-operative, "When you come the next time, we'll sing again." The tape recorder, with its immediate feed-back, is an ideal tool because it establishes good learning relationships. By playing back a piece of music or speech one can demonstrate what one is trying to understand and this then turns the 'objects of observation' into 'teachers' (Lydall/Strecker 1979a: 138-39).

Thus, learning and using the tape recorder went hand in hand, be it in situations that were light and playful as in the instance above, or be it at times when people were more composed and serious. Furthermore, while recording the verbal—or rather mental—ingenuity of my friends, I began to anticipate a kind of "ethnographic exegesis" that would do justice to the power of expression that is characteristic for Hamar culture. Here is the passage where I first speak of this:

> In the afternoon I ask Baldambe and Choke to tell me about the cattle exchanged in bond-friend relationships. The 'seminar' turns

out to be as informative and lively as last night's instruction on the stars. I have now reached a new stage of fieldwork. The skill consists of choosing the right situations of 'live' talk and the right topics for group interviews, each with the aim of getting normative accounts of social phenomena that are still problematic and need more adequate documentation. It is the wealth of information that lies in small linguistic details that excites me and leads me to use the tape recorder so extensively. At school literary criticism was my forte, and I envisage that much of my writing-up will be in the same vein. First I will translate many of these rich texts and then embark on exegesis (Lydall and Strecker 1979a: 200).

Although the essays assembled below are in one way or another the result of an anthropological stance, which I developed during fieldwork, it took me a while to put a name to their common feature. First, in order to indicate that much of my writing consists of a "gluing together" of separate texts (generated on the one side by the Hamar and on the other side by myself) I thought of "The ethnographic collage" or "The ethnographic pastiche", but this would miss the dynamics of trans-cultural understanding that characterise the ethnographic endeavour, would just indicate a joining, composing without drawing attention to discourse, rhetoric and mutual persuasion. "Collage" and "pastiche" would miss the movement, the thrust, the collision of mind and emotion involved in the encounter between the ethnographer and the cultural "Other".

Faced with the challenge of finding a more appropriate characterisation of my essays I eventually thought of *The Ethnographic Chiasmus*, for nothing would attend better to the fact that trans-cultural understanding can only be partial, can only come about as a "meeting", "touching", or "crossing".

The notion of chiasmus derives from the ancient Greek letter *chi* and denotes an inversion of parallel elements of expression— A : B :: B : A —like in the opening lines of Macbeth where the witches chant "Fair is foul, and foul is fair!"

(see Anthony Paul's masterly study *The Torture of the Mind*, 1992). Nothing is more surprising and moving than when the opposite of what one holds to be true turns out to be the case. Chiasmus is therefore a prime mover in human thought and history.

Like metaphor, chiasmus is a rhetorical figure that helps us to "control the world that we make for ourselves to live in" (Richards 1965: 136). More precisely, it is active in communication not only as a form of "elocutio, the part of rhetoric that studies the choice and arrangement of words (where chiasmus normally belongs), but as a feature of dipositio, the arrangement of the parts of an argument, and above all inventio, the invention of subject matter and the logical arguments that give form to it" (Wiseman 2009: 87).

One can go even further and find chiasmic features in the world as such, especially in social relations. To provide an observation from Hamar:

> As evening comes I sit outside in front of the house on my cowhide. Soon the goats will come and later the cattle. Already even before it really gets dark, the moon and the male and female stars become visible. They have been sitting in a semi-circle as in a public meeting and that means trouble. They would not sit together like this if everything in the country were fine, for then there would be no reason to hold a meeting. In the silence of the night Baldambe, contemplating some deep-seated conflict with his brothers, suddenly exclaims, "The hyena—its son is a lion; the lion—its son is a hyena" (Lydall/Strecker 1979a: 226).

On the one side this is a proverb and therefore an element of *elocutio*, but on the other side one can hear—so to say—life itself. Baldambe expresses the agonising experience of conflict between generations. Magnificent fathers who are like lions beget sons who are miserable like hyenas, and then— mysteriously—the hyenas again beget lions, and so on.

In the light of this observation it is interesting to note how Boris Wiseman has analysed the way in which the "figure of chiasmus plays a key role in shaping Lévi-Strauss's conception of the anthropologist's relationship to his object of study and, by extension, of what constitutes a specifically anthropological form of understanding" (Wiseman 2009: 87). Lévi-Strauss, he says, "construes anthropology itself—the process of anthropological understanding—in terms of a figure of chiasmic inversion... [where] the anthropological journey, real or in the mind, is construed in terms of a switching of positions of self and other" (2009: 93). Further, "It is this chiasmic switching of positions—other becomes self, self other—that explains the contradiction inherent in anthropology: if the other remains other, I have no way of understanding him/her; but if I understand him/her, he/she is no longer other" (2009: 99).

The essays that follow below are all characterised by this dilemma inherent in the ethnographic chiasmus, and in order to provide an example of how I expressed this problematic in the field, I quote here from a diary where I first tell of the feeling of closeness and mutual understanding that emerged between me and my friends Choke (also called Kairambe), Bali (also called Lokangare) and Banko (also called Burdimbe) when we were travelling and hunting in the savannah plains adjacent to the Lower Omo, only to suddenly turn into its opposite: a sense of estrangement, and a feeling of despair which made me question whether we could ever really understand each other:

> 17.1.1974 Morning in the cool shades of tall trees at Dus by the Omo. We came here yesterday evening when we had run out of water. The Omo is now low and its slow-moving waters are clear, pleasant to wash in and good for our black tea... While I have been writing, the sun has been rising higher. Choke emerges from the green-gray-white sorghum fields flooded with sunlight, bringing me a bowl of coffee. He wears his blanket like a Roman toga and walks slowly and upright, the feathers of his red and violet clay cap are sparkling, "Theoimba, this is the coffee which

Lokaribuk has sent you." Being 'on the road', detached from normal social life we are continually doing things for one another without ever questioning one another's independence. Hamar men like Choke and Lokangare and Banko have never been made to question their power to manage their own lives, they are confident and competent and that's why doing ethnographic work with them is so satisfying (Lydall/Strecker 1979a: 255–56).

18.1.1974; Early morning in the yellow plain in the long shade of the Land Rover: The recent intimacy with my friends has become too much! I want to be alone, just by myself. I am sad. I realise once again that our intimacy exists only on one level: that of adventure, ethnographic co-operation, the sharing of food, caring for one another etc. That's great and beautiful—but there is also another level, one on which we are so infinitely separate, the level of general concepts of understanding. I still have not grasped the really fundamental intellectual concepts of the Hamar; I mean those general notions that are related to the social cosmos of the past and present and future, concepts like *barjo* and *rukunti*, ideas relating to the ancestors, the sky... and to the precedents of countless rituals... Similarly, the Hamar don't share my abstract concepts, such as dialectic for example... This all came to mind when Choke and I were talking last night after Banko and Lokangare had fallen asleep. We talked about greeting and the variability of greeting customs. Choke told me how he and Lokangare observed greeting customs in Addis Ababa. He certainly has a great interest in this and I don't doubt that his observations are governed by an implicit theory of greeting behaviour. But this theory is very different from mine, and I just can't put my theory in Hamar words. How does one say that social life is an interconnected whole where the hidden shows itself through the obvious, i.e. shows itself to those who have discovered the interconnections? After all, anthropology is a highly specialized European enterprise, it bridges big gaps at times, but the bridges cover only certain points—and even lapse with time, crumble away.

My father's eyes come to mind. How warm and mild they used to look when he watched us children, and how cold and sharp and devastating when he directed them at the objects, apples, stones, pots, flowers, glasses, that were the subjects of his still-lives. Would any Hamar understand this look? Yes in his terms. But he could not possibly know that my father was examining the relationships between the objects in front of him, and not only this, that he was examining these relationships and transforming them into the two-dimensional totality of a picture existing independently of the objects. Two-dimensional? No, multi-dimensional, because there are the dimensions of colour, temperature, and intensity, light and heavy... The dialectic of visual contrasts, of 'a priori' forms and individual historical experiences... How am I to share this with my friends, friends who through common experience and interest have become extremely close to me? In theory, the gulf is not unbridgeable, but practice works against it. Now it is almost four years since I first came to Hamar, and still with each new phase of achieving intimacy with the Hamar I become aware of another abyss that separates us (Lydall and Strecker 1979a: 257–59).

This alternation between feelings of mental and emotional closeness and distance has remained with me ever since. By the time the present collection of essays goes into print it will be not four but almost forty years that Jean Lydall and I have been studying and writing about Hamar culture, have enjoyed good days and suffered bad times together with our Hamar friends, have witnessed the success and failure of various Ethiopian governments, have seen our children grow up and the first Hamar enter college and take up posts in the government and so on, but in spite of all this the feeling of only partial understanding has remained. The ethnographic chiasmus simply does not allow for any stable sense of knowing, only instant moments of insight, each akin to a spark, to a flash.

The book begins with a prologue and ends with an epilogue, which are both devoted to Balambaras Aike Berinas, better

known by his family and friends in Hamar as Baldambe—
Father of the Dark Brown Cow. For twenty-five years,
Baldambe was our host, friend, teacher and mentor in Hamar,
and he has deeply influenced the course of our ethnographic
work.

Although written after Baldambe's death, the prologue tells
of our first encounters with Baldambe, of how he invited us to
his homestead (Dambaiti), of how sickness brought us all closer
together, of our many conversations around the coffee pot, of
our systematic ethnographic work, of how Baldambe joined us
on a trip to Europe, and of how we ended up in silence when
we contemplated the limits of our mutual understanding, when
we realised "that it is impossible fully to understand the reality
of another culture. Hamar is too much for me; Europe is too
much for Baldambe. The only thing that is true and tangible is
our friendship, which has moved through and become strong in
each of our separate worlds".

The epilogue asks about the causes of Baldambe's death not
because I, the ethnographer, have posed the question, but
because after Baldambe died people were eager to relate to me
the dramatic, incongruent and agonizing tales about the events
that were said to have led to his death. This brought
Baldambe's problematic relationship with other Hamar elders
into sharp relief and paid—at least in my view—homage to
Baldambe's sincerity and sense of justice. In his search for truth
Baldambe was deceived and in the end could not see clearly
anymore what was true and what was not. Here he faced a
dilemma, which also characterizes the ethnographic endeavour.
As I put it in the epilogue, "We all are confined to particular
deictic fields, to singular contexts of time, place and action that
allow no overarching, 'objective' knowledge. We can see and
evaluate events only from our individual perspectives, and like
the witnesses in Kurasawa's film *Rashomon* we are bound to tell
conflicting, contradictory, open-ended stories that leave us
unsatisfied and haunt us in our dreams".

Chiasmus characterises anthropology not only on the plane of ethnographic practice but also on a general level of theory where the chiasmus concerns the relationship between culture and rhetoric and says that just as culture structures rhetoric, rhetoric structures culture. This view—formulated in "Rhetoric in the creation of Hamar culture" (first essay of Part I)—emerged slowly during my long years of fieldwork. It developed further when I was writing up research results (Strecker 1988) and when I began to teach and work with a team of graduate students at the Johannes Gutenberg University of Mainz. But it shaped up fully only in the context of the international *Rhetoric Culture Project*, a project dedicated to a long overdue reunion of rhetoric and the study of culture with the aim to position, or rather re-position, culture within the realm of rhetoric, and... to explore how culture and rhetoric are co-emergent, how persuasion pervades all forms of social life, and how human existence is neither fully free nor completely determined (Strecker and Tyler 2009).

Another essay concerned with *Rhetoric Culture Theory* is "Hamar rhetoric in the context of war." Here I acknowledge Stephen Tyler as the scholar who has most deeply influenced my work, saying: "Like so many other post-postmodern anthropologists I have been searching for a new paradigm for the study of culture. Two great teachers and friends have most inspired me in this, Baldambe (Balambaras Aike Berinas) from Hamar and Steve (Professor Stephen Tyler) from Rice University, Houston, Texas. Both have pointed to the same direction—rhetoric. Rhetoric is the key to a new (and one can say also very old) theory of culture."

"The *genius loci* of Hamar" is similarly influenced by Steve and—in a way—is meant as homage to his thinking, especially to his epistemological stance, which alerts us against the dangers of inappropriate literalness and acknowledges "a certain 'looseness' about all of our conversational rules and our rules of social life generally, so that anyone who follows the rules literally, destroys the normative character of interaction and induces social paralysis".

"The predicaments of war and peace" and "The temptations of war and the struggle for peace" also follow Steve's lines of thought. In his great book *The Said and the Unsaid* he had insisted on a vision of social life, which is neither anarchic nor fully determined, and which could be seen as a process emerging from the "intentional acts of wilful egos constrained by convention" (Tyler 1978: 135). I took these ideas seriously and applied them to an analysis of armed conflict between the Hamar and their neighbours. In addition, "To share or not to share: Notes about authority and anarchy" pertains to *Rhetoric Culture Theory* as the essay listens, as it were, to the voices of the Hamar—their monologues and dialogues—to show how culture specific notions of property and authority are established discursively.

Related to *Rhetoric Culture Theory* are symbolic theory and the theory of tropes, especially metaphor, and several essays focus on these topics. "'Face' and the person" is one of them, but "Do the Hamar have a concept of honour?", "*Michere*: How the whipping wand speaks", "Lomotor's talk or the imperial gerund", "Meanings and rhetoric of the *barjo aela*", and "Magic and the rhetorical will" also dwell on questions of figuration. However, "Speech situations and social control", "Political discourse in an egalitarian society", and "Rhetorics of local knowledge" are more concerned with the rhetorical use of language and focus on concept formation and the richness of Hamar ecological knowledge.

Finally, the concept of 'self', also has a close affinity to *Rhetoric Culture Theory*. By using it, I follow Stephen Tyler's advice to keep an eye on the "wilful egos"—men and women alike—who are the inventors of culture (see above). Thus, Part I (Rhetorical Creation of Culture and Self) shows how Hamar social values and notions of personhood are rhetorically created, sustained and at times contested. Figuration plays a central role here, including the metaphor of 'face' with its culture specific variations of name, whipping wand, word/mouth, big toe, forehead, and good fortune.

An understanding of the Hamar concept of the person provides the springboard for Part II (Rhetorics of War and Peace) that explores different kinds of interpersonal, gender and inter-group conflicts characteristic of Hamar society. It begins with an essay on speaking as a means of social control ("Speech situations and social control"). Then follow chapters that show the role of rhetoric in the practice of herding and gender relations (*"Michere*: How the whipping wand speaks"), in politics ("Political discourse in an egalitarian society") and in economics ("To share or not to share: Notes on authority and anarchy"). A detailed analysis of an account of peacemaking ("Lomotor's talk or the imperial gerund") provides the background for further essays dealing with present day warfare and the impossibility—as it seems—to secure lasting peace in the regions of southern Ethiopia ("Predicaments of war and peace", "Temptations of war and the struggle for peace" and "Rhetoric in the context of war").

Part III (Rhetorical Articulation of Knowledge and Belief) tunes in with the 'spirit of place', the environment and the physical as well as the mental and emotional climate of Hamar country ("The *genius loci* of Hamar"). It demonstrates the rich and meaningful relationship between the Hamar and the world they inhabit ("Rhetorics of local knowledge"). It probes into transcendental notions that aim at orientation, identification and control of both nature and society ("Meanings and rhetoric of the *barjo aela*"), and it explores how in Hamar—like in so many other cultures—emotion rules over mind, will over reason. Thus, mantic and magical dispositions are found in almost all domains of Hamar life ("Magic and the rhetorical will" and "Mantic and magical confidence: The work of persuasion").

Our *barjo* brought us together!
Obituary for Baldambe

I cannot as yet speak of you in the third person. I cannot think or speak of you as "he" but have to address you directly, you, my dear *misso* Baldambe. We used to call each other "hunting friend" although we never killed any game together. What we hunted were not animals but the "lies" of people. You compared my tape recorder to a trap and often gleefully told me to get it ready when a social drama was in the making: "*Misso, donzana ni'idine, budamo kissa zaninka wo kaze*" (hunting friend, the elders have come, let's catch their lies in the snare).

When we first crossed the river below Arba Minch hospital, there was no bridge there, and we drove the car off the dusty road into the shallow stream. We splashed the children, Theo and Rosie, with water and then left them to play while we washed ourselves, you, Jean and I. You came over to wash my back, and I in return washed yours. "Rub harder," you said, "and use some sand." So I rubbed harder, and when I had finished your back I poured water over your head and rubbed it too. This head, strong as granite and of such beauty!

I did not kiss your forehead then. I kissed it only recently, twenty years later, on the afternoon of the 28th of March in Arba Minch hospital when you had stopped fighting, when quietness had returned to your face and when I thought you had fallen asleep.

But your son Gauaimba knew more about death than I and turned away and cried. Also his friends who were with us knew at once what had happened and roughly told me: "Go and get a car, go and get a car quickly." This was their way of telling Jean and me that you had died and that it was now for us to quickly find a car in which we could bring you back home and bury you in the mountains of Hamar, next to your kin.

It was a great comfort to be with you in the hour of your death and later to be present at your burial, surrounded by your friends and relatives. Sarinde was most persistent in her wailing and sang most beautifully day and night, remembering you: "Father of the brown cow, hunting friend of Theo's father." Your children and we held each other and cried, but we also felt that life will go on and will draw us together like when you were alive. Perhaps from now on even more so because now that you have gone Jean and I feel more responsible for your children who have come to call us *indo* and *imbo* which means "mother" and "father".

Today I have returned to Europe and am now to talk to my age-mates about you and explain how you used to say that our *barjo*, our good fortune, had brought us together and how you were elated to find in us people interested in anthropology just like you. At our first encounters you chose to speak indirectly to us. A great distance had to be mediated and you did this by means of tropes, by metaphor, synecdoche and metonymy:

First you stumbled into our camp, "drunk and delightful", carrying a branch of a tree which you called *biri*. It was night, and in the light of the fire you showed us the different divisions of the branch and related yourself to them, but what you meant eluded us then. Later we understood, that the branch was from a tree from which stirring sticks are made, sticks to stir blood, meat broth, beer and sorghum gruel. Both the tree and the tool are called *biri* and at the same time they were the name of your grandfather Biri.

Biri was the father of the great Hamar spokesman who became known as Birinas, son of Biri, and you, whose childhood name was Aike (locust), were the son of Birinas. With the help of the *biri* branch you had tried to show us these genealogical relationships and also to explain how you were the oldest son of the third wife of Birinas. This, then, was how you introduced yourself to us by means of analogy, or, if one likes, by means of a model or metaphor.

The second time you visited us again at night, and again you were intoxicated. You took from your pocket a handkerchief with little medicines which we understood to be particular to your clan Karla. We ate together and then smelled your various medicines. Were you offering some of them to us? We did not ask then, but today we know that had we demanded any you would have given them to us. So, in the second meeting you turned to synecdoche, offering us a significant part of your whole.

The third event, which I remember vividly and also have recorded in our journal is my visit to your homestead in Dambaiti. I came to ask you whether you would accept us as guests. But you did not answer. You took an axe instead and began cutting a path through the bush so that we would be able to reach Dambaiti with our motorcycle. You talked and laughed a lot while you cut trees and brushed thorny branches away from the path. This was your answer to my question: you went ahead and taking the cause (our metonymic coming) for granted, turned to the effect (the need for a path). In order to tell what happened once we had moved to Dambaiti, I will constantly refer to what I wrote in our work journal. Firstly there were those cases of illness, which drew us together. I remember how after several months in Dambaiti, I felt exhausted and ill. You looked at me and said that I was weak because I had lost so much weight. Therefore you arranged that

I received a share from a sheep, which was slaughtered for Gadi who had just given birth to a boy (Lydall/Strecker 1979a: 43).

And later you were the first to notice that Jean had jaundice and you asked your brothers Kairambe and Makonen to slaughter a sheep and cut its stomach open so that Jean could inhale its content. Let me quote what I wrote the day after Jean had fallen ill, for the lines show how concerned you were and how you taught us to be perceptive:

> At night I give medicine to Ginonda and her son Gino who are both not well and I again realize that we are getting closer to each other here in Dambaiti through sickness, sickness we share. Everybody gets sick at times, our children, our Hamar neighbours and now Jean. We all are a "community of suffering" in Turner's sense. Baldambe tells me that he was bothered one night when Theo was crying badly. Why was he crying? He was not ill. He sensed that illness was coming in his family. "You see, now Jean has fallen sick." Theo was like the cattle and goats who also sense sickness: "When the cattle walk straight home, the bells ringing strongly and regularly, that's a good sign, but if the herds don't want to enter the gateway, when they have to be driven in by repeated hitting, that's a bad sign, then there will be illness" (Lydall and Strecker 1979a: 53)

Not only your hospitality and the security and shelter which you provided drew us together but also, of course, your magnificent mind and your marvellous ability to explain Hamar culture. When we showed you the book *Conversations with Ogotemmeli* and said that you were like he whose words Marcel Griaule had collected, you agreed and laughed, and later, often clownishly, sat down like Ogotemmeli on the cover of the book, and folded your hands over your forehead.

There were many in Hamar who helped us, but there was nobody equal to you. I soon realized that your great ability to explain Hamar culture should find expression in its own terms, that your voice should be heard without anyone interfering.

This project I formulated already earlier on when, on the 18th of September 1971, I wrote in the work journal:

> In the evening, as Baldambe and I talk and I record his narratives, the project of our first Hamar book takes shape in my head: Baldambe describing his country, his people, his family, his father and himself. There is so much poetry and expression in his descriptions. These and the rhythm of his speech should be reproduced in a book: the fast passages and interludes, the accelerations, the lingering of his voice. What a job it would be to translate such tapes! But if we were able to manage the translation without losing the quality of the actual speech, then something beautiful could result (Lydall/Strecker 1979a: 53).

In the end not just one but two books resulted from this project, *Baldambe Explains* the second volume of "The Hamar of Southern Ethiopia" (Lydall/Strecker 1979b) and "Berimba's Resistance" (manuscript not yet published).

You also delighted in etymological puzzles and anything having to do with hidden and multiple meanings. You were like Muchona who helped Turner to look through the Ndembu "forest of symbols". Let me quote what I wrote in the work journal when my feelings were still fresh and full of amazement about you:

> We have a lively and at times rude conversation. We discuss the difficulty of finding out the connection between different things of the same name and different names for the same thing. We take the "prick" as an example, called *sama* in Hamar, which also means "fat", the fat tail of a sheep in particular. But what about the fact that *sama* becomes *banzi* when it is cut off an enemy? *Banzi* is also the name of a ritual object used in the initiation ritual of the young men. I follow this chain of related meanings up to this point and then Baldambe suddenly has one of his characteristic "dictionary" moments: Yes, I have thought about this connection between *banzi* (penis) and *banzi* (ritual symbol). There is truly a connection between them because just like the warrior who has killed an enemy, the initiate who has received the *banzi* may not

be touched by a woman. But not only this: the penis of the enemy is sewn onto the tail of a stolen cow with the bark of the *martso* tree whilst the thorns of the *martso*-tree are used when the *banzi* is sewn onto the initiate's little finger. In both cases only *martso* may be used!" Fieldwork can be really satisfying at times when emotional excitement and cognitive achievement fall together, and such moments occur most often when we work with Baldambe. For some time I have wanted to write about this, yet it is difficult to say what I mean: The greatest satisfactions of ethnographic work here in Hamar have mostly centred round Baldambe. Living in Hamar always means *kau* (bush), i.e., confusion and the inability to see far. The customs, ideas, values and most of the concrete historical events evade us... and then amidst our confusion, we talk to Baldambe and suddenly things fall into place. Each time when something "clicks", when separate things suddenly relate, then we are excited and happy and feel more confident of being able one day to look through the forest of Hamar symbols (to paraphrase Turner) (Lydall/Strecker 1979a: 62-63).

While you were a blessing for us, we wonder whether we were not at times something of a curse for you. True, you were obviously happy to have us with you and engage with us in a discourse about Hamar culture which only anthropology can generate. This is why you said that our good fortune had brought us together.

But there were also costs and unintended consequences which Jean and I noticed already quite early in our fieldwork and mentioned in the work journal as follows:

In spite of our generally good relations with the Hamar certain rancour exists at times. This is not surprising, for working almost regular hours, having a project, our travels, our comparative wealth, our use or modern goods and equipment etc. makes us different. But not just different, also exclusive, whether we want it or not. We can only work regularly if we send away people who intrude on us when we want to work. We can only carry ourselves, and very few others, in our Land Rover. We can only feed a very few in our house … and then, after all, we always look on events rather than really take part in them. This applies to Baldambe as well as to us … he always was to a certain degree an outsider in Hamar, being the son of a deceased great political leader and having worked at times with the Ethiopian Government in the administration of Hamar. His new job as "anthropologist" has not changed this, perhaps it has even increased his isolation at times, not so much from the outside but, psychologically, from the inside. That is why Baldambe so often has a sharp tongue and is so critical of Hamar (Lydall and Strecker 1979a: 61).

But your "bitter voice" (*apho tsakama*) of which you yourself were well aware, and which you attributed to your clan Karla, did not stop you from being genuinely concerned about the welfare of the Hamar. In fact Jean and I constantly witnessed the contrary, like at the beginning of that dry season where I wrote:

The dry, strong winds and the hot sun during the day make Baldambe worried, not for himself, but for the "yellow land" which is a metaphor for the country and its inhabitants. I have come to appreciate his sighs and lamentations more than I used to. He is really sincere. He is a born leader, like his father Birinas, and has a capacity for compassion that goes beyond the normal egocentric concern for one's fellow men. The sincerity of his worry strikes me most forcibly tonight as Baldambe talks with old Sago whose sincerity is beyond doubt. In the dark moonless night, coffee bowls in hand, they join in each other's lamentations about the harshness of the season. Before, I always used to listen to Baldambe's lamentations with the feeling that he was blowing himself up, for he would show concern about matters that were beyond anybody's control, such as the weather. Tonight I see that Baldambe is genuinely concerned for his fellow human beings and knows what suffering in the dry season means. The thought that one should not talk about it because one cannot change the situation would be alien to him. It is typical of his complex nature that, having evoked a dark picture of the future, he points to the dry leaves on the ground saying, "Look here, the goats will clean all this up, it's their food; they will sweep up the leaves in every corner of the bush, they will always find something to eat." (Lydall and Strecker 1979a: 204-205)

Jean and I did not always work closely together with you. Sometimes we turned to other Hamar and spent most of our time with them, like when we had embarked on a survey of Hamar. Then we noted that you were slightly at a loss because the survey had put you out of work. But we also hoped that when our research reached a new stage, this would fully occupy you as our teacher and make you feel at ease with us again (Lydall and Strecker 1979a: 82).

Also, there were many occasions, when other Hamar friends were with us. I liked this work in small groups especially well, and in my slightly alienated and academic style I wrote about it as follows:

I have now reached a new stage of fieldwork. The skill consists of choosing the right situations of "live" talk and the right topics for group interviews, each with the aim of getting normative accounts of social phenomena that are still problematic and need more adequate documentation. It is the wealth of information that lies in small linguistic details that excites me and leads me to use the tape recorder so extensively (Lydall/Strecker 1979a: 200).

Here are some descriptions of such work in small groups, which I came to call "seminars":

In the afternoon I ask Baldambe and Choke to tell me about the cattle exchanged in bond-friend relationships. The "seminar" turns out to be as informative and lively as last night's instruction on the stars. Their account will furnish a "conscious model" of this system of distribution and insurance. But the recording is interesting at more than the purely normative level; both my teachers recount examples of how the system works in practice. Moreover, at one point Baldambe explicitly relates the system to the anarchy of Hamar life (Lydall and Strecker 1979a: 200).

It is still night when Baldambe and Sago rise to settle down again for coffee and conversation (and I record). Baldambe tells Sago what was said during the big public meetings at Kizo where he and the other spokesmen of Kadja stopped the fighting with the Galeba. This is my favourite theme again: socio-linguistic awareness, speaking about speaking; the intellectual background of the use and manipulation of language in politically important situations. Both Baldambe's and Sago's command of the language is great. They delight in recreating all the single features of an argument which they have heard about, re-enacting the situation so that you can visualize them listening, answering, shouting, rising, sitting down, coming to conclusions, leaving something in the air....

When the conversation has run on uninterrupted for a long while, the same thing happens as last night: the coffee being almost finished, Ginonda is called to join the coffee drinkers. Not as a serious talker, but rather as "fool" or "clown" who gives the serious play a funny ending (Lydall and Strecker 1979a: 206).

At night, drinking Ouzo, I continue the kinship seminar with Baldambe, Wadu and Choke. I am unable to describe fully how inspiring it is to work with these three men. They are imprinting my enterprise with their own character, they lead me intellectually through the labyrinth of their institutions, they are also teaching me something about their own morality. For example, through our discussions they show a curious recklessness and lack of false concern that I have come to appreciate very much. Death, equality, honesty, all these I was taught to fear and esteem. But these men teach me the value not of life or death, but of good fighting or good resting, not of honesty but of lively arguments and entertaining tales, not of equality but of rewarding encounters ... (Lydall and Strecker 1979a: 214).

So much about systematic work and recordings. But much, or even most, of your teaching and enriching contributions came almost in passing at odd moments during the day, like in the following example:

> At noon I feel hungry and Baldambe and I feast on some dry *muna* and two cups of milk. How satisfying this simple food is... As we chew our *muna*. I reflect on my attempt to work during the morning. I sigh and tell Baldambe that if I were a proper anthropologist, I would be writing from now on, writing without respite, so that the books would grow fat whilst I myself grew thin. My youth would go into the books and my eyes would darken, I would need glasses, my hair would grow white and with a whisper I would talk to my students. I imitate the speech mannerism of an old professor talking Hamar. "*Nananoto, kami wodimate...*" I relate what I would say about Hamar and when I reach the institution of bond-friendship, pointing out that it is in this way that a young man builds up his capital, Baldambe suddenly interrupts my imaginary lecture. "And by giving his cattle away to his bond-friends, he makes sure that none of his relatives and affines comes and takes them away from him unexpectedly." I had always thought that this "hiding" was one of the most important reasons for the institution but I had never heard a Hamar state this clearly. "Thank you, *misso* Ogotemmeli" (Lydall/Strecker 1979a: 221).

Also, the deepest thoughts and the most complex exchanges developed spontaneously, almost casually and in ways, which cannot be planned. They were, of course, philosophical and had to do with the limits of our mutual understanding. There is a long passage in the work journal which starts off with the feeling that we would never be able to grasp each other's views fully but ends on a surprising note of understanding:

> At night, Baldambe and I lie in front of our house and watch the sky. I tell Baldambe that it is now Christmas Eve in Europe and that Meuder, Baka, Ali and others must be thinking of us resting on our cowhides exactly as we are doing (they had visited Hamar the year before!). We recall memories of last year when we were in Europe and participated in the rituals of the Christmas tree.

Baldambe comments that the lights symbolized how the hearts of the people should burn, they represented the flames of their lives. We enumerate in detail the food we ate, the drinks we drank, whom we were with… But we give up our reflection, realizing that it is impossible fully to understand the reality of another culture. Hamar is too much for me, Europe is too much for Baldambe. The only thing that is true and tangible is our friendship, which has moved through and become strong in each of our separate worlds. After a while I slowly pick up the conversation again, embarking on an odd epistemological theme. As with everything abstract I have to use metaphors to explain myself: if you are born in a hole, you think that you know much and are ignorant of very little. When you move out of your hole and find yourself in a valley; you think that you know more now, but also realize that there is a lot you don't know. When you then climb a mountain and see the world around you, you hardly think of what you know anymore, but are impressed by what you don't know. Does Baldambe understand what I want to say? I think he does and we say to one another that one has to be strong to continue on the path of knowledge since it is a path with no end. This makes me think of my sensitive, tired eyes, my aching shoulder, my bleeding gums… and from there my thoughts wander to Thomas Mann. I tell Baldambe that there was an older brother of Sigmund who would not tell stories like the Hamar do, but would write them down. The point of his stories was that sickness and good talk are complementary rather than contradictory. I say that Thomas Mann would tell of a raid preceded by a public meeting in which two men were talking. One of them had malaria but despite his weakness, he said the right things, whilst the other, strong and healthy as he was, spoke badly… At this point Baldambe interrupts me, "Just as in Hamar!" He adds, "We say that the strong and the young are blunt and stupid. But we don't think that the sick are wise. It's the old who are wise, the ones who have survived all sickness, those who have grown thin and weak from a long life of suffering." Baldambe transforms Thomas Mann's distinction between health and disease into a distinction between youth and age. This pleases me very much since I was trying to bring together two separate strands when I used the term "good talk". Good talk is an art and it is art to which Mann's distinction between health and disease refers. But "good talk" also represents wisdom or "science" and it is this that Baldambe's distinction between youth and age refers (Lydall/Strecker 1979a: 219-220).

This was the way we used to talk, and how we noticed that we could understand at least part of the differences of the worlds in which we had grown up, like when you agreed with Thomas Mann that health does not lead to wisdom, but then went on to equate wisdom not with disease but with old age which has weathered all storms of sickness.

We talked and talked, and as we kept talking together, Jean and I with you, our closest friends like Sarinde, Ginonoda, Choke, Wadu and so on, we experienced already in Hamar a sense of exclusiveness and a thrill of complicity which went with it. Were we not exposing "the lies of the Hamar" and did we not together try to look behind the appearance of Hamar life and "untie the knots of custom" as you used to call it? Anthropology was the good fortune, which had brought us together in this.

Our exclusiveness increased outside of Hamar during our many travels in Ethiopia. People would wonder who you were as they watched you talk animatedly with Jean and me. Were you from Kenya, Uganda, America? Surely, you could not be Ethiopian. And then in Europe, how great was your delight to chat with us in public, be it at Frankfurt airport, in the streets of London, at a bar in Lyon or a conference hall in Berlin. You liked it when people were amazed about our conversations, and you commented: "they wonder about us three Hamar here."

When you were in Germany for the second time, I asked you to help me in courses at the Johannes Gutenberg University of Mainz. You soon had a group of admirers and friends, and I was struck by the fact that, after awhile, the students felt closer to you than to me. This showed that cultural differences should not be mistaken for social distance. You came from a different world but everyone could immediately see that you knew much more about life than I, and that you were broader minded and more ready to understand others, no matter who they were and what they were trying to say. Raymond Firth once mentioned that Malinowski always gave his students the feeling that he had understood them, even when they were confused and incoherent. You, Baldambe, had a similar gift, and gave the students the chance to understand themselves in the very process of formulating their questions and listening to your answers. Accordingly, the students felt very close to you.

There are many more memories that come to my mind when I think of you, especially memories of our joint effort to do practical work and help the Hamar and their neighbours during the recurrent periods of drought. Our mad activities in the heat and dust of the Woito valley forged lasting bonds of friendship, first when we tried to reactivate old irrigations channels and later when we held a peace ceremony in Arbore at which more than a dozen languages were spoken.

Now your death has come suddenly and as a complete surprise, for together with some students I had visited you in Dambaiti not long ago, and you had promised to spend one more semester with us in Mainz. First you would have to perform the funeral rites for your mother and your older brothers, you said, but then you would be free to come. So Jean set off eight weeks ago intending to return with you for the summer term. However, before she could reach you she heard that you had fallen ill and had been brought to Arba Minch hospital by your son Awoke. So she rushed to meet you and spent three days by your side, but as your condition did not improve, she called me in Europe. I sensed immediately that your life was in danger, took the next plane to Addis and arrived just in time to be with you at the hour of your death.

Jean had told you that I was coming, and you had waited for me.

When I entered the room and sat by your side, you said, "hunting-friend, I have died, what can we do?" Then you looked at me closely and said that you could not recognize me anymore. I had changed. This disturbed you as well as me until tenderly you added that my hands and teeth were still the same. They were the hands and teeth, which you knew from before and proved that it was really I who had come.

I gave you my glasses and this improved your vision so much that you sat up and looked around you. You could see us all more clearly now. This raised your spirits, and we began to talk of the past and of the future. You would get better and visit all our friends in Europe again. Like so often before, you mentioned them all and were proud that you had not forgotten their names. Your eyes and ears were failing, but your brain, you said, was still intact.

This was your last moment of strength. Then you lay back and the final battle between life and death began. You let us know what happened by lifting and lowering and opening and closing your right hand, saying *yeda* (hold), *piska* (let go), *yeda*—*piska*, *yeda*—*piska*, and your last word was *piska*.

In between there were moments when you mentioned my dead father Sigmund and my sister Susanne whom you were to join now, and once you turned to me and mentioned my hands: "here they are, the hands of Sigmund." So our good fortune brought us together even in your last moment when I could experience once more your tenderness and witness how you intertwined our lives beyond death.

With this I have come to the end of my account and now want to turn to my age-mates with one final remark: I keep thinking about the figures Baldambe used in our last conversation. What was he doing when he mentioned my teeth and my hands? Why did I find this so touching?

I venture the answer that not metaphor but metonymy and synecdoche are the most endearing tropes. Metaphor distances while metonymy helps you to draw the other close to you. Although all of us may know this intuitively, usually we are not aware of it. Let me explain:

The discourse of everyday life can be envisaged as a line of plain speech from which we deviate now and then to express something in figures. One way to deviate is towards specificity (metonymy and synecdoche) and the other is towards generality (metaphor). In metaphor we liken one thing or person to something else, as in Stephen Tyler's example of metaphor where someone is equated with the whirlwind (1978: 322). Tyler's theory is not only fitting here because it stresses the emphatic and affective element in metaphor, but also because his prime example, the "whirlwind", was used by Baldambe to describe himself. "I am a whirlwind" (*saile*) he used to say, "I am like the flood" (*meri*). I am irresistible and take everything away with me.

Thus metaphor is suitable for exhilaration, praise, blessing, and also swearing, and so on. It is a means to point beyond the person and relate her or him to the world. This is the enriching power of metaphor! But it is also its weakness, because metaphor necessarily involves two different semantic domains and shifts the attention away from the term with which it has started.

It is telling that Kövescses, in his study of metaphors of anger, pride and love (1986), only gives examples that do not really show love but are flattery, praise, and rather conventional expressions of admiration. And, of course, how could it be otherwise, for love turns to synecdoche or metonymy to find its expression. It draws attention to a significant part of the other and in this way evokes the whole. Like when Baldambe mentioned my teeth and implied, "I like your teeth and what they show about you", and by mentioning my hands he meant, "I know your hands and I like them just as I like you as a whole person and your family as well."

So I learnt in my last conversation with Baldambe that to attend to the particular is to elevate the whole. But in order to be tender, the attention to the particulars of the other must be given lightly, almost fleetingly, so that it does not destroy the feelings, which it tries to evoke.

Part I: Rhetorical Creation of Culture and Self

Rhetoric in the creation of Hamar culture

In this essay I want to show how Hamar culture is created rhetorically. To substantiate this view I proceed in three steps. First I introduce the notion of "internal rhetorics" without which no understanding of the rhetorical nature of culture is possible; secondly I outline some of the basic ideas underlying rhetorical theory of culture; and thirdly I substantiate my thesis with results of fieldwork with the Hamar of southern Ethiopia.

Internal rhetorics

Rhetoric is generally understood as the art of public speaking, but in her beautifully written book *Internal Rhetorics*, Jean Nienkamp has shown that "from the earliest sources in which public rhetoric is depicted self-persuasion is also portrayed" (2001: 9). She provides striking examples of internal rhetoric in very early Greek texts such as the *Iliad*, which are of particular interest here because they throw light not only on rhetoric but also on "figuration in thought and action". Thus, when Agamemnon threatens to take Briseis from Achilleus, the latter's thoughts are portrayed as follows:

> And the anger came on Peleus' son [Achilleus], and within his shaggy breast the heart was divided two ways, pondering whether to draw from beside his thigh the sharp sword... or else to check the spleen within and keep down his anger. Now as he

weighed in mind and spirit these two courses and was drawing from its scabbard the great sword, Athene descended from the sky (Nienkamp 2001: 11).

Note the centrality of tropes in this characterization of Achilleus internal rhetoric: the role of the heart as the source of deep thought and deliberation, and the spleen as the seat of anger so widely reported in anthropological literature. In another example we hear Odysseus talk to himself in the midst of battle:

Now Odysseus the spear-famed was left alone, nor did any of the Argives stay beside him, since fear had taken all of them. And troubled, *he spoke then to his own great-hearted spirit*: "Ah me, what will become of me? It will be a great evil if I run, fearing their multitude, yet deadlier if I am caught alone; and Kronos' son drove to flight the rest of the Danaans. Yet still, *why does the heart within me debate on these things?* Since I know that it is the cowards who walk out of the fighting, but if one is to win honour in battle, he must by all means stand his ground strongly, whether he be struck or strike down another. *"While he was pondering these things in his heart and his spirit..."* (Emphases by Nienkamp 2001: 12).

From an anthropological perspective it is interesting that Nienkamp finds it important to emphasize that these examples show how rhetoric is an almost timeless general human disposition, and to witness how she applauds Susan Jarratt for arguing that, "mythic discourse is capable of containing the beginnings of a 'rhetorical consciousness'" (Op. Cit.: 10).

There is no room here to do justice to Nienkamp's fine-grained analysis of the relationship between "internal" and public rhetorics, but it is important to note that she distinguishes between the time honoured orthodox position that restricts the definition of rhetoric to oratory, and another rather recent position that sees "all human meaning-making as rhetorical", and which she calls "expansive" (Op. Cit.: 3).

Proponents of the latter view are for example Lloyd Bitzer and Edwin Black (1971: 208) who include in rhetoric all forms of human communication, as well as all symbolic expressions that have the capacity to influence human life. The ubiquity of rhetoric postulated by "expansive" rhetoric theory has led John Bender and David Wellbery to speak of the "rhetoricality" of modernism:

> *Modernism is an age not of rhetoric, but of rhetoricality*, the age, that is, of a generalized rhetoric that penetrates to the deepest levels of human experience... [Rhetoricality] manifests the groundless, infinitely ramifying characteristics of discourse in the modern world. For this reason, it allows for no explanatory meta-discourse that is not already itself rhetorical. Rhetoric is no longer the title of a doctrine and a practice, nor a form of cultural memory; it becomes instead something like the condition of our existence (Nienkamp 2001: 3; emphasis in the original).

Nienkamp finds that this:

> distinction between rhetoric and rhetoricality is a useful way to think about traditional and expansive rhetorics", and she adds that, "in a sense, rhetoric has come full circle in its expansive manifestation: the broader sophistic concern with all of *logos* (language, speech, reasoning, thought) that was codified into the art of persuasive speaking and writing is now being broadened again to cover the contemporary equivalent of *logos*: a concern with how language in all of its manifestations influences humans (and sometimes other sentient beings) (Nienkamp 2001: 3).

This accords well with the position taken by rhetoric culture theory, which says that our minds are filled with images and ideas, but these remain unstable and incomplete as long as we do not manage to persuade both ourselves and others of their meanings. It is this inward and outward rhetoric that allows us to give some kind of shape and structure to our understanding of the world, and which becomes central to the formation of individual and collective consciousness.

Rhetoric culture theory

Rhetoric culture theory as developed by Stephen Tyler, myself and others aims at establishing a new paradigm for anthropology that retrieves, explores and makes full use of the ancient insight that just as rhetoric is founded in culture, culture is founded in rhetoric.

Thus, rhetoric culture theory sets out with a chiasmus, which starts from a familiar mental territory, for we all know somehow that all successful rhetoric make use of the cultural contexts of speakers and hearers. But from this well-established position rhetoric culture theory then ventures out to claim that also the opposite is true, namely that culture is produced rhetorically.

Critics have objected to an unmediated juxtaposition of rhetoric and culture, arguing that the juxtaposition of these two nouns without linkage leaves the reader wondering whether rhetoric and culture are meant to be one, which would require "rhetoric-culture" (and would grievously impoverish the concept of culture) or whether the distinct concepts are thought to be linked by constitutive interplay. In that case one would need "rhetoric and culture" to make the interplay possible (F.G. Bailey 2002, personal communication). But to this one may reply that although it may be safe and fruitful to keep both concepts separate and analyse their interplay, Bailey himself has shown in much of his work how rhetoric is inherent in culture and culture is inherent in rhetoric (see for example Bailey 1983). The two fuse in infinite ways, are saturated with each other, and their currents and counter currents create a field of forces that encompasses both.

Everything would be easy if we were to re-insert "in", "and" or "of" between "rhetoric" and "culture", which would how-ever weaken the intellectual challenge entailed in the un-mediated collocation of "rhetoric culture" considerably. The boldness would disappear like when one moves from metaphor to simile. As pointed out already above, the relationship between rhetoric and culture needs to be understood as a kind of *chiasmus* where thought (and practice) move from rhetoric to culture and from culture back to rhetoric. Both phenomena interact in what one might call a "chiastic spin".

The relevance of rhetoric culture theory becomes further apparent when one considers the way in which rhetoric culture theory gains its momentum from a treasure of rich and exciting research on metaphor that began with Ivor Richards and Kenneth Burke in the middle of the twentieth century, speeded up in the 1960-70s and has continued until today. Victor Turner, Paul Ricœur, Max Black, David Sapir, Christopher Crocker, George Lakoff, Mark Johnson, Stephen Tyler and, of course, James Fernandez are some of the most outstanding names to be mentioned here.

Related to the study of tropes is the aim of rhetoric culture theory to highlight the *fantastic* elements in culture. Here—like so often—it draws on Stephen Tyler's *The Said and the Unsaid. Mind, Meaning, and Culture*, which shows that a wide margin of indeterminacy and interpretative leeway exists in communication, because "our sentences—and their interpretations—are syntheses, emerging from the interaction between intention, convention, and performance, and this is consistent with our common-sense notions that we think before we speak, and that there are slips between the tongue and the lips—and that our speaking often fails to convey what we had in mind" (Tyler 1978: 137). People do not and cannot always know how to say properly what they think, and they do not and cannot always know what others mean by what they say. These seeming shortcomings in natural communication can in turn be—and in fact often are—exploited rhetorically. The use of tropes is a prime example for this, because when people create tropes they create semantic collocations that resist any univocal interpretation and therefore have an element of the "fantastic". In other words, the figures we live by, to paraphrase Lakoff and

Johnson, imply that we also live by the fantastic. It is from here that rhetoric culture theory launches its enquiries.

The constitutive role of rhetoric in Hamar culture

When, more than a quarter of a century ago, I asked my friend Baldambe (Father of the Dark Brown Cow) to provide us with an explanatory account of Hamar culture, I was miles away from rhetoric culture theory. But I felt then already that I needed some rhetorical skill—would have to take recourse to tropes—in order to express what I wanted to convey. This is how I formulated my request:

> "*Misso* (hunting friend), we have seen how you Hamar live and what you do. For many months we have talked with you about Hamar customs. Yet our eyes don't see and our ears don't hear. We feel as if we have been handling separate pieces of wood, poles and beams. You know how the poles and beams fit together. Please take them and reconstruct for us the house to which they belong." Upon this, Baldambe answered "*Eh, eh*", which meant that he had understood and agreed (Lydall and Strecker 1979b: x).

Looking back at what I thought and did then makes me feel awkward now because of the hyperboles I used ("our eyes don't see, our ears don't hear") in order to emphasize total dependence on our Hamar host. Also my metaphors aiming to evoke a picture of a *Gestalt* or meaningful whole look dated now, remindful as they are of the heydays of structural anthropology when culture was still seen mainly in terms of structure or system, that is of logical and functional order. There was in this exchange no inkling, as yet, of the non-determined, rhetorical, tropical, multi-vocal, even fantastic nature of culture.

My understanding changed only slowly—and is in fact only gradually developing now—as I re-read *Baldambe Explains*, which Jean Lydall and I transcribed, translated, annotated and published so many years ago. In what follows below I will analyse some passages of Baldambe's text to show empirically how culture is based on rhetoric, and how people may talk themselves and others into adopting and adhering to particular, "fantastic" ways of life.

The text begins with a "view from afar" (Lévi-Strauss 1992), that is a seemingly detached:

> Long ago, in the time of the ancestors, the Hamar had two *bitta* [ritual leaders]. One was Banki Maro, one was Elto. The first ancestor of Banki Maro came from Ari [a country to the north] and settled in Hamar in the mountains. He, the *bitta*, made fire, and seeing this fire, people came many from Ari, others from Male, others from Tsamai, others from Konso, others from Kara, others from Bume, and others from Ale which lies beyond Konso. Many came from Ale (Lydall and Strecker 1979b: 2).

Shortly after this first passage, the mode of Baldambe's account changes, gets charged with more "emotional energy" (Kennedy 1998) and turns into mimesis. That is, Baldambe now uses direct speech, a command: "The *bitta* was the first to make fire in Hamar and he said: 'I am the *bitta*, the owner of the land am I, the first to take hold of the land. Now may you become my subjects, may you be my dependents, may you be the ones I command'".

After the command, which heralds a usurpation of power, verbal exchanges—dialogues, conversations, arguments—follow that can best be understood as forms of *tacit collusion*. Summarizing the work by R.P. McDermott and Henry Tylbor (1995), Denis Tedlock and Bruce Mannheim have written about *tacit collusion* in social life as follows:

> All events require the *tacit collusion* of the participants, who implicitly agree that they are interpreting the events within the same general framework. This interactional collusion is not socially neutral; rather it involves a carefully crafted set of social re-positionings in which dominance hierarchies emerge with the collusion (though not necessarily the consent) of the dominated (Tedlock and Mannheim 1995: 13).

Although Mannheim and Tedlock, as well as McDermott and Tylbor never speak and seemingly never even think of rhetoric, the notion of *tacit collusion* is eminently rhetorical and leads us deeply into all and everything that concerns figuration in thought and action. The "play of tropes in culture", as James Fernandez has called it (1986); or, in Paul Grice's parlance, the "creativity of conversational implicatures" (1975) all are based on myriad forms of *tacit collusion* where interlocutors may safely say what they don't mean, and mean what they don't say—and it is here where the gates to the realm of the fantastic open, and where the creation of cultural fantasies and fantasy cultures begins.

Collusion theory is thus very well suited for an understanding of Baldambe's account of the rhetorical emergence of Hamar culture. To bring this out clearly, I will subsequently quote and interpret further episodes of Baldambe's—at times highly mimetic—representation of the conversation between the *bitta* and the people.

Colluding with the *bitta*, the Hamar answer his command saying: "Good, for us you are our *bitta*". Then the *bitta* asks the newcomers one by one from where they come and what they want. They all answer by giving the names of their clans and their country of origin, and add that they want land, as in the following example:

"From where do you come?"
"I am Karla, I come from Kara."
"Eh! What do you want?"
"I want land" (Lydall and Strecker 1979b: 2).

After people have told who they are and from where they have come, the *bitta* asked: "What are your marriage ways?" and then the following dialogue developed:

"Karla and Gulet marry each other. Dila and Gulet marry each other."
"Eh-eh! So you are mother's brothers and sister's sons?"

"We are each others marriage partners, marrying each other we
came."
"*Eh-eh!*"
Then the *bitta* said:
"I have no wife, I would marry a woman."
"Whom will you marry?"
"The people of Gulet who came with Karla will provide my
wife."
"*Eh* good, you marry Gulet girls" (Lydall/Strecker 1979b: 3).

Later on, Baldambe recalls how the *bitta* not only usurped the
land but also the people and their herds.

"Let these people be mine. Your *bitta* am I. Herd cattle for me, herd
goats for me."
"*Bitta!*"
"*Woi!*"
"We don't have any cattle, only a few clans have cattle, only a
few men have some What shall we do?"
"You have now cows?"
"We have no cows."
"You have no goats?"
"Only one or two men have goats. Most of us are poor."
"If you are poor collect loan cattle and cultivate your fields so you
can bring sorghum to those who own cattle. Herding the cows drink
their milk."

Upon this follows a passage where the *bitta* promises to
protect the Hamar against their enemies, sickness and drought.
So, according to Baldambe, people began to collect animals and
then said to each other:

"The poor should not go down to the waterhole with nothing. The
bitta told us that those who have cattle should share some of
them, calling those they give cattle to, *bel* (bond-friend)."
"Whose cattle are these?"
"These are the cattle of so-and-so."
"And yours?"
"I have a cow from a *bel*, an arrow from which I drink."

Here, for the first time a figure comes in, a metonymic expression, which Baldambe is quick to explain as follows:

> "A cow from a *bel* is called 'arrow' because one takes the blood letting arrow to draw blood from the jugular vein of the cow, and mixing four cups of blood with one cup of fresh milk, one feeds the children."

Then Bladambe continues to imitate how the people spoke to each other:

> "Whose cattle are these?"
> "They are the hair of so-and-so."

As this exchange yet again makes use of a figure, this time a synecdoche, Baldambe enlightens the listening ethnographer by saying:

> "That means, they belong to so-and-so like his hair belongs to his head."

No mode of subsistence comes as natural as we may think, even the consumption of grain and its products may need persuasion, like the following example shows, where the *bitta* encourages the people to practice agriculture. Note how he uses the rhetorical figure of *analogy* to convince the people that sorghum is edible:

> "Dig fields. When you have done that, here is the sorghum. *Barjo* [creator, creative power] has given us sorghum. Sorghum is man's grass. As cows eat grass so shall man eat sorghum. *Barjo* gave us meat and milk of cattle long ago, saying: 'Drink milk of cattle and goats and eat their meat. Cattle and goats shall chew leaves from the bushes and cattle shall graze grass'" (Op. Cit.: 7).

Figuration increases when discourse reaches into the realms of social relations, morality, ethics and—in a way—also magic. One can see this very clearly in Baldambe's account of the rhetoric relating to marriage procedures. People addressed the *bitta* asking him about the proper way to marry:

"Some men are bad and troublesome, always beating their wives and then abandoning them. *Bitta*, tell us what to do."

The *bitta* replied:

"A man of Gulet should become a 'butter man'. When the country is dry and there is no butter, cow dung and the dung of sheep shall become butter" (Lydall and Strecker 1979b: 6).

Here the "moral imagination" (Fernandez 2009) of the Hamar increasingly makes use of figuration and expresses the wish to cause well-being by using butter and if this is not available by using appropriate symbolic substitutes like cow dung or the dung of sheep. These are, as David Sapir would say, metonyms that express one cause by way of another, or cause for effect (efficient for final cause), container for contained, and such variants as instrument for agent, agent for act, etc. (Sapir 1977: 19-20). There is also analogy involved, for a marriage should be fertile, should produce offspring, should lead to abundance, should be rich like—yes what?—like butter.

Baldambe goes on to say that for a marriage ceremony a cattle gateway has to be erected. This is, of course, again a trope. Gateways refer to the act of entering or leaving and therefore can express an important aspect of marriage, the fact that a new period of life will begin, and that the bride will leave her home to join her husband's family. In addition Baldambe mentions that a right-handed bowl should be used in the ceremony. Here one would expect that right-handedness is saturated with the figurative meanings observed and analyzed by Hertz (1909), Rodney Needham and others (1973) long ago. That is, physical right-handedness expresses social righteousness, the will to do what is morally right and according to custom.

To show how figuration inescapably leads into the realm of the fantastic I quote Baldambe once again at length as he lets the people instruct the 'butter man' how to perform a proper marriage:

Here is the bowl, if a *maz* [neophyte] comes to you rub him with butter. Before this, the girl should take the headdress of the *maz* and throw it into a *giri* tree and the *maz* should lap milk from a cow's udder saying: 'From now on I will never again lap milk from a cow's udder.' Then they should come to the 'butter man' and put four sorghum rolls in his bowl. Let the girl bite the sorghum first and you, the *maz*, bite second. Next, butter shall be put on to the hands of the girl and the boy and they shall rub each other's hands. After this the girl shall take the belt from the waist of the boy, and he shall take the string skirt from the girl and they shall put them into the bowl. Finally the boy shall take the string skirt and the girl the belt and they shall return home. From now on for good or bad they will never leave each other. There will be no divorce, it is forbidden. Whether they bear children or not they will always remain together until the grave (Lydall and Strecker 1979b: 6-7).

All the strange objects, substances and actions mentioned above—the butter, the head dress, the *giri* tree, lapping milk from a cow's udder, the number four, the sorghum rolls, the exchange of the belt and the string skirt—carry symbolic meanings that express, as Dan Sperber has said, "a commonality of interest but not of opinion" (1975: 137). That is, the bewildering "displacements" (Sperber 1975) or "artful placements" (Strecker 1988) we are witnessing in the ritual prescriptions for the 'butter man' are the work of figurative imagination aiming at getting things done in the world. Or, to put it differently, they are a product of rhetoric, which in turn is hard to distinguish from magic.

Anthropological theory holds that magic "is based on the belief that both nature and man can be brought under compulsion and controlled by psychological means," and that art (including all forms of figuration) has a magical quality too, for "when we say that we are 'under the spell' of beauty or great music, or call a view of a work of art 'magical', we are acknowledging the existence of magic, in the extended sense of non-rational, emotional and often unconscious formalizing or patterning forces, which are essential for all transcendent experience" (Huxley 1966: 264-265).

This goes well with Kenneth Burke's observation that the magical use of symbolism to affect natural processes by rituals and incantations can be understood as a kind of transference where the hortatory use of language "to induce action in people" is extended to a magical practice that aims "to induce motion in things" (Burke 1950: 45).

In other words, the use of symbols is indistinguishable from magic. The rhetorical will creates, as it were, figurative express-ions that act as means of inward and outward persuasion and lead to fantasies of power, of powers that are able to control not just single objects and events but even the whole cosmos, not just individual actions of people but even their whole destiny. Thus, after they have completed all necessary ritual actions under the supervision and with the blessing of the "butter man", Hamar husbands and wives "will always remain together until the grave".

To round off this essay let me now return to some of my earlier thoughts about the art of figuration, which might be of relevance here. As I have said above, the objects, substances and actions mentioned in Baldambe's outline of a Hamar marriage ceremony appear to be in some way "displaced". They have their proper places in other domains and other context of the order of things in Hamar. People know of these placements, and they also know that other people know of them as well. Given this shared background knowledge about the practical order of things, people may then deliberately place things where they—strictly speaking—do not belong. Here people do on an action level what they also often do on a verbal level. Metaphors, for example, are created in a similar way, for they bring together terms that belong to different semantic domains (see Sapir 1977: 6).

But not every kind of displacement has the potential to carry figurative or symbolic meaning. Only "artful" displacements engage mind and emotion, and in *The Social Practice of Symbolization* (1988) I have used the displacement of sand to illustrate how a particular displacement may have the power to lead to rich fields of culture specific evocation. My argument went as follows:

In one episode of the Hamar rite of transition in which a young man leaps across the cattle in order to be allowed to marry, the initiate enters a gully and is 'washed' with sand. Baldambe has described this as follows:

> Then he [the initiate] runs off, over to a gully, a *barjo* (creation, creator) gully which he and his washer [ritual assistant] enter. The washer washes the *ukuli* [initiate] with sand, sand, sand, sand, his head, his back and his front. He washes away all badness. He washes away all that was bad in his childhood, his intercourse with donkeys and relatives, saying: "May all go away with the flood of the gully". Then they step out of the gully and run to the homestead (Lydall and Strecker 1979b: 81).

Now, why was sand used here? I have answered this question by pointing out that in light of the culturally specific experiences and memories of the Hamar, the displacement of sand (from the river-bed on to the naked body of the initiate) at the particular moment when it occurs in the ritual can be understood as a successful move to create symbolic condensation. The condensation entailed in the displacement is in turn achieved through multiple forms of figuration as follows:

> The displacement may be interpreted (by actors and ethno-graphers alike) in terms of *metaphor*, for the mountains of Hamar contain much quartz which makes the sand in the dry river beds look very light, and after each flood the sand is washed anew, getting a strikingly fresh, white and 'virgin-like' appearance. Thus, the sand in a dry riverbed is an impressive example of something recently cleaned. The flood removes filth; it erases all traces of human and animal use so that ... the sand of an untouched

riverbed epitomizes any physically clean state and any kind of erasure of past states of pollution, which one has observed in the world. And this metaphorical extension also reaches into the social and moral realm so that one can say that in the ritual the initiate is brought into contact with sand in order to become socially as unpolluted as the untouched sand in a dry river-bed (Strecker 1988: 216).

Furthermore, "Watching the sand being *poured* over the body of the initiate, one may say that the sand is poured *like* water. Sand, resembling water in that it is pourable, would thus stand metaphorically for water". One could go on to argue, using a synecdochial mode of thought, that the sand may be seen as a part standing for a whole. In Hamar the mixture of sand and water is a widely used cleaning agent, the abrasive part of which is the sand. Knowing of no other technical term, I suggest we call the replacement of a mixture (sand and water) by one of its components (sand) an 'ingrediental' synecdoche. The replacement of a mixture by a component has what Sapir calls a 'particularizing' character, like the replacement of a whole by a part in the anatomical mode, and the replacement of genus by species in the taxonomical mode of synecdoche (see Sapir 1977: 13).

Note that the use of only water would been a much weaker displacement here, "because it would not have evoked the emphatic (abrasive) removal of dirt. In fact it is the very absence of water, which counts. The absence of water makes the displacement "speak" and provokes one to enter the metaphorical realm where physical acts and agents make one think of non-physical referents—for example, social and moral purification (see Strecker 1988: 216-217).

One could add further figurative meanings to the displacement of sand, but I think the examples given above are already persuasive enough to suggest that "the analogies which are possible, which make sense in the context of the situation, are not only multiple but also condense into one general intended meaning. It is this condensation, which makes displacement such a powerful tool of intention and here lies both the artfulness and the effectiveness of symbolism (see Strecker 1988: 217).

By way of conclusion

As the saying goes, "ethnography is stranger than fiction", or at least it may acquire qualities that outdo fiction in that ethnography may lead us into patterns of signification—or better of fantasy—which we could not possibly imagine at home, for even our dreams are constrained by cultural conventions (B. Tedlock, ed. 1989). Who on earth would think, for example, that one would need to leap over a row of cattle in order to ensure a successful and fertile marriage, and that before doing so one would have to be purified by means of sand poured over one's back and shoulders?

As my ethnographic examples have shown, the Hamar themselves understand very well that culture is the product of rhetoric, emerging as a continuous process of mutual persuasion, and they are also aware of the fact that culture involves figuration, that is the use of tropes which open the gates to the realm of the fantastic, the mysterious, the magical.

'Face' and the person

'Face' in the theory of politeness

The concept of 'face' has come to play an important role in politeness theory. Brown and Levinson (1978; 1987), for example, have chosen it as the central notion for their study of universals in language usage and politeness phenomena. They have paraphrased 'face' as the public self-image that every member wants to claim for himself (1978). However, obviously they prefer 'face' to 'public self-image', for throughout their text they almost exclusively use the term 'face', only occasionally mentioning 'public self-image'.

Brown and Levinson (1978: 66) say that they have derived the notion of 'face' from Ervin Goffman and "from the English folk term which ties face up with notions of being embarrassed or humiliated, or 'losing face'". In the process of their analysis they have come to distinguish between negative face and positive face, which they have defined as follows:

(a) Negative face: the basic claim to territories, personal preserves, rights to non-distinction i.e. to freedom of action and freedom from imposition.

(b) Positive face: the positive consistent self-image or 'personality' (crucially including the desire that this self-image be appreciated and approved of) claimed by interactants.

That is, negative face and positive face may be expressed as wants. Negative face: the want of every 'competent adult member' that his actions be unimpeded by others. Positive face: the want of every member that his wants be desirable to at least some others.

In the 1987 reissue of their work, the authors have stressed the abstractness of these definitions. They say that central to their theory is a "highly abstract notion of 'face' which consists of two specific kinds of desires ('face wants') attributed by interactants to one another; the desire to be unimpeded in one's actions (negative face), and the desire (in some respects) to be approved of (positive face)" (Brown and Levinson, 1987: 13). I think the emphasis on abstractness here is misleading. Firstly, the definitions of 'face' given above are hardly abstract but, on the contrary, very concrete. People want to be respected (unimpeded) and loved (approved of). Secondly, by stressing abstractness, Brown and Levinson run the risk of forgetting that 'face' is, after all, not an 'etic' but an 'emic' category and should be studied as such.

'Face' is "a metaphor we live by", as Lakoff and Johnson (1980) would say. It allows us, actors and observers alike, to grasp some essentials of politeness phenomena. It evokes the danger inherent in social interaction, the possibility of threat and assault on one's social standing or personal integrity and, above all, it reminds us of the fact that social vulnerability is mutual. As Brown and Levinson (1978: 66) have pointed out, everyone has face and "everyone's face depends on everyone else's being maintained, and since people can be expected to defend their faces if threatened, and if defending their own, to threaten other's faces, it is in general in every participant's best interest to maintain each other's face".

The insight into this kind of reciprocal interest and the co-operation which it generates lie at the heart of Brown and Levinson's theory of politeness and have inspired their brilliant analysis of the strategies by which various forms of face-threatening acts (FTAs) can be performed. However, abstractness has played little role in this. Rather, the authors have used the metaphor of 'face' to think through the dialectics of politeness and then have transformed this metaphor into a series of subsequent ones. This helped them to define positive and negative face, that is, metaphors of action (claim), of legal and spatial domains (territory, preserve), of appearance (image) and of evaluation (appreciation, approval).

Brown and Levinson do not characterize their analyses as consisting of a transformation or extension of a powerful initial "root metaphor" (Turner 1975). Rather they stress, as I have said, that their notion of face is highly abstract. Also, when they ask the question of how different cultural notions of face can be studied, they think first and foremost of the different ways in which FTAs may be performed, and how the parameters and variables within their scheme of politeness strategies may be differently utilized in different cultures. They ask, "what the exact limits are to personal territories, and what the publicly relevant content of personality consists in" (1978: 66-67), and "how confrontations or shamings are managed, how people gossip... how they clear their name from disparagement, and how face regard (and sanctions for face disregard) are incorporated in religious and political systems" (1987: 14). Their discussion of interactional ethos is also along these lines. They note that in some societies the ethos of interaction is friendly, warm and easy going, while in others it is distant, stiff and irksome. In some societies people are allowed, even encouraged, to show off and brag, while in others they must be deferential and modest, and so on. The task of cross-cultural studies of politeness is, as Brown and Levinson have convincingly shown, to describe and explain such cultural variations in the performance of FTAs.

Yet, there is also another and closely related task. Brown and Levinson (1987: 14) have mentioned it in some very suggestive lines. They have said, for example, that "notions of face naturally link up to some of the most fundamental cultural ideas about the social person," and they have called for "more in the way of ethnographic descriptions of the way in which people articulate face notions."

However, they have never spelt out clearly what a truly cross-cultural analysis of variations of the metaphor 'face' would look like. The face is a very significant part of the human body. As such it is part of a universal analogical repertoire, which can be used for metaphorical production in all cultures. How is this repertoire actualized? Do all cultures use 'face' as a metaphor, or is 'face' not universal? What are the cultural variations of face metaphors? Which features of the face are stressed when people think and speak of 'face', and what do the varieties of 'face' tell us about the cultures and societies in which they occur? Surely, these are interesting questions and must be part of any cross-cultural study of politeness. Furthermore, if there are differences, even striking differences, in the ways in which people conceptualize 'face', will these differences not illuminate a common ground? Will a comparative study of 'face' not enhance our understanding of politeness phenomena in a similar way as our folk term 'face' first inspired Brown and Levinson? The more metaphorical meanings of 'face' we know, the better we will be equipped to think about a general theory of politeness.

The coercive power of 'face'

I will present a specific cultural variation of 'face', that is, the Hamar concept of *woti* below. But before I do so, let me say a few things about the way I understand our own metaphor of 'face'.

I think that the evocative power of 'loss of face' derives from a clever exploitation of conceptual part-whole relationships. The first is a synecdoche: a significant part of a person, that is, the face with which one faces others (or which one hides from others) is taken to represent the whole person, that is, the whole character, social standing, moral values, etc. Then, in turn, a single act or single acts are used as an index where metonymically an effect stands for a cause. A bad deed, it is said, reflects a bad person; a bad result reflects a bad cause.

Or, to see the same thing synecdochically, a bad part (morally bad act) represents a bad whole (bad person). Thus, when people warn each other not to risk loss of face by doing this or the other, they say implicitly that there will be people who track back the path of the synecdoche contained in the notion of 'face'. The unspoken argument is: if you do not do what is publicly expected of you, then you will lose your face and will be declared bad *in toto*. This totalizing effect seems to be the central motive of the metaphor 'loss of face'.

Also, if 'face' is a supreme value and everyone in the social hierarchy has 'face' and is forced to 'save face', then this must necessarily strengthen the status quo. Thus 'face' acts in favour of existing social inequalities. It binds people to their different domains in the social hierarchy. All those who would perhaps like more freedom, fewer impositions, more opportunities to be admired and held in esteem by others are restricted by 'face' and are inhibited from aspiring to anything lying outside the confines of their narrow and conventionally defined realm of action.

'Face', then, is a coercive social concept and indirectly speaks of social chains. Because you have 'face', you always have to be afraid of losing it. This feature of 'fear of loss' is shared with a number of other terms used to express the social worthiness of a person. But interestingly, one does not have a 'sense of face' nor does one compete for 'face' as one does for honour and also for 'name', fame, regard, esteem or respect. This comes out most clearly in the fact that one does not qualify anyone's 'face' as being 'great', 'high', 'rich', etc. One cannot accumulate and compete for it. There are many more facets to 'face' that need to be explored. But here I want to mention only one more feature that plays a significant role in our understanding of 'face'. When we speak of 'face', we envisage the central part of the face. We see especially the mouth and the eyes, which are so prone to reveal a person's inner feelings, often even against one's own will. For us, 'face' is closely associated with the self, with inner feelings, emotions and desires, and with cultural notions of sin, guilt and shame.

The Hamar

The Hamar of southern Ethiopia are the southernmost group of Omotic speaking peoples (see Bender 1976). They number between fifteen to twenty thousand people and practice a mixed economy based on pastoralism (goats, sheep, cattle), agriculture (sorghum, maize, various beans etc.), apiculture, gathering, hunting and raiding. Settlements are dispersed, and their location is usually chosen as a compromise between the need to be near the fields (slash and burn cultivations in the bush), near a waterhole, and near good and healthy pasture.

Within a settlement area there will be a number of home-steads, varying considerably in number (from less than ten to more than thirty), but each homestead always follows the same layout and consists of a cattle kraal, goat enclosure and one or more houses, which belong to the married women, who, with their husbands, jointly own the herds.

The homestead is often inhabited by a widowed mother and some of her sons and their wives, or by a group of siblings under the ritual authority of the oldest brother. Descent is patrilineal, but lineages are shallow. There are twenty-four clans, which again are divided in two moieties (see Lydall and Strecker 1979b). Also, their territory is divided by one basic division, one part of the country being under the ritual authority of a man from the clan Gatta and the other under a man from the clan Worla. Each half of the territory is again split into segments, which have, however, no single ritual functionary responsible for them as a whole.

Although the Hamar practice a mixed economy, they do not rely on all the different resources in the same way. Most important for their survival are the goats, and they themselves stress that goat husbandry is the backbone of their economy: *Kuli edi zani ne*, people with goats are like ropes or leather straps; their life is well secured, it will not snap". The management of goats inhibits the formation of large corporate social groups and encourages individualism with much spatial mobility. Goat herds always fluctuate in size and, above all, allow a quick build up. One does not need the cooperation of different age groups and generations as one does to build up herds of cattle or camels. The management of goats is more efficiently carried out by small and largely independent units, which perhaps in crisis lend each other support, but do not have to cooperate continuously over any length of time. The individualism of goat herding is deeply ingrained in Hamar culture and has led to a very thorough rejection of authority. True, the Hamar *donza*, that is, the married men who are the basic agents of Hamar politics, have delegated some responsibilities of decision making to individuals. First, there is the hereditary office of the two *bitta*, who are ritually responsible for the health, safety and general well-being of the Hamar. Then there are the *gudili*, who look after the well-being of the fields, the *kogo*, who bless the homesteads, the *jilo*, who magically lead dangerous enterprises like raiding or hunting, and there are the *ayo*, who have been elected to speak in public for their respective territorial segments. But the Hamar watch these men carefully, and the closer an office is to any truly political activity, the more the *donza* are ready to check their ambition for power.

Terms referring to the persona

If one wants to understand the Hamar concept of 'face', it is best to look at the wider semantic field of which it is a part. There are several Hamar terms that refer to the persona. I outline them here, before turning to 'face' itself.

Barjo ('good fortune')

In Hamar, the most important aspect of the persona is its *barjo*. *Barjo* may be defined as a concept of continuous creation. According to the Hamar, creation goes on continuously in the world, and human beings have an active part to play in it. Every living being needs *barjo* to exist and achieve its natural state of well-being. Even such phenomena as clouds, rain, the stars, etc. need to have their *barjo* to appear in a regular and ordered way.

People can actively engage in producing and augmenting the *barjo* of people, animals, plants, the soil, the seasons, etc., by calling *barjo*. Here is an abridged version of such a *barjo aela*:

> *Eh-eh!* The herds are carrying sickness
> May the sickness go beyond Labur, may it go,
> Cattle owners you have enemies,
> May the Korre who looks at our cattle, die, die,
> May his heart get speared, get speared,
> *Eh-eh!* My herds which are at Mello,
> May my herds come lowing, come,
> May the girls blow the flutes, blow,
> May the women dance, dance
> May the men rest, rest
> (Lydall and Strecker 1979b: 14-15).

Both men and women have *barjo*, but only the *donza* call *barjo* in the emphatic and stylized way of the example given above. Women call *barjo* in a quiet and unobtrusive way, for example, by sweeping the entrance to their goat enclosure and by putting on a belt that is decorated with cowry shells. As one old woman once told me, she causes others to be well (have *barjo*) simply by wishing them well; she does not need any words for this.

The Hamar elders, on the other hand, stress that they need to meet and chant together in order to call forth *barjo*. They carry their own *barjo* with them wherever they go, and whenever it seems necessary to cause well-being, they get together and call *barjo*. Often they delegate the leading part of the chanting to men who act in a specific office, for example, as *gudili* (guardian of the fields), *kogo* (guardian of the fires of the homesteads) or *bitta* (guardian of all of Hamar country). When older and younger brothers are present, it is always the older one who leads the chanting.

By means of the *barjo aela* the elders try to exercise control over each other and especially over women and children. It is the old who call *barjo* for the young, and it is the men who call *barjo* for the women, not vice versa. But having said this, one needs to stress that the concept of *barjo* and the practices associated with it lack any competitive or aggressive element. People never do anything great and outrageous to achieve *barjo*, nor do they boast about their *barjo*. In fact, the concept is of such a kind that the greater anyone's *barjo* is, the more that person will be harmonious, non-aggressive, non-competitive and non-problematic. Anyone who has great *barjo* will be able to act well, will not collide with others and will be agreeable in the eyes of others and his (or her) own.

Now, if the Hamar concept of the persona is grounded in the concept of *barjo*, then it is interesting to view *barjo* from the viewpoint of politeness theory. If every adult member of Hamar society claims *barjo* for himself, and if the Hamar are concerned to call *barjo* for each other, does this not mean that they are constantly attending to their negative and positive "face wants" (as defined by Brown and Levinson)?

Their desire to be unimpeded by others (negative face) is expressed in terms of *barjo*. Often I have heard people say to each other, *"issa barjon saesan gara"* (Don't spoil my good fortune).

To claim *barjo* for oneself is the supreme expression of a Hamar's want for freedom of action, or more precisely, for the potential to act or simply exist freely. The calling of *barjo* for others is, on the other hand, a most emphatic form of positive politeness. Those who get blessed are positively attended to and assured of their intrinsic social value.

Nabi ('name')

The Hamar concept of *nabi* closely resembles our literal and figurative use of the term 'name'. Like 'face', the metaphor 'name' acts by exploiting a part-whole relationship (see my analysis of 'face' above). The name is an intrinsic part of a person, and the social worthiness of a person accumulates in the name. To have a good name is like being a good person; to have a bad name is like being a bad person. In this way 'name' in our own culture and *nabi* in the culture of the Hamar can be used for coercive rhetoric, which is very much like the rhetoric of 'face' and honour. If you do not behave properly, you run the risk of losing your good name.

'Name' already acquires some coercive force by the simple fact that by giving a name to someone, one usually implies the recognition of her or his social value. Naming is equivalent to valuing! People are given names in order to be or become socially valuable.

Typically, in Hamar, people are given several names during the course of their life cycle, each name signifying some specific aspect of their persona. Also, the giving of a new name is always associated with blessing. You are blessed to become worthy and great like a big mountain, like Mount Bala, as the Hamar say. This blessing is an emphatic act of positive politeness, but it is also coercive in that a person is named and given a value precisely to enter the social domain and aspire to social worthiness. The name is given in order that the owner may guard, keep and enhance it and fulfil all the social expectations that are connected with it.

Michere ('whipping wand')

In the same way as the Hamar may say, "Don't spoil my *barjo*" or "Don't spoil my name", they also say, "Don't spoil my whipping wand".

The whipping wand is the most significant tool for herding in Hamar. It is long, light and flexible and ideally suited to act as an extension of the arm of the herdsman, or, more often, the herding boy or girl. "At the nose of the whipping wand there is butter," goes the saying, and indeed in the long run, no survival would be possible if the Hamar did not manage to use their whips well. You can herd cattle and camels with sticks, but for small livestock you need the whipping wand, especially for the goats who tend to spread as each goat wanders off to satisfy its individual taste. Sheep are easier to handle because they tend to stay together in a close group, but goats need constant attention. The art of herding, then, involves the voice (all sorts of hissing, whistling, shouting, singing), gestures (especially with the arms) and the whipping wand, which is used not only as an extension of the arm but also as an extension of the voice, because one can produce a variety of sharp noises with the whip and can use it to hit the ground, leaves, grass, branches, and thus attract the attention of the goats and lead them in the desired direction.

As goats provide the backbone of the Hamar economy (see above), and as the whipping wand is the most important tool for herding the goats, it is understandable that the use of the whipping wand has, to some extent, been ritualized, and has been metaphorically exploited to speak of the social wants of the person.

The ritualization already begins in such small acts as when a father hands a new whipping wand to his son in the morning. He usually does this after some accident has happened, for example, a goat may have been lost or eaten by a hyena. After such ill luck, the father hands a new whipping wand to the herding boy, who then uses it throughout the day, and in the evening, when the whole herd has entered the homestead safely, places it over the gateway of the goat enclosure. As time goes by, many dry old whips accumulate here and grow into a big bundle, which is evidence of the problems of looking after the herd and how those problems were overcome. Further forms of ritualization are found in the rites of passage into manhood (Lydall and Strecker 1979b: 76, 83) and in the burial rites (ibid: 41, 57).

The whipping wand, however, is not only a tool to herd animals; it is also a tool to control people. Typically, boys and young men shift their attention away from the goats and cattle when they come to the homesteads, the fields and the water holes, where they meet girls with whom they flirt. Then they express their liking for the girls not so much in sweet words but in mock assaults in which they use the whipping wands in their gestures of attack. Later, when they have married, men sometimes use their whips in earnest in order to subdue their wives. Men use the whip towards women but not vice versa, except during the harvest celebrations when women mockingly whip men. The degree to which its use is based on provocation comes out most clearly in the ritual of manhood, where the girls (possible future wives) provoke the initiates (their possible future husbands) to whip them in public (see Gardner 1972; Leach 1976: 48; Lydall and Strecker 1979b: 45, Lydall 1994).

Men also use the whip on other men. This begins as early as childhood when older brothers often threaten or actually hit their younger brothers with the whips, which they are constantly carrying. Later in life, youths may sometimes be severely whipped by their 'older brothers' (men senior to them) as a punishment for some offence like thieving or going on a raid without the consent of the elders. The elders (*donza*), however, are never whipped, but punished by other means, for example, by the fine of an animal.

This asymmetry in the use of the whip is ritually expressed in an institution called 'whipping wand' (*michere*). Every year, shortly after the crops in the fields have ripened and the young men have, as the Hamar say, become so well fed that they question the authority of their seniors, the 'older brothers' get together, equip themselves with bundles of fresh whipping wands and chase after the most provocative youths in order to beat them. After they have caught them (some of them) and have given them a real or token beating, the men are served food and drink in the fields by the women (some of them the proud mothers of the delinquents), and there is much talk, feasting and fun where the general authority of the senior men is asserted. In older days, when the Hamar age-set organization was still functioning, ritual whipping of young men also occurred at the formation of each new age-set.

In a sense we can speak here of the expression of negative face wants, that is, the want to be unimpeded by others (see above). Note that here the one who has been threatened defends himself by using an off-record strategy which hides his personal interest behind a metaphor. Here the metaphor of *michere*, in other contexts the notion of *barjo*, and, as I will show below, in still other situations, the metaphors of a*pho* ('word'), *dumai* ('big toe') and *woti* ('forehead') are used to speak indirectly about one's claim to be unimpeded by others.

Apho ('word')

In order to show how the notion of *barjo*, the institutionalized whipping and the Hamar concept of the word (*apho*) all tie up in one single social practice, let me quote the following two statements:

> Now it is time for the herds to leave for the distant grazing area. The elders hold a meeting where they bring their whips and whip the young men: "What are you doing here, lazy fellows, go and herd the cattle. Look the Korre are coming, the Galeba are coming. Go and look after the herds." So they whip them and then they call *barjo* and hand a whip to the spokesman of the new age group: "Take it, herd the cattle with it and when any man talks badly or works badly hit him with this whip." The new spokesman is an intelligent youth who can talk well (Lydall and Strecker 1979b: 124-25).

> So the fellow draws forth service. Such a man is an *ayo*. If those who go don't kill the giraffe, the buffalo, the lion, the ostrich, the leopard, but if they meet the enemy and one of them dies, it will be said: "His word is bad, his command is bad. Stop him."

And he will be stopped from taking command. Someone else will be selected to take his place (Op. Cit.: 109)

The two texts show how in Hamar the word and the whip are given to exercise authority, but both your whip and word will only be accepted by others if they lead to good fortune. Only a person with great and strong *barjo* can be a leader (*ayo*). If his *barjo* is weak, then his word will cause bad luck for those who listen to it. One can often hear in Hamar the statement, *"apho barjo tau"* (The word is *barjo*). The Latin proverb *nomen est omen* comes to mind, and the almost universal belief in the magical power of words. The word is always a very critical extension of the persona, and it inescapably affects both the speaker and the world around her/him.

The ultimate expression of this mode of thinking is the Hamar *barjo aela*, which I have described above. Here the human voice is used to invoke well-being. In a continuous process of giving and receiving *barjo*, people bless each other by means of their inherent power of speech. As speech is such an intrinsic part of people's social and moral being, it also lends itself for the production of metaphors that refer to the social and moral side of a person. When the Hamar say *"apho issa saesan gara"* (Don't spoil my word), they do not mean this literally but think of much more complex meanings like, "don't spoil the good influence which my words usually have on the world", "don't interfere with my will", "don't attack my *persona*."

When the Hamar judge each other and assess their respective social values, they constantly refer to the sincerity or insincerity of a person's word, and to whether it is truthful or false. They say *"apho kissa tipha ne"* (His word is straight), or *"apho kissa koara ne"* (His word is bent). Typical attributes used for judgement are:

Positive:	**Negative:**
gon (true)	*budamo* (false)
daetsa (heavy)	*sholba* (light)

> *durphi* (fat)   *gancha* (meagre)
> *kadji* (cool)   *oidi* (hot)

As speaking is such a significant social activity, to speak truthfully is like being a good person, and to speak falsely is like being a bad person. No wonder then that in Hamar *apho* has been exploited for metaphoric production and has received a meaning which pertains to the whole person.

Dumai ('big toe')

It may sound odd that the Hamar consider the big toe and, by extension, the shin as important aspects of the persona. But a brief moment of reflection is enough to grasp the logic of this train of thought: the Hamar move constantly on foot through difficult terrain. When they go to their fields, when they follow their herds, when they go scouting or hunting or raiding, it is extremely important that they do not hurt their feet and legs. But there are many thorns, hard pieces of wood or sharp stones, on which people hurt themselves even if they are careful and experienced (see Strecker 1979a: 175). Therefore, people are very much aware of the importance of their feet and legs and the need to keep them safe from damage.

"May your path be free (of obstacles)" is one of the ways in which the Hamar wish each other well. Also, when they call *barjo*, they wish each other to move like baboons, for baboons move lightly and never hurt themselves as human beings do (see 1979a: 3). The big toe is thus, in practical terms, a very significant part of the body, and it makes sense that the Hamar have used it as a metaphor of a person's competence and freedom of action. But there is also more to it, an almost magical element, which is also present in the notion of *barjo* and in the metaphors of 'whipping wand' and 'word', but which comes out more clearly here. In order to demonstrate the thinking which is associated with the *dumai* ('shin' in general, 'big toe' in particular) let me quote directly from my notebook:

Lalombe, Makonnen's older brother, tells me without me asking more than what the name for 'big toe' is: "The right big toe is very bad (that is, very good). It leads you to success, to success in raiding, in hunting and so on. Your right big toe is fat. If I go to visit a homestead and my big toe hits hard against an obstacle on the path, then I ask myself whether the homestead will be well. If I stumble with my left foot I will meet well-being, much food and good fortune. If I stumble with my right foot this will lead me to suffering, lack of food and misfortune. When I encounter such obvious bad luck or good luck I say to myself, isn't it the stumbling which has caused this affair?"

Lalombe does something here, which is typical for the Hamar: he not only speaks of a predictive sign but also of a cause for bad (or good) luck. When he stumbles on his way, he does not know whether the stumbling initiates anything. Only when he arrives at his destination and finds there that he is not welcome, or that there is simply nothing to eat and drink, or that people are sick or have died, does he say, "Things are bad here because I have stumbled".

What is happening here? I think Lalombe is playing a rhetorical game that helps him uphold the illusion of his power and competence. To be part of a situation where misfortune has occurred is always in some way damaging, even to the witness who may not be directly concerned. Therefore it makes sense to develop strategies that help one to escape or at least cover up one's helplessness. What Lalombe does is to exploit the ambiguity inherent in language. More precisely, he exploits the lack of deictic clarity that characterizes much of everyday speech. For a sentence to be deictically clear one needs an anchorage of space, time and actor action.

In "Isn't it the stumbling which brought about the affair?" there is an ambiguity about the relationship between time, action and place. This comes out most clearly when one visualizes the three domains involved in the sentence: the person, the obstacle and the destination with its good or bad luck. It remains an open question whether the speaker is conceptually separating three domains or is thinking of two domains where either the hitting of the obstacle or the meeting good or bad luck are merged into one domain. Finally, he may not distinguish between any domains at all, thus merging time, space and action in an unspecified way.

The person, the obstacle and the house in these figures are both separate and related entities. Lalombe alludes to some necessary connection between all the three entities as soon as some significant lack of control has occurred. Stumbling is involuntary; it escapes one's control, and like the twitching of a part of the body often 'tells' something. And so does the prosperity and well-being of others towards whom one is heading. Will their house have coffee? If one goes somewhere and people are not prepared for one, if they lack something, which is essential to the visit, then both parties, the host and the guest, lose out. They allow some weakness to manifest itself. Not only does the host lose in social standing, but so does the guest who wrongly assumed that there would be coffee in his host's house: each has obviously miscalculated the situation.

This is why 'causes' are invented which explain why it is not the people concerned but something else, which has caused the threatening situation, a stick or stone on the path, for example. Those who aspire to influence social standing must never show themselves as being unable to control things. This is why people use strategies of diversion which are ultimately nothing more than strategies of politeness, and which shield them from the critical view of others (and of themselves).

Woti ('face', 'forehead')

I have so far examined the notion of *barjo* and the Hamar metaphors of name (*nabi*), whipping wand (*michere*), word (*apho*) and big toe (*dumai*). *Barjo* is the most general of these concepts. It exists wherever there is well-being, harmony, good-fortune. When well-being disappears, *barjo* has disappeared. Therefore the physical and social health of a person is a direct expression of his or her *barjo*. According to the Hamar, without *barjo* no development and continued existence is possible. This is why the notion of *barjo* is found at the top of the list of all the Hamar concepts related to the persona. Name, whipping wand, word, big toe and, as we will see, also face (*woti*) are nothing but particular manifestations of the general *barjo* of a person.

Which part of the body do the Hamar have in mind when they speak of *woti*, and which are the metaphorical meanings associated with it? When one asks the Hamar to point to their *woti*, they first move their hand up to the forehead and subsequently let it pass down slowly towards the chin. Similarly, the verbal explanations of the term *woti* first focus on the forehead. *Woti* is part of the head as the carrier of the brain. Behind *woti* there lies thought and reflection. Conversely, *woti* is the place where a person's worry and sorrow show, that is, the informed concern for others. Also, *woti* is the part of the body with which you meet and confront others, rather like the goats and cattle that typically meet head on in play and in earnest. Thus, by metaphoric extension, boldness and courage, as well as thought and reflection, are stressed when the Hamar speak of a person's *woti*. The following figure summarizes this argument:

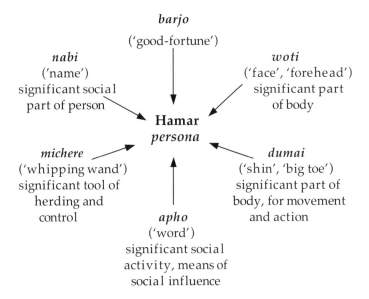

Interestingly there is no Hamar word which focuses, like our word 'face', primarily on the area around the eyes and the mouth, which so easily betrays a person's inner feelings and, concomitantly, can be used to express them. The face of the Hamar is not one that could be hidden behind a veil. *Woti* does not focus on a person's concern for his/her own self but on his/her concern for others. Therefore it is not associated with shame. In fact, the Hamar have no word for 'shame', nor do they have one for 'sin'. What they are concerned with in social life is not to speak of failure but of success, not to humiliate others but to elevate themselves. Theirs is a culture of boasting and not of humility (see Strecker 1988: 87-88, 187).

Everything I have said so far about *barjo*, whipping wand, word and big toe has also pointed in this direction. The Hamar claim freedom of action for themselves. This is what they fight for: *"issa wotin saesan gara"* (Don't spoil my forehead—my 'face!'). The forehead refers here to a person's sphere of action, the world, which he 'faces' and wants to control. The forehead, the word (voice), the whipping wand and the big toe all have a similar directional and outward element. They are metaphors of intention and action. They embody the will to confront, reach, influence and control others. What distinguishes *woti* from the other metaphors mentioned so far is the fact that it lends itself for the celebration of the social worthiness of a person.

In a literal sense the forehead of the Hamar is often anointed in precisely the way Brown and Levinson (1978: 75) have described positive politeness which 'anoints' the face of the addressee by indicating that, in some respects, S wants H's wants, for example, by treating him as a member of an 'in group', a friend, a person whose wants and personality traits are known and liked.

Such anointing of the *woti* is ritually done as a celebration of a man's proof of his competence and courage. In Hamar a man should prove himself before he marries, by hunting dangerous game and/or killing an enemy. Once he has done this, he is applauded, his 'positive face wants' are satisfied and he is ritually anointed. To give a lively and authentic picture of how this ritual celebration of the person is integrated in Hamar life, I quote here at length from a Hamar text:

> Now: "Has so-and-so's child killed a hyena?"
> "He has killed a hyena."
>
> When someone kills a hyena he shaves off all his hair. He takes some pure white paint and smears it on his head. Another person has killed an elephant. He smears red ochre on his forehead. A man who kills a lion puts on red ochre. He who kills a leopard puts on red ochre. When a rhinoceros is killed, red ochre is put on. Red ochre with butter.
>
> "Who's that?"
> "See he has white paint, he has killed a hyena."
>
> The paint is white like hyena shit, it shows, and so the girls know. Another man puts on red ochre and sticks a white feather in his hair. Another, after he had shaved his head, used to put a

smooth plate on his forehead here, with flaps over his ears and white paint on his head. After four days like this he washed off the white paint on his head and put on red ochre. Another had no plate but had a *kalasha*, a white thing made from an elephant tusk and placed on the forehead. At the back of his head is a brass plate. That man has killed an elephant. That one has killed a lion. That one has killed a rhinoceros. That one has killed a man, maybe a Borana, maybe a Korre, maybe a Mursi, maybe a Maale, maybe a Karmit. After he has killed some fierce animal or a man, then:

"Take the *boko* stick".

Otherwise: "*A, a!* I have not killed a hyena, I have not killed a lion, so I will not marry a woman. Only when I have killed a hyena will I marry. Only when I have killed a lion will I marry. Only when I have killed a leopard will I marry. Only when I kill an elephant will I marry" (Lydall and Strecker 1979b: 74).

We can see here how highly the Hamar value their freedom of action. The most emphatic proof of this freedom is to kill. By killing dangerous game or humans who are traditionally the enemies of the herds and social group, men show that they are able to defend their 'basic claim to territories, personal preserves, rights to non-distraction' (see the definition of negative face).

For this achievement they receive (and demand!) the attention of their group, are appreciated and approved of and are blessed and ritually anointed. But their forehead is not only anointed; they may also put on a *kalasha* as the text says. The *kalasha* is an ornament, which used to be worn by men who had killed dangerous game and/or human enemies. It was common among many cultures of southern Ethiopia before the area was conquered by the troops of Emperor Menelik II at the turn of the century. It belonged to the regalia of the old kingdoms of Kaffa, Dauro and Wolamo as well as to Oromo groups like the Borana, and to the Konso and Tsamai (Jensen 1936; Haberland 1963; Baxter 1965).

Interestingly, outside observers have often found it difficult to assert what kind of object the *kalasha* represented. Bartels' comment sums up the situation very well:

E. Haberland speaks without a shadow of doubt always of a phallic ornament (1963: 51, 305). P. T. W. Baxter in his article 'Repetition in certain Borana ceremonies' speaks of a 'white metal horn'. But he assured me personally that the Arsi Oromo gave him only a phallic interpretation. The form of this *kallacha* is, indeed, evidently phallic. For the rest, a symbol can have many associations (Bartels 1983: 146).

For the present purpose it does not matter whether that 'white thing made from an elephant tusk and placed on the forehead' was shaped like a phallus or like a horn. The Hamar use the same word for 'to kill with a spear' and 'to copulate' (*uka* 'stab'), therefore the horn and the phallus must both be viewed as having an element of forcefulness. It is force that is symbolically represented on the forehead, the force to act independently and to such an extent that one is able to destroy or create the life of others.

The English term 'bully' comes to mind, which is derived from 'bull' and speaks of the domineering and self-assertive character of a person. Like a bull, the bully pushes others around, faces them aggressively and incapacitates them. In Hamar this image of facing someone like a bull has fewer negative and many more positive connotations. Indeed, it is part of the general ethos of personal independence and equality. People can only hold equal rights if they are ready and competent to fight for them. Also, everyone concerned must be outward oriented. They must show others what they want and articulate their negative as well as their positive face wants. An egalitarian way of life demands that all the 'equals' expose themselves to each other to a certain extent. No one is allowed to hide behind modesty and mask his/her real competence.

Thus, at their public gatherings and in their public speeches (as well as in their informal conversations) the Hamar often reprimand each other for pretending to be incompetent, in-experienced, not well-informed enough, etc., to act in matters of public concern. In their eyes, false humility is the greatest enemy of equality, and this is why they encourage boasting and self-elevation. Every *donza* should think of himself as great and capable and act accordingly. At the same time, if he fails, if for some reason he does not reach the intended goal, he should not feel guilty or despised.

This is why the Hamar have no concepts of sin, shame or honour. A person should not be inhibited by the fear of losing face if he/she fails. The consequence of failure should only be positive, that is, that the person does not continue doing what he/she is not good at. In Hamar people always make a clear conceptual separation between what someone is and what he/she does. The practice of calling *barjo* is closely related to this: by calling *barjo* people bless each other. They do this especially after conflicts have occurred among them. When a bad deed has been done, it is not the offender who is con-demned, but the deed, and both the offender and the offended are subsequently blessed. No one speaks of 'loss of face', 'shame' or 'sin' in such situations. What counts is the *barjo* of people, that is, their well-balanced and harmonic power to live. If your *barjo* is rich, you will act well. You will be socially competent and able both to assert your own sphere of action as well as to respect the interests of others. The metaphor for this necessary measure of self-assertion and readiness to fight for your rights is the metaphor of *woti*, your forehead.

Conclusion

The picture which I have drawn here of the Hamar notion of 'face' is far from complete. But I think it has become apparent that their 'face' is very different from ours and that this cultural variation is related to variations in social organization. Perhaps it is possible to generalize and formulate an as yet, untested (but testable) hypothesis which says that societies with long lasting social inequalities and asymmetries of power (as in feudalism, monarchism, absolutism) tend to develop concepts of 'face' which focus on the inner self, on a person's feelings of guilt, sin and shame, and conversely, on a person's sense of honour (Bourdieu 1979). Such concepts would logically also focus on the openings of the face, especially the mouth and the eyes.

In egalitarian societies one would, on the other hand, expect a tendency towards concepts of 'face', which do not have an inward but an outward direction and are less concerned with the self than with the other. Such concepts would stress impenetrable parts of the face and would be used as metaphors for unimpeded action and the confrontation of others. Also, while the inward notion would be associated with humility, the outward notion would be associated with assertiveness and culturally controlled ways of boasting. The following table may summarize the argument:

Cultural variations of 'face'

Stratified societies	Egalitarian societies
Responsibilities and opportunities are evenly distributed among men	Responsibilities and opportunities are unevenly distributed among men
Many adult men show humility towards others	Many adult men boast in front of others
Concepts physical face stress penetrable and revealing parts like the mouth and eyes	Concepts physical face stress impenetrable unrevealing parts like the forehead
Metaphors of 'face' stress inwardly directed feelings of guilt, sin and shame, and the need for self-control	Metaphors of 'face' stress outwardly directed want of action and control of others
'Face' motivates negatively as fear of loss of social standing, and constant reminder of the power of the opinion of others	'Face' motivates positively as hope, social gain of freedom of imposition by others

We need, furthermore, to examine the hierarchy and order of the different concepts relating to the *persona* in any particular culture. As we have seen, in Hamar the perception of the person as a socially sensitive being happens first and foremost in terms of *barjo*. *Barjo* is the most general aspect of the person. If I threaten the 'face' (*woti*) of someone I also threaten his *barjo*, but if I threaten someone's *barjo*, this need not necessarily involve his *woti*; the focus may well be on other aspects like, for example, the *nabi* ('name'), *michere* ('whipping wand'), *apho* ('word', 'voice') or the *dumai* ('shin', 'big toe'), which all emphasize different sides of the *persona*.

To me the data from Hamar suggest that if a Hamar were to develop a theory of politeness, he or she would not base it on 'face' and the 'face-threatening act' but would probably speak of the '*barjo*-threatening act'.

As *barjo* is the power of life, the well-being, the good luck and good fortune of a person, this central notion would inspire the Hamar theory of politeness. Also, negative and positive politeness would be expressed in terms of *nabi*. Strategies of negative politeness would say, 'I do not want to threaten your well-being', while strategies of positive politeness, 'I wish you well'.

I find this more widely cast approach, which is inherent in the Hamar concepts relating to politeness, very attractive. It is not moulded by a feudal, monarchic or bourgeois past and is not overburdened by social fear and painful introspection. If one wants a democratic theory and practice in which human rights and the concern for others have a place, then one's thoughts and actions should not be dominated by notions of fear and threat, but should be matched with hope and the confidence that one may have the courage to 'face' others and speak one's mind. Therefore, the Hamar view of politeness phenomena seems to be more timely than our own (and of other 'civilized' societies), which still has to extricate itself from a non-egalitarian past.

Do the Hamar have a concept of honour?

In an interesting essay on honour and shame Unni Wikan has noted that, 'Honour is a word with a very special quality. Unlike most of the words used in anthropology, it holds an alluring, even seductive appeal. I think its spell derives from its archaic and poetic overtones: it harks back to more glorious times when men were brave, honest and principled' (1984: 635). The term honour has certainly a long history and evokes a whole lot of sentiments. Of all the related terms like prestige, esteem, fame, glory, respect, face, name etc., honour is the only one, which allows the phrase, 'she or he has a sense of …'. We speak of a 'sense of honour' (Bourdieu 1979), but we don't speak of anyone's 'sense of name', 'sense of face', 'sense of fame', etc. As the phrase 'sense of' indicates, honour refers particularly closely to a person's inner self. In my native language, German, the nexus between honour and personal sentiment comes out in a similar way. We speak of *Ehrgefühl* (sense of honour) but not of *Ansehensgefühl, Rufgefühl, Gesichtsgefühl*, etc. The latter compound words, though grammatically correct, are semantically unacceptable. From where does the sentimental charge or impact of honour and *Ehre* come? Historical linguists tell us that the ancient Indo-Germanic root *ais* from which *Ehre* derives points out an emotionally charged act of veneration. Some people must have once shown deep reverence to someone or something. They venerated and worshipped and their acts of *ais* were inspired both positively by admiration and negatively by fear. In addition to this there was the act of pleading. People pleaded to those whom they admired and feared. This act of submission to some superior power lies at the heart of the Gothic term *aiza* and the old Greek term *aidos*. Later an interesting change occurred: the concept *ais* moved from the perspective of the honourer to the perspective of the honoured. That is, the Old Saxon term *era*, the Anglo-Saxon term *ar* and the old Nordic *eir* don't speak of veneration and worship anymore. They speak of granting peace instead, and of protection and luck. They embody the beneficent will of superiors towards their dependents, who, by providing peace for others, gained honour for themselves. For them honour was also heavily charged with emotion. The superior who gave peace and protection was proud of his strength and ability. He risked his life for others by doing chivalrous deeds, and therefore he received glory, fame, praise and all the wonderful attention, which makes the heart beat faster.

The Roman use of *honos* and *honestum*, which later was strongly coloured by *era*, *ar* and *eir*, involved yet a third party. This third party was the public, which judged the performance of the honourer and the honoured. *Honos* was a result of virtue: persons who adhered to the publicly defined and sanctioned code of morals were also publicly honoured (given *gloria, decus, reverentia*). This public attribution of social worthiness was eminently political because it was the basis on which people were granted political offices. The holding of an office in turn led to that strong personal sense of socially accepted dignity which in European culture has been a defining element of honour until today.

In the past, the concept of honour like its counterpart *Ehre* was always emotionally charged. To varying degrees, three different parties were involved in the process: the honourer, the honoured and the public. Unni Wikan is right when she speaks of the allure of honour, but when we meet that word, we do not just project our ideas of a heroic past onto it. Rather, the term honour has always spoken, and speaks still today, of contexts in which sentiments play an important part. Honour is not simply a detached anthropological category. It is not an observer category but an actor category, which evolved under specific social conditions and had its function in specific places and times.

What are the conditions that give rise to the concept of honour and in what kind of social formations does honour have a place? These are the questions we should try to answer. But to do so we need a general and historical theory of the formation of social concepts. More specifically, we need a general theory of honour phenomena. Such a theory is still missing today. There have been a number of detailed studies of how the concept works or has worked in particular societies, especially in the Mediterranean area, but no one has approached the topic within a general theoretical framework. The spell of Peristiany seems to have had a lasting effect. He wrote in his introduction to *Honour and Shame: The Values of Mediterranean Society*: 'If honour and shame are universal aspects of social evaluation, the polarity of the sacred and profane is equally common. But our concern is not with the universal causality or logic of these phenomena but with their relevance to a particular social system and to the search for correlations which might provide an index to the classification of these social systems' (1966: 11).

Why should we not concern ourselves with the universal causality or logic of such concepts like honour? Surely, we can only fully assess the relevance of specific social (and moral) concepts once we have understood what objective conditions and what kind of subjective reasoning cause them to arise. Also, why should we assume that concepts like honour and shame are culturally universal? Peristiany has neither offered a theory, which allows him to deduce that the concept of honour should be found in every society, nor has he offered any comparative evidence, which would prove its universal occurrence.

In fact, in this paper I argue that honour is not a universal concept, and in many societies, like for example the Hamar of southern Ethiopia, it has no place. To sustain this argument, we first need a definition of honour, which goes beyond the one provided by Unni Wikan. Drawing on earlier studies by Blok, Campbell, Herzfeld, Peristiany and others, she has defined honour as 'the value of a person in her or his own eyes but also in the eyes of her or his society' (Wikan 1984: 649). From this minimal definition many of the components are missing which have given terms like *ais, aiza, aidos, era, honos* their particular colour. All we are left with is the 'value of a person'. This value is both assessed by the public and by the person's inner self. How can we complete the picture and capture the semantics of honour related terms? In order to know what honour is, we also need to know what it is not. We need to focus on the differences which separate 'honour' from similar terms like 'dignity', 'respect', 'name', 'regard', 'reputation', 'esteem', 'fame', 'face', 'merit', 'pride' and so on. All these terms have to some extent to do with the value of a person in his or her own eyes and also in the eyes of others. But how do they differ?

A first step to visualize the differences is to draw a horizontal line and call the left end self and the right end others. As we know from Unni Wikan's definition, honour should be placed in the middle of the continuum because it belongs equally well to the domain of 'self' and 'other'.

Pride and fame are also rather easy to place because they each belong to one of the extreme poles. 'Pride' belongs closely to the domain of 'self' while 'fame' belongs closely to the domain of 'other'. Your pride belongs more closely to you than to others because you may believe in your own value while at the same time knowing that others don't value you highly. Your fame, on the other side, is always in the hands of the others. You may wish and work for your fame, but it is up to the others to notice you and make you famous. Dignity should also be plotted near the pole of 'self', but unlike pride it always involves the recognition of the judgement of others. Persons act with dignity when they think they have reasons to believe in their own social worthiness. As the self is involved so much, it would be a pleonasm to speak of 'self-dignity' and so this possible linguistic form is not found. With 'regard', 'respect' and 'esteem' this is different. 'Self-esteem', 'self-respect' and 'self-regard' are linguistically acceptable expressions, and this points to the fact that 'regard', 'esteem' and 'respect' are closer to the domain of 'other' than that of 'self'.

'Face' and 'name' are used in a figurative sense and we need to have a closer look at them before we can place them on the continuum. 'Face' as a metaphor for public 'self-image' draws its power from a clever exploitation of part-whole relationships: First, a significant part of a person, that is the face which one shows or hides from others, is taken to represent the whole person, including character and social standing. Secondly, acts are used to deduce causes from effects. Bad deeds, it is said, reflect a bad person, to break a social norm is a sign of bad character. Thus, the threat behind the notion of face is that if you don't do what is publicly expected of you, you will loose 'face' and be declared bad *in toto*. The metaphoric meaning of 'face' is in this way a reflection of the influence of others and the self. Like 'honour', it lies in the middle of the continuum. But as it is less abstract than honour, and as it is physically associated with the body, it should be plotted towards the side of 'self'.

Like 'face', the term 'name' is used metaphorically to say something about the social worthiness of a person, and like face it exploits a part-whole relationship. In all cultures people are named, and their name is an intrinsic part of their social existence. Social standing and worthiness accumulate, as it were, in the name of a person. To have a good or great name is to be good or great. However, in this mode of thought the opposite is also true: to spoil a name means to spoil the whole person. Therefore 'name' has a coercive aspect like 'face' and 'honour', for if you don't behave according to the moral values of your society you risk your 'name'. But 'name' reflects more the influence of others, while 'face' reflects more the influence of self. To think and to speak about someone's name always implies a fine distinction between self and the public image of a person. While face points to the affective involvement of a person, 'name' speaks of a label which itself is an object of manipulation and reflects the social skill and power of a person or that of others. This attempt to differentiate honour from some of the related terms may be summarized in the following diagram:

Diagram 1: **Honour and related terms**

I place the concept of honour in the centre because it is determined as much by the private and the public. The individual and society merge here more closely than in any other related term. Above all, honour is a coercive concept. 'Honour lost, everything lost' the saying goes. You cannot escape the power of honour because it is neither your own, nor yet not your own. Honour welds self and other together and this gives it its special effectiveness for social control.

People tend to overlook this darker side of honour. They rather think only of brighter aspects such as praise, adoration, applause etc. and don't notice the coercive aspect of honour. But those who have honour are also always in the danger of loosing it. That is, those who live in honour also live in fear. In fact, all the terms included in Diagram 1 are terms which share the feature 'fear of loss': you don't want to loose your 'face', 'respect', 'name', 'fame', 'esteem', 'dignity', 'pride', or 'honour'. To bring this out more clearly, let me introduce a further term: 'merit'. 'Merit' differs from 'honour', 'face', 'dignity', etc., in that it is an intentionally neutral category which evades the 'self—other' polarity and the social struggles which go with it. Like money, 'merit' refers to objective scales of judgement and does not speak of the social bartering that goes on between 'self' and 'other'. Ideally, an objective third party, preferably God, would measure the merits of women and men and award them accordingly. 'Honour' and the related terms mentioned above do not make any such claim to objectivity. Rather, they are radically subjective and express the emotive and political side of social and moral judgement. A further noticeable feature of 'honour' is that you may qualify it by speaking of great or small honour. With 'face' this is different. You may loose it or keep it, but you don't try to increase your face like you try to increase your honour or the respect, which you command, your name, fame, regard, esteem or dignity. Also, you don't speak of a person's 'sense of face' (or 'sense of' respect, name, fame, regard, esteem). Only 'honour' and 'dignity' (and to some extent 'pride') allow the gloss 'have a sense of'. But what distinguishes honour from dignity? In terms of the rhetorical definition of honour which I am aiming at, the crucial difference lies in the fact that dignity is a concept which does not lend itself for social coercion because anyone who thinks of himself as having dignity and acts dignified, does so because he thinks he has reasons to believe in his own social worthiness. Dignity reflects the recognition of right social conduct, and either you have it or you don't. You cannot spoil your dignity nor can it be spoiled by others. Therefore, you cannot properly reprimand anyone saying something like 'think of your dignity'. Such a reprimand would sound comical and utterly insincere, for the one who has dignity should know best what his social conduct should be. Lastly, dignity is not a competitive concept like honour. One does not compete for dignity as one does for honour. In a sense, dignity is the peaceful and mature companion of honour. You don't incite people to die on the 'field of dignity'. No, you incite them to die on the 'field of honour'.

This leads me to the following definition of honour: Honour is the value of a person in her or his own eyes and in the eyes of others. Its loss entails grave social danger. It may be qualified by attributes like high/low, great/small, etc. One has a sense of it, and it may be increased through competition.

The following diagram locates the various concepts as they fall between the value of a person and honour:

Diagram 2: **Honour and the value of a person**

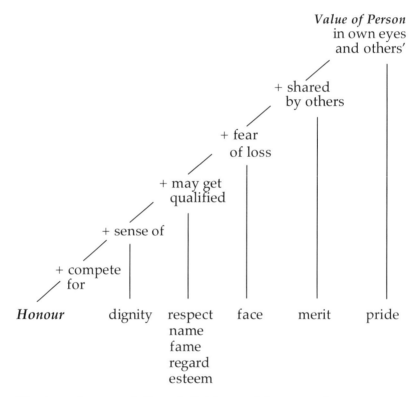

Having given a fuller definition of honour, let me now continue with the theory. The reasoning involved in the discourse of honour is that if an effect is bad (or good) then the whole must be bad (or good), or if the part is good (or bad), then the whole must be good (or bad). If you do a bad deed, then, not only that deed, but your whole person gets condemned. The condemnation is in turn justified by the argument that the individual is a part of a whole (society). The rules of conduct have been established by society, and to break them is like rejecting society. This, of course, is an insult. Here lies the special twist in the concept of honour: it transforms social conventions into subjective feelings. Those who act against existing codes of conduct can therefore be met with indignation, scorn, anger. In short, they can be morally coerced (see Abu Lughod 1986).

It is important to note that for honour to work as a coercive concept people must live under social conditions, which do not allow them to move freely away from the contexts in which they are living. If people can move away freely from one other, and if they can live to a large extent independently of each other, the power of public opinion and ostracism is weak.

There are many societies with predominantly face-to-face social relations where mobility is high and the power of social ostracism is accordingly low. Such mobility exists typically among hunters and gatherers, but it also occurs among a number of pastoralists, cultivators and people practicing different varieties of mixed economies. The Hamar of southern Ethiopia with their reliance and different resources (sorghum, cattle, goats, sheep, apiculture, hunting, gathering, trading and raiding) are a case in point. Their whole economy is based on the ability of people to move and exploit their environment optimally in this way. No large corporate groups and no large permanent settlements exist, and for this reason alone we should be able to predict, that the concept of honour has no important part to play in the politics of the Hamar.

Also, in my own native Western society, honour has hardly any coercive power because many options for mobility have drastically reduced the effectiveness of public opinion. For this and other reasons, the concept of honour has become virtually obsolete (see Berger, 1970 for an interesting analysis of this topic).

So where should we expect the concept of honour to flourish? We should expect it in societies with restricted spatial mobility, prevalent face-to-face relations and a significant division of labour and social stratification. The prototype would be feudal society with its social organisation based on the homage and service of vassals who have been granted holdings of land or fiefs as spheres of operation and control. Here politics of honour are part and parcel of the formal public acknowledgement of feudal allegiance, of the acknowledgement of the lord's superiority, and of the demonstrative fulfilment of duties.

In feudal society honour was used by the powerful as a weapon in the class struggle. The superior who delegated a responsibility to an inferior (who in turn was the superior of some other inferior) forced the other by means of the concept of honour to act honestly and not to betray his oath of allegiance. When a vassal was entrusted with a task, honour demanded that he did what had been delegated to him. And once he had done the task, he was honoured and gained honour. In this way honour converted the exploitation by others into the pleasure of doing one's duty. In the extreme case the superior honoured his vassal and then let him die on the 'field of honour'. Ironically, many of the oppressors within a feudal system were also oppressed. They, the 'courageous' were in constant fear of loosing their honour or being surpassed by others in their battle for honour.

The Hamar of southern Ethiopia have no feudal past, and they do not have the degree of social differentiation and the asymmetries of wealth and power, which would motivate any strategies of honour. There are no kings, lords and vassals, no patrons and clients, no competing social classes or corporate groups. As I indicated above, the Hamar economy is based on pastoralism, slash and burn cultivation, gathering and hunting, apiculture etc., and these diverse modes of production require small groups, which can quickly change their residence and adapt to changes in environmental conditions. Their repertoire of moral and ethical concepts, beliefs and rituals is geared to the practical problems of living in an unpredictable transitional zone, which lies between the well watered Ethiopian highlands and the semi-desert of northern Kenya.

The Hamar have no single political leader but delegate responsibilities for decision making to single individuals. But while this means to allocate a certain amount of power, they are careful to distribute it evenly and constantly check it. Also, people may never show their political power directly but hide it behind the guise of ritual. There are two *bitta* who are ritually responsible for the well-being of two parts of Hamar territory; there are the *gudili* who are ritually responsible for the well-being of the fields in their own settlement areas; there are the *ayo* each of whom speaks for his respective territorial segment at public meetings; there are the *jilo* who magically initiate and supervise dangerous enterprises like raiding; and there are the *moara* who divine by means of throwing sandals, reading the entrails of goats, sheep or cattle, etc., and in this way influence public and private decision making. But these functionaries are jealously watched by the *donza*, the Hamar married men who, each in his own independent way, shape the politics of Hamar every-day life (see Lydall and Strecker 1979b for a more detailed description of the offices mentioned here).

If there is any axiom that characterises Hamar social life then it is the rejection of authority outside the domestic sphere. This feature is so striking that I used to call it Hamar anarchy and filled many pages of my diary on this topic when I began to study Hamar culture and society (see Lydall and Strecker 1979a).

The insistence on the primacy of the individual and its concomitant rejection of the influence of others can also clearly be detected in the use of language. Remember the self—other continuum and how the terms relating to the value of a person can be plotted on it (Diagram 1). We saw that the heaviest moral coercion lies in the middle where the domains of the 'self' and 'other' merge. In Hamar, where such a merging is rejected, we simply have a blank here. There are plenty of terms which refer to the value of a person in his or her own eyes, and there are plenty of terms which speak of the value of a person in the eyes of others, but there are no terms which attempt that curious merging of perspectives which is characteristic for honour.

Typically, in Hamar one does not swear by one's honour or something similarly intrinsic to one's self. Rather, one swears by something that is close to oneself but extrinsic. The women swear by their *bakulo*, the three stones which constitute their hearth. The *bakulo* signify that a woman is married and a house of her own. The hearth stones are the symbol of her adult, married status. So when she says *'issa bakulo ne'*, she means 'I swear by my hearth, by my house, my children and all what I value highly'.

Also the man swears by something, which is not intrinsic to him. He swears by his *garo*, the calf, which played a special role at his initiation rite and became his first symbolic child, long before he brought home his wife and could have children with her. The *garo* is taboo for him. He should not drink its milk, nor eat its meat. He should not even rest on its hide. If he swears by his *garo* he says, 'I swear by my calf, by my child, by my elder-hood, that what I am saying is true'. So both men and women say they would risk something which is external to their selves (yet at the same time dear to themselves) should they not tell the truth.

It goes well with their rejection of authority that the Hamar not only have no word for 'honour' but also none for 'shame', 'duty', 'sin', 'devil' and not even for 'god'. They don't pray but call forth *barjo*. Jointly and individually they call forth what they want the world to be: 'The rain shall fall, the children shall play, peace shall be in the land', etc. As long as a person is alive and healthy, she or he has *barjo*, only when one dies is one's *barjo* finished. People speak of other people as having rich (or poor), small (or big) *barjo* and select their spokesmen and ritual leaders accordingly. And as soon as the luck or good fortune of such a leader begins to wane, they say that his *barjo* is not rich anymore and they withdraw the tasks, which they had delegated to him before.

If the Hamar do not play the game of sin, god and honour, this does not mean that they are morally insensitive. Quite the contrary! Their egalitarian ethic forces them to scrutinize one another carefully and constantly. In order to check the power and aspirations of others you have to know them and keep a discourse alive which has a rich social and psychological vocabulary. In Hamar, people forever discuss the strength and shortcomings of others, and their language abounds with metaphorical inventions which give colour to their expressions. Metaphors for character traits come from diverse domains, as the following examples show:

Animals:

gaia (baboon) — playful, irresponsible

kofini (ground squirrel) — clever, unbeatable, trickster

guni (snake) — traitor

Body parts, substances or gender:

kanta (joint) — ruthless

woilem (heart)   concerned, thoughtful

pii (excrement) — coward, disgusting

angi (male) — competent, strong, reliable

Elements:

nu (fire) — engaged, spirited, successful

gibare (wind) — unreliable, insincere

Natural attributes:

cherengi (clean) — no social offence

kadji (cool) — peaceful, tempered

tipha (straight) — truthful

Such metaphors are often used to judge persons, and they may be grouped into good/bad pairs:

good traits	bad traits
kabo (thoughtful)	*barri* (mad)
gon (truthful)	*budamo* (deceitful)
kadji (peaceful)	*palli* (quarrelsome)
burda (generous)	*bancho* (mean)
zia (courageous)	*pi* (fearful)
tipha (straight)	*koara* (crooked)
cherengi (clean)	*mingi* (polluted)

Interestingly, the Hamar also have terms for the lack of developed character traits. They call such persons *dudi* (closed), *daega* (dumb) or *mume* (full). Significantly, Hamar people are not judged much in terms of physical strength and wealth. What counts and is prominent in their assessment of others are qualities pertaining to the mind, temper, generosity, courage (which must not be mistaken for physical strength!) and the general ritual state a person is in at any given time.

There are several words in Hamar which refer to the acts by which people show appreciation for each other:

walsha (praise deeds of others in song, especially those who return from hunting or raiding);
sada (celebrate your kin and dear ones in song);
shekinda (to get adorned with beads, cauri shells, etc., for having killed big game or an enemy);
ganata (address others endearingly).

Just as there are terms for acts of appreciation, there are those for rejecting other persons like in the following three examples:

bagga (reject, dislike, break with a person);
boia (despise, deride, reject, look down on);
ishimba (don't take the other seriously, don't listen).

This shows that the Hamar are not morally indifferent and that they judge each other, applaud and criticize, and certainly also guide and control each other. But they don't do so by means of concepts that could be translated as 'honour'. There is simply no concept which fuses 'self' and 'other' in the way 'honour' does. Hamar terms relating to the social value of a person always keep 'self' and 'other' nicely distinct from each other. To bring out this point more clearly, let me turn to the two concepts of *k'aia* and *goshpa*, which come closest to honour.

A word that is constantly used in Hamar everyday conversation is *kaia*, 'get lost, disappear'. More rarely one hears the word *k'aia*, which begin with a imploded /k/ [k'] and means the opposite of *kaia*, i.e. 'to appear, become known, become visible and manifest'. When I asked the Hamar about the meaning of *k'aia*, they gave me examples such as the following:

1. A tree may become known because it is very high, has an important shade, is a good one to place beehives in, etc.
2. Big herds of goats or cattle.
3. A person may become well known for many different reasons, good ones and bad ones, especially if the person is a leader and speaks at public meetings, initiates raids, etc.
4. Fields become known for their good harvests and the social events have taken place there.
5. A family or homestead.
6. A settlement area, a territorial segment, the whole land.
7. An important event like a raid, a public meeting etc.
8. Dances, songs, fashions...

There is also a Hamar saying which throws light an the concept of *k'aia*: *'wodemo k'aio ne'*, 'The rich are maggots', that is their cattle and goats multiply quickly like the maggots in a piece of fat, and as their animals become many, they themselves become widely known. Just like the maggots appear over night and multiply with great speed, so a person, an object, a group, a place or event appears and becomes visible and known to everybody. Interestingly, neither the 'self' nor the 'other' is particularly involved in the concept. *K'aia* differs from 'fame' in that it does not involve rumour, gossip and praise. No one says admiringly of someone else, *'kissi k'aiditai'* (Hasn't he become well known) in the sense of 'He is admirable that he has become so well known'. Rather, such a sentence is said in a matter of fact way, with perhaps an element of surprise and envy in it. Whatever the case, *k'aia* cannot be translated as 'honour' because it would be impossible to have 'a sense' of it, and it lacks the dimension of social coercion.

The concept of *goshpa* is difficult to grasp and it took me a while to figure out its full meaning. Literally it means 'to cause to look beautiful, to adorn'. *Goba* is 'to be furnished with ornaments' and therefore 'walk about looking beautiful'. Women are adorned with butter and red ochre, iron rings on arms and legs and around the neck, with ostrich feathers, beads, etc., and men are similarly beautified with beads, bracelets, feathers, special hair dress and so on. But the term *goshpa* has also received a metaphorical extension that pertains to the social domain: you may adorn someone by accepting her or him. You beautify others by expressing your liking for them. Furthermore, *goshpa* has a reciprocal element because it applies both to the host and the guest. The guest gains by the good things the host does for him, and the host gains by the good sentiment he creates in the guest.

To give some colour to what I have said and show how I discovered the social meaning of *goshpa*, let me quote directly from my notebook:

1.   Sarinda's son Kaala explains *goshpa* to me as simply 'the act of dressing and adorning someone with clothes and beads'. But Sarinde likens *goshpa* to *shoshinsha*, 'the act of receiving a guest'. You *goshpa* someone by giving something to him, a goat, a cow, grain. You worry: *'edi shoshi niade amaekoato?'*, 'Will they say that a guest has arrived?'. *Goshpa* expresses the fact that you are recognised as a worthy guest. In Hamar, the guest never brings anything (except within some clearly defined situations like

marriage negotiations). Therefore a person exposes himself (or herself) when he goes to visit. He can not force anyone to accept him by offering a gift first. He has to wait until he is recognised and accepted as a guest and is given things freely by the host. Then he has been *goshpadada*, 'beautified by acceptance'.

2.   Merrie explains *goshpa* to me differently from Gardu. He says that you *goshpa* a host by acknowledging his good hospitality and generosity. I ask if those who eat like hyenas and don't say that they have been treated well also *goshpa* you. 'No, they don't; only those who say that you have treated them well *goshpa* you'. Before he departs, I give Merrie a Konso blanket. I also ask, 'Who is doing *goshpa* here, do I *goshpa* you or you me?' He answers, 'I will *goshpa* you later when, at home, I say that I have received the blanket from you'. What is happening here? First I *goshpa* someone by accepting him or her as a guest. Gardu from her socially weak perspective (she is a widow with four children to look after, stresses this point. She gets *goshpa* when she comes somewhere and is accepted. As people know that she does not come just so, and that she will take something away, they *goshpa* her, value her highly, by accepting her as a guest. Once she has been accepted, it is her traditional right not to just remain passive but to tell the host what she wants, or rather what she needs. She is allowed to demand and argue toughly with the host. She uses all sorts of ways including a lot of clever talking, to make the host give as much as possible. In the end, there is no direct thanking and expressions of thanks towards the host involved. Rather, the thanks return indirectly, that is via the *goshpa*, which happens when she has returned home. Here she praises or at least comments on the generosity of the host. But she does not really have to do it because the gifts speak for themselves and *goshpa* the person who has provided them!

3.   Haila comes and shows me his stick, which indicates that he has entered his rite of passage into manhood. I give a present, as is customarily expected, which he later will pass on to the girls who will come to attend his ceremony. I ask whether I *goshpa* him

or he me. He answers that he will *goshpa* me when he later
recounts that I gave him the present. When Haila tells me of
goshpa, he makes gestures, which imitate generous and completely
devoted giving. It seems that there exists an ethos of giving in
Hamar that I still have not yet understood well. Here, in a
society where all people know each other, it makes sense to give
away all you have, especially not completely necessary goods,
because you will get things back eventually in the endless chain of
demands and counter demands. At least this is what Haila seems
to suggest to me. To be ready to give is held to be of great value.
But you don't count the returns, you don't think like a merchant.

In an ideal world, we would never be in fear of others. We
would do things freely for each other and because we positively
want to. Also, in this ideal world we would all have equal
rights to personal preserves, non-distraction and claims to
spheres of action. We would accept each other in our respective
individuality. Unfortunately, many historically known societies
were far from ideal, and many of their members could not
satisfy their basic wants of freedom. They were forced to
accept impositions by others and were cognitively controlled by
concepts such as honour. Therefore, when I ask: 'Do the Hamar
have a concept of honour?' I also ask about their social chains.
Isn't it telling and also encouraging that here some of the more
insidious ones are missing?

Part II: Rhetorics of War and Peace

Speech situations and social control

Emergence of an individualistic society

The Hamar live in southern Ethiopia in the mountainous region between the Omo and the Woito valley, north of Lake Turkana (Rudolf) and Chew Bahir (Lake Stefanie). Their past lies in the dark, but according to tradition Hamar originated as a composite society unified through ritual leadership:

"Long ago, in the time of the ancestors, the Hamar had two *bitta* (ritual leaders). One was Baki Maro, one was Elto. The first ancestor of Baki Maro came from Aari and settled in Hamar in the mountains. He, the *bitta*, made fire, and seeing this fire people came, many from Aari, others from Maale, others from Tsamai, others from Konso, others from Kara, others from Bume, and others from Ale..." The *bitta* then told the immigrants: "You who have came from Maale, leave the customs of your fathers and listen to my word. You who have come from Konso, leave the customs of your fathers and listen to my word"(Lydall and Strecker 1979b: 2).

Lexicostatistical evidence points to an element of truth in this tradition, for the strongest linguistic influence most certainly comes from Aari. Yet, there is quite a difference between Hamar and Aari languages and customs. How long did it take for the authentic cultural configurations of Hamar to develop? I cannot even guess at this, and equally mysterious as the history of

Hamar is that of three other groups who also speak Hamar (i.e., dialects of Hamar) and whose customs are, together with those of the Hamar, variations of a single theme: the Banna who live to the north, the Bashada who live to the west, and the Kara who live down on the east bank of the Lower Omo.

Oral tradition and ecological evidence suggest that the Hamar had established themselves in their mountain range by the nineteenth century. At that time they lived a relatively stable social life, which was less hazardous, had less sickness, and experienced fewer external conflicts than today. This ended with the advent of Emperor Menelik's troops at the turn of the twentieth century. Then, many Hamar were enslaved or killed, and those who escaped fled south to the Arbore in the delta of the Woito, to the Dassenech (Galeba) by the shores of Lake Turkana, and to the Kara by the banks of the Omo.

Only slowly, after their dispersal, did they return to their country, and it is this reoccupation of their territory that became the basis of modern Hamar social structure. The return was characterized by a high degree of individualism. Strong-minded persons, who were no longer prepared to stand the humiliations of life in exile, returned with small herds of goats, sheep, and cattle to their former grazing grounds an the wide plateau that extends west and south of the Hamar Mountains. Here they lived a semi-nomadic life, which was full of physical hardship, but free from the strains of living in exile or of enslavement by the Amhara, who had established themselves in the higher altitudes of the Hamar Mountains.

The defeat spoiled the mystical power of the ritual leaders, and through the deaths of countless members of the society the old age-set system fell into ruins. Instead, each man performed by himself the rituals he considered necessary, and rejected all external authority. The newly emerging pattern of individual-ization was further enhanced by raiding. Since the cultivation of fields and the reliance upon crops made the returning men and their families vulnerable to attack and exploitation by the

Amhara intruders, each economic unit tried to build up a large stock of animals in order to gain independence. The quickest means to this end was raiding (mainly of the Borana to the south and the Gebra in Kenya), and from then until today, successful raiding as the strongest expression of personal achievement and economic independence, has reinforced the individualistic (and often anarchic) pattern of Hamar life.

By 1920 most Hamar had returned to their country, but they never again settled in large, compact settlements, and they continued to shift towards a reliance on pastoral resources. This proved to be an asset during the potentially hazardous time of the Italian occupation, and it has kept them relatively safe from any outside exploitation until today. The shift towards pastoralism was a matter of degree. As I infer from my studies of ritual, the Hamar economy must have been based for a long time on three main resources: the herds, the fields, and the bees. However, the degree to which any one of these resources was exploited has been changing over time and space, in response to political and ecological pressures.

In the nineteenth century, when, undisturbed, the Hamar cultivated their mountains, the economy may well have been 80 per cent based on agriculture; by around 1920, when they had returned from exile, the pattern was reversed, i.e. 80 per cent pastoralism and 20 per cent agriculture. Today, as a *modus vivendi* has been established between the Hamar and the Amhara, the Hamar are showing a tendency to return to their original mountain homes and to shift back again towards a higher reliance on agricultural products. Hamar, then, is a relatively new society. Not one which has adopted much from the outside (except superficial features much as hairstyles and songs), but one which, in response to strong external pressures, reshaped and is reshaping itself, building on the old matrix of its indigenous culture.

Hamar speech situations

Before I describe each of the selected speech situations separately, I summarize them here:

Reciprocal speech

pen gia – telling the news

hakati – playful talk

palli – argument, quarrel

irima, atap – insult, swearing, negotiation

baida, k'ara – noisy talk

kurkum, kubai – important discourse

assaua – private negotiation

kemo dalk – marriage negotiation

Non-reciprocal speech

kilima – instruction

elkima – last will

osh – public meeting

Reciprocal speech

The Hamar have one term, *dalk,* which signifies talk and reciprocal speaking generally, and there exist at least eight different specific situations of *dalk*, as follows.

Pen gia

The central locus of Hamar domestic social discourse is the coffee pot. A woman brews coffee in a large round clay pot that she has put on her fire place, and then she serves it in large gourd bowls to her husband and his neighbours and guests who sit in a semi-circle around the fire place. The coffee is made with the whole beans, husks and all, and is so weak that it would not be recognized as coffee by an uninitiated Western observer. Large quantities are drunk, perhaps more to replace bodily water lost in the hot climate than for its stimulant value.

A good visitor in Hamar is expected to arrive at a homestead either early in the morning or early in the evening, at a time when (ideally) his host's wife has put on a pot of coffee. The guest is invited to sit down on a cowhide and then, when the coffee is served, his host will ask him: "Tell me the country" (*pen gia*). The guest answers: "No, no, I have heard no bad", or he uses a metaphor like: "No, no, the wind has not whispered" and he adds: "Tell me yours". Upon this the host replies: "No, no, the country is well".

Then there's a pause after which the guest slowly begins to tell the news which he has brought. He always has something to tell, and unfailingly begins his talk by telling what he himself has been doing, from where he has come and which way he took, etc., and into this account of his private actions he weaves public events, news of the country, the description of rituals and oracles he has encountered, the news of raids in which he has participated or of which he has heard, the rains that have fallen or failed to fall, the state of the pastures and the fields.... No one interrupts him while he talks. There is only a certain 'echoing' by the host to whom he addresses himself, and there are spontaneous reactions by the audience, e.g., laughter and exclamations of disbelief or anger.

The length of a *pen gia* varies depending on the extent of dramatic events happening in the country, on the speech competence of the speaker, on the sympathy and interest of the audience, and other factors. Over a period of three years, I have listened to countless *pen gia* which extended over more than half an hour, sometimes even over more than an hour, and I was always struck by the excellent memory of the speaker, his sense for detail, his minute reconstruction of time sequences and, above all, by his dramatic reconstruction of social arguments.

The *pen gia* is a complex process, which contains several elements that directly and indirectly relate to social control:

1. Certainly the most important element in the situation is that the speaker is telling factual news. Responding to

ecological and external political pressures, the Hamar have developed a fragmented, dispersed, and highly individualized society. These loose organizational features would not help them survive, if they did not constantly pass vital information from one fragment of the society to the other. It is this manifest function that has turned the *pen gia* into an institution in Hamar.

2. A second important element is that the speaker evaluates news. He not only passes on factual information, but also evaluates it. When his rational and moral evaluations concern his fellow countrymen or women the *pen gia* turns into an explicit agent of social control. In Hamar, like in many face-to-face societies, each word said in favour or disfavour of a particular individual affects that person's social credit and with it his chances to achieve the goals to which he aspires, i.e. to collect large herds, to perform memorable rituals etcetera.

On one level the *pen gia* is, therefore, institutionalized gossip. The element of social control in gossip is well known to comparative anthropology and it is interesting to note that the Hamar themselves often refer to the *pen gia* as gossip. They call it *mermer* (murmur) if the *pen gia* contains neutral gossip; and *wupha* (gossip) if it contains gossip full of malice and slander.

3. The *pen gia* always reflects back on the speaker. If he tells the news well, he gains social esteem, if he speaks badly he loses it. This is well understood by the Hamar. So much so that many speakers turn the tables and use their *pen gia* offensively, trying to impress upon the listeners their general social competence by means of magnificent speech performance. This can reach bizarre, even pathological dimensions.

I have witnessed *pen gia* the therapeutic element was paramount. During such therapeutic *pen gia* the sympathetically listening audience allows the speaker to embark on 'far-out' monologues in which he tries to develop – for himself and for the audience – a unified image of himself and of his actions. I think that this need for self-repair results from the frustrations that Hamar anarchic social structure creates in the individual. A Hamar who was wronged by one of his countrymen usually has no immediate means of direct redress. His only avenue is talk – talk not only to muster social support to repair broken social relations, but also to repair his disturbed inner self.

4. To tell the news, the speaker uses numerous stylistic features and a host of bodily motions. He does not so much talk about events but rather tries to recreate them dramatically for the benefit of the audience.

But, important as this artistic element is, it is enjoyed with a divided heart, for the Hamar know too well that the speaker's verbal art is closely related to aggression and social domination. So, whenever a speaker excels in poetics, delight in the pure artistic forms is sometimes curbed by the cruelty of the message.

Hakati

When the *pen gia* proper is finished, the conversation around the coffee pot acquires new features. The speaking patterns become more fragmented and diffuse, and more people enter the conversation.

If the group has good spirit, or someone wants to generate such good spirit, a speech-situation may develop which the Hamar call *hakati*, "playful talk". In Dambaiti, the small settlement in which most of our research was conducted, the *hakati* situations were typically initiated by Ginonda, a women who exercised the largest influence in the domestic sphere of Dambaiti.

Usually Ginonda would join the speaking group at a point when the men had satiated their initial thirst for coffee and news. She would sit down quietly apart from the men, and after she had had a sip of the remaining coffee she would, at a convenient moment, enter the conversation by offering a joke about seeming trivialities. Never would she give herself an air of importance, never would she try to impose herself on anybody.

Yet, after a while I detected method behind her *hakati*. She was not imposing herself but rather exposing others. Through her playful talk she was exposing the weakness of those who participated in the world around her. Through joking and laughter, which the others usually were happy to take up, she skilfully operated a powerful mechanism of social control: ridicule.

Palli

Sometimes a situation may develop which is called *palli*, an argument or a quarrel. Yet, during all my fieldwork I never witnessed a quarrel in which people shouted angrily at each other or used physical threats.

I see this as related to the anarchic social structure: life is so precarious for an individual that he does not dare to assert his claims and interests by forcing an argument. Direct opponents suppress their anger when they are face-to-face, and only after they have moved out of each other's presence do they separately muster support and plot against each other.

In fact, the *palli* that I witnessed never lasted very long, for when the open antagonism of the speakers was realized, the conversation was soon turned to different subjects, and non-adversaries took the word.

Irima and atap

Part and parcel of any conversation around the coffee pot are insults (*irima*) and swearing (*atap*): not in their direct form, however, for insults and swearing belong first and foremost to action. Hunters, herdsmen, and especially raiders delight in insults at crucial points of their actions, and the speaker who recreates a certain event turns this phenomenon into a stylistic asset by calling out insults in such a lively and dramatic manner that it looks as if he himself had performed the action that went with it. The audience always welcomes such indulgence and 'good' insults are retold again and again.

Such insults are usually very short and distort the normal articulation of the words used. When someone exclaims for example *sephi assa* ("your cunt") he will hold his breath and then violently eject the "*s*" and blur all the subsequent syllables into one almost indistinguishable sound. Most insults allude to sex.

It is only age-mates who insult each other directly, for if you insult someone who is not close to you, there is the danger that your insult will turn into a curse. So, paradoxically, the direct insult is a sign of closeness rather than of separation. It is used as an emphatic signal with which pals correct each other's behaviour.

Although there is a notable absence of direct swearing, the conversations around the coffee pot abound with indirect swearing. *Yir kon njarsh* ("may something destroy it") and the *aino kossa tsaerk* ("curse its sun/day") can be heard again and again.

With this the speaker expresses his discontent with a certain state of affairs, and he admits his impotence—his inability to control the world around him. With this the swearing is, of course again related to the social structure in which everybody rejects the direct exercise of authority of everybody else. But the relation is dialectic: through his swearing the speaker attempts to absolve himself from responsibility for a particular unsatisfactory event, while at the same time retaining an acceptable claim on the general control of societal affairs.

Baida and *k'ara*

The conversation around the coffee pot moves from being highly structured to being diffused. After the most important news has been told, possibly three to four different conversations may develop at one and the same time. The Hamar refer to this situation as *baida* or *k'ara*, using terms that they otherwise apply to the noises goats, sheep, and cattle make in their kraals. The Hamar listen carefully every evening to the sounds of their herds, for these sounds tell them whether the

herds are well or not. And in the same way as the head of a
family listens to his herds, he listens to the *baida* or *k'ara* of his
people.

Kurkum and kubai

The terms *kurkum* and *kubai* are rarely used, and I heard them
only after I had stayed a long time in Hamar. One evening,
when I was the only grown-up male person present at the
conversation around the coffee pot, Ginonda, in her playful
way, said that because of my presence we still were able to
keep a *kurkum* going. When I asked her what she meant, she
told me that a *kurkum* (or *kubai*) is a 'heavy conversation in
which important matters are discussed'.

Later inquiries substantiated the way in which the terms had
first come to my ears: a *kurkum* is not an explicitly aimed-at
speech situation, like for example the *pen gia* or the *assaua* (see
below), it is rather a welcome result, a state of discourse that is
achieved in the process of speaking. As such it is an interesting
facet of Hamar speech classification, and it throws light on the
general value attributed to well-organised speaking.

Assaua

In Hamar, where hardly any social relationship can be
axiomatically trusted, the *assaua*, which may be translated as
'private negotiation', has an important inter-personal control
function, and people meet constantly to conduct *assaua*. If
nobody else is present, an *assaua* may be held next to the coffee
pot, but usually the men who want to negotiate in private take
their stools and dissociate themselves from unwanted listeners
by settling down in the shade of a tree outside the homestead.
During the first phases of fieldwork, I observed such *assaua*
situations only from a distance. The secretive air which
surrounded them and the low voices of the speakers made me
feel that something special, almost asocial, was going on.

All the *assaua* that I witnessed had the same tenor. I had
expected that certain forms of etiquette would be dropped and

that there would be a loosening of talk and a tendency to be more outspoken. Nothing of this was the case—if anything, the speaking was rather more guarded than usual. After some reflection this certainly made sense to me, for in the private negotiation and political plotting that go on in an *assaua*, each participant faces not only the promise of economic and political gain, but also the risk of exposing himself and making himself vulnerable.

The precariousness of the *assaua* situation is reflected in the use of indirect talk and metaphors to test whether or not your partner is in tune with your own personal interests.

Kemo dalk

The Hamar marriage negotiations range from informal talk to highly ritualized speeches. The negotiations fall into two stages: the cautious ones initiated by the wife-takers, and the aggressive ones initiated by the wife-givers.

When a couple seeks a wife for one of their sons they send a go-between who carries a thin straight stick, which signifies his office. The go-between conducts his negotiations secretly before dawn outside of the homestead of the oldest male member of the wife-giving group. Once a marriage has been agreed on, the wife-givers unfailingly come 'enraged' to demand bride wealth from the wife-takers, and their aggression must be checked by public social control. They arrive as a group early in the morning, heavily armed with fighting sticks, spears, and guns, and they stop the herds from leaving the kraal. Sitting down by the gateway, they threaten to take by force the cattle and goats which they consider their due, if the owner is not willing to give them freely.

They wait till the elders of the surrounding homesteads have arrived and then their leader formulates their demands. Upon this the most competent speakers of the neighbourhood answer one by one and the ensuing discussions may last for several hours, each speaker taking the welcome opportunity to formulate not only his opinion about the immediate situation, but also about Hamar social life and lore in general. During the course of the negotiations, each party retreats at certain points and assesses among itself the state of the discussion and the strength and the weaknesses of its own and the opponent's arguments.

Although these retreats are manifestly aimed at sharpening one's renewed attack and defence, I have found that they gradually de-escalate the arguments and furnish a decisive contribution to the final decision-making. They allow a calming-down of emotions and a psychological adaptation to newly created situations. The wife-takers usually sit apart and let the neighbours act as their verbal armour.

Non-reciprocal speech

I now move on to describe non-reciprocal speech situations, which differ from those outlined above in that they are asymmetric: they consist of single speakers, or a series of single speakers, and a listening audience. Also, they are more explicitly aimed at social control than any situation described so far.

Kilima

A *kilima* is an instruction. Most instructions that I witnessed happened in the private sphere and were practical and specific. Usually a father would instruct his sons, or an older brother his younger brothers, telling them, for example, in detail how they should go about defending their herds against the Galeba (Dassanech), how to collect debts from such and such a family, how to go on a trading expedition to Banna, how to prepare such and such a ritual. The *kilima* usually happens in the early morning before people go to work or embark on travelling or other activities. A *kelima* situation may develop towards the end of a coffee session. More often, however, the man who wants to instruct his sons or younger brothers asks them to sit with him slightly apart from the stage of every day social life. I found that a preferred place for a *kilima* was the seclusion of the cattle kraal.

During his instruction the speaker talks more slowly and quietly than usual and he often pauses for a long time. To give his instruction an air of authority, his voice carries a heavy moral element. Not a moral element of outright command, like "I have told you how to do things, now I order you to go and do exactly as I told you", but rather the inverted form of lamentation like: "I have told you how to do things, but who listens these days to his father or his older brother?" The use of lamentation rather than command in instruction is related to the anarchic social structure of Hamar.

Less frequent than the private, specific, and practical instructions are the public, general, and moral instructions. They usually happen when there has been a quarrel and someone is made to pay a goat or sheep as a fine. After certain rituals have been performed and the meat of the slaughtered animal has been consumed jointly by all the young and old male members of a settlement, one of the oldest and most competent speakers will get up and, with a voice that rises slowly till it gets loud and articulate so it can be heard from far away, he will lecture to the young and old alike, summarizing for then the most general social values that should govern their lives. Occasionally he refers to the quarrel in question, but he will not accuse a single individual. If he utters accusations of violation of codes of proper social life, he addresses the community as a whole.

After the first speaker, there may follow a second, a third, and so forth. The speaking will be terminated by men getting up and saying that through speaking there has now developed a state of 'good creation' (*barjo*), and that the men should stop talking before they destroy with their words what they had caused to be by speaking.

Elkima

The *elkima* is the last speech that a man gives to his close kin shortly before his death. One could call it the 'last will' if one conceives of a last will as going beyond the limited instructions concerning the distribution and administration of property. An *elkima* moves from a sorting-out of private family affairs to comments on the public spheres of the society, and then finally to a blessing of the whole world surrounding the dying man, including not only his family and society at large, but also the herds, the game, the bees, the crops, the grass, the water.

The *elkima* is an element of a 'rite de passage', and must be seen in the light of Hamar ancestor-worship. The man who formulates his last will is not abdicating from social control. On the contrary, in his final speech he sets his seal under a charter by which his descendents should rule after his death. This is the reason why the *elkima* are retold widely and repeatedly by the descendents of the deceased.

Osh

In the eyes of the Hamar their most powerful speech situation is the public meeting called *osh*. The outward sign of the importance of an *osh* is the slaughter of animals. If an *osh* is small and local a goat will do, but if it is held by one or several territorial segments one, two, or more oxen will be slaughtered. The roasted meat will be laid out on freshly cut branches in a large semi-circle at which the men sit and feast while the orators speak to them.

Not every grown-up man is allowed to speak. There is a form of election, which reduces the number of orators to about five per cent of all married men in Hamar. The orators compete with each other, and there is an ever-shifting hierarchy that changes not only over time but also over space so that, for example, a man who ranks high in a predominantly agricultural setting may rank low in the pastoral setting of the cattle camps, and vice versa.

Since the hierarchy at an *osh* is open to question, the speakers decide among themselves beforehand who will speak first, their choice being an acknowledgement of the outstanding quality of that speaker.

Every speaker owns a special spear which signifies his privilege, but during any one *osh* only one spear is used, the spear of the speaker who has been chosen to speak first. Before he starts speaking, he unlashes the leather casing that usually covers the sharp edges of the spearhead, and then walks over to the centre of the semi-circle of seated men, where the ox has been slaughtered. He takes some of its stomach contents and rubs it on to the spear, his legs, his chest and his forehead. Then, according to his temperament and his message, with a fast or slow stride, he walks back and forth in front of the semi-circle of men and begins his speech: "*Hai!* Hamar, lend me your ears!"

The first speaker usually performs the first blessing, which is an integral part of any public meeting. In doing so he will pause at a certain point in his oratory and then, with a slight upward shift of register, he will call out: "*Eh, eh!*", and enter the chant of a blessing. With the open palms of his hands he will call the rain to fall, the bees to return, the sorghum to grow, and by jabbing the pointed metal tip at the end of his spear shaft he will send away sickness, the enemies, etc. The audience acts as chorus echoing his calls.

From the blessing the orator will return to his speech and continue until one of his colleagues rises, walks over to where the ox was slaughtered, and rubs himself with the contents of its stomach. With this he announces his intention to speak. He is, however, not allowed to speak until the former speaker has offered him his spear. After the second speaker, follows a third and so on, depending on the importance of the meeting. If is not much to say, a public meeting ends when the men have finished the meat. They will call for one more blessing and then they leave.

However, if important issues are at stake, for example, war or peace with the Galeba, Arbore, or Bume, then an *osh* may continue for many hours. Typically such long public meetings are not isolated events, but links in a chain of interrelated meetings. Long though some meetings seem, they contain only a fraction of the total amount of speaking that goes an.

Before an *osh* happens, for several hours while the animals are being slaughtered and roasted at the fire, the men cluster together in the shade of trees and talk. Here, on an informal level, political views are articulated and decisions are made that will later be expressed publicly at the *osh*. Then again, when the *osh* is over and the men have returned to their different homesteads and cattle camps , they will repeat and discuss what was said at the *osh*, and begin to formulate their political stance for the next meeting.

The public meetings are in fact nothing but a public exhibition of points of view, which were arrived at through discussions on an informal level. The public meetings are not 'debates', for in their speeches the speakers rarely refer to each other, and never do they criticize each other. Each speaker exhibits his own view only, and if there is criticism and disagreement, these remain implicit.

It is the Hamar philosophy of the power of the word, which forbids public debate. There should be no argument on the public stage of the *osh*, because speaking by itself influences the social and the natural cosmos. At an *osh* each orator sums up what is of central value to him, and what he thinks people should do in response to the problem which the *osh* is trying to solve.

If the views of the various speakers overlap, then the power of their common word will become evident both in the social and the natural world. If their views diverge, however, then the power of the word, being divided, will not be strong enough to influence either the social or the natural cosmos. Ideally, public meetings should be repeated till in the end the speeches achieve a unison which lifts them not only to a level of social causation (bringing harmony within the group), but also to a level of natural causation (causing the rain to fall, the enemies to go blind, etc.).

Conclusion

All culture is communication, but societies differ significantly in the modality and frequency of their speaking activities. The emphasis placed on speaking in Hamar is, as I see it, related to one basic feature of their social structure: the absence of any institution of centralized social control, or, expressed more drastically: the permanence of anarchy. Frequently social control is not effectively achieved at all, but inasmuch as it is attempted and achieved, it always involves extensive speaking. In this chapter I set out to indicate how this happens.

Michere
How the whipping wand speaks

Anyone who has ever worked in an ethnographic museum knows the dilemma of providing too much or too little information about the material objects that are on display. Too many texts, pictures, diagrams and the like destroy the autonomy and evocative power of objects and are incompatible with the visitor's wish to gaze at them and contemplate their meanings without interference.

On the other hand, there are many stories of production and use, which are so exotic, so fantastic that they are far beyond anyone's imagination. One characteristic of ethnography is, after all, that it provides tales 'stranger than fiction'. Therefore an exhibition that lacks such enriching background stories would fall short of its mission. The present essay is devoted to this theme and deals with the abundance of meaning enshrined in just one, unobtrusive, small material object: the whipping wand (*michere*) that a Hamar herding boy carries with him when he herds his goats.

In 1971 I assembled a collection of Hamar material culture that was meant to be as complete as possible. Yet, when the objects arrived at the Ethnographic Museum of Goettingen University the whipping wand, *michere*, was missing. This was, no doubt, because a *michere* is only an attractive object when still in use, fresh, green and elastic. As it dries up it shrinks in size and begins to look more like a thrown-away twig than an object used for a significant purpose. Also, the making of a *michere* is a very simple, casual affair: You tear off a straight shoot of a *baraza* bush (Grewia mollis), rip off the leaves with your hands, smooth its thicker end and the sides with a knife—and the *michere* is ready. Hence, when making the collection, I completely overlooked this object, which plays such an important role in Hamar culture. It was only much later, when I tried to explain to my students how various objects of Hamar culture embody different kinds of social conflict, that I noticed I had forgotten to collect the *michere*.

In order to understand how the *michere* plays a role in various forms of social conflict one needs to know something about its practical use in every-day life where it is first and foremost a tool for herding goats. Cattle and sheep tend to keep together in a single herd. They are slower and more predictable in their behaviour. This is why a stick will do to herd them. But the fast, erratic movements of goats ask for the whipping wand as an extension of the herding boy's arm, plus his gestures, whistling and constant bodily presence. While herding, it is important to allow each goat its own feeding habit, its particular browsing escapades into the bush, its individualistic search for the grass, herbs and leaves it prefers. But then again, the goats have to be brought together to move on through the terrain as a single herd. So the herd disperses, joins together, moves on, disperses, joins, moves, disperses, moves and so on until the evening when it returns again to the homestead.

Furthermore, the goats are moved at different speeds at different times of the day. First, when they leave the homestead they should move relatively fast—but not too hastily—in the direction of good pasture. When they reach it, they should make optimal use of the available feed. Therefore, they are made to slow down, and care must be taken to stop them from wandering off. Thus, a herding boy constantly influences the direction and speed of his goats. With his voice he calls, whistles, sings and hisses, and in the course of time the goats learn the meaning of these sounds. Certain songs and whistles mean something like, "It is good to browse here, let's stay for a while." Other sounds, especially whistles and hisses say, "Get

going again, it is time to move on!" This is supported by movements of the *michere*, which can be used to produce sharp,
snapping noises in the air, and to hit on leaves, branches, the
earth or the animals themselves in order to alert them. In the
dense, thorny bush it is often difficult to get close to the goats,
but a long *michere* helps to reach them.

Even the most attentive and bright herding boy occasionally
looses a goat, and it is then that conflict is prone to arise,
especially between a father and his son. As the conflict is
predictable—fathers regularly get upset about the negligence of
their sons—we should expect some ritual practices here, like
Malinowski suggested long ago (1948). Although theoretically
we anticipate some special ways of reducing conflict, we could
hardly imagine the strange and 'fantastic' ritual practices that
the Hamar have developed in this context. The rest of this
essay is devoted to the 'ethnographic surprise', which, in my
view, is the most interesting part of anthropology.

When a herding boy has been struck by ill luck and one of his
goats gets lost and devoured by hyenas during the night, it is
the custom that next morning his father will go and fetch two
fresh *michere* from the bush and bring them to the homestead.
There he hands one of them to his son, shaking it as if he were
herding goats and blessing his son by spraying saliva from his
lips. The son carries the new *michere* when he goes off with the
goats, while the father places the second *michere* horizontally
above the gateway (*kiri*) of the goat enclosure. In the evening,
when the son returns with the herd, he too places his *michere*
above the gateway. From now on, the Hamar say, the boy will
not loose any of his goats anymore. But later, if for some reason
an animal of his herd should get lost again, the ritual will be
repeated.

A careful herding boy will always place his *michere* over the
entrance of the goat enclosure when he returns in the evening.
Not only is he certain to find his whipping wand there when he
needs it in the morning, he can also leave it there for good when

it has become too dry to serve its purpose of herding the goats. Thus, the *michere* becomes part of both the boy and the herd. In rhetorical parlance, it is metonymically associated with both boy and herd in that it 'causes' each to be well. Without *michere* no prosperous herd, without herd no prosperous boy. An object imbued with so much *barjo* (good fortune, well-being) must not be carelessly abandoned but carefully kept where it belongs, that is across the top of the *kiri*. Here the bundle of *michere* grows and grows until at last it is so big that it is transferred to and buried in the mound of dung and rubble (*tukare*) that surrounds the lower part of the cattle enclosure (see also Lydall and Strecker 1979b: 190).

As the *michere* is of such great importance it is used in many rituals to metaphorically express the act of herding, the goats themselves, the herder, and the results of successful herding, that is milk, butter, meat and the like. Here are some examples:

The blessings of a dying father

Now the funeral of an elder. When a father falls ill and feels that he will die he demands: 'Call my children.' And the children are called. 'Call my father's sister's son.' And he is called. 'All your children have come.' 'Bring me the milk container, milk the cows and bring the milk to me.' They bring the milk to him and he fastens on a handle made of *baraza* bark, and holding the milk container he tells his children to come. 'Come children, hold the milk container. I am dying. When I have died, herd the cattle, herd the goats.' Then he tells his children to bring him four whipping wands of *baraza*. Holding these and the milk container he calls the *barjo* of the herds, calls, calls, calls, calls, calls, calls, calls. He gives his children milk and tells them to herd the cattle and then his illness kills him. (Lydall and Strecker 1979b: 37).

Bond friends

Now the oldest son goes and pulls off two branches from a *baraza* tree. He places them in the cow dung of the cattle kraal and treads on them so that they are damp and full of cow dung. Then he touches the backs of the cattle that the bond-friend has brought and blessing them in this way, he hands them over to the bond-friends. The bond-friend will give some cattle and goats and honey to the dead man's sons. (Op. Cit.: 41).

At a father's grave

Next, the oldest son goes and pulls off branches of *baraza*, and if he is of the Galabu moiety he collects quartz stones and if he is of the Binnas moiety he collects black stones, they represent cattle. These he gives to the sons and the sister's sons of the dead man, to one five stones, to another three stones, to another four stones, to another five stones, to another ten stones. Thus they are shared out. Then carrying the whipping sticks they shake them as they go around the grave, 'shi shi shi shi shi shi.' They also carry a horn of butter, 'shi shi shi shi shi.' The sister's sons are behind, the mother's brothers in front, as they circle four times: one, two, three, four! Then the stones are placed around the *baba* stone. They are his cattle. The cattle are mixed, mixed, mixed, mixed together. Then butter is emptied out of the horn and rubbed on the cattle.

"Father, keep away the sickness of the cattle."
"Mother's brother, keep away the sickness of the people."
"Father, keep away the sickness of the people."
"Mother's brother, take our sickness away with you."
So his cattle are put on the grave; then the whips. (Op. Cit.: 57).

The rites of initiation

When the father gives the *baraza* wand to his son at the gateway, he first offers a goat to his own dead father. If he had an older brother who has died, he will also offer one goat to him on the following day.

"Come so that I may give you a *baraza* wand."

The father brings the *baraza* wand and shaking it as when herding the cattle: *zig-zig-zig*, he hands it to his son: "Take it." (Op. Cit.: 76).

Because it provides the *michere*, the *baraza* tree (Grewia mollis) is considered to bring good fortune, and its wood is used in many rituals that are meant to ensure fertility and prosperity. Here the father's gesture means firstly that he blesses his son who should grow up and successfully herd goats, sheep and cattle. But the wand also stands for the ritual staff (*boko*), which is carved out of *baraza* and which the initiate carries with him when he goes to call his relatives to attend his initiation, throughout which whipping wands are used to bless people. When, for example, the initiates encircle the cattle, the women and cattle are blessed with songs and the rhythmic movement of bundles of *michere*.

This use of *michere* in blessing derives, as I have said above, from the fact that whipping wands help the goats to feed well, help them to give plenty of milk, which in turn feeds the children and allows the making of butter, which is a symbol of well-being, abundance and fertility. A proverb sums up the beneficial power of the *michere* as follows: "*Michere sa nukä'ate kurri, mea kissa gidä'ate wokati.*" "At the tip of the whipping wand is honey, along its sides there is butter." In their commentaries about this proverb the Hamar say that *michere* are not only important for herding animals but also for guiding, controlling, and looking after people. Here they use the same verb for humans and animals, *gisha*. That is, you *gisha* animals and human beings by using the *michere*.

There are many situations of social conflict in which the *michere* plays a role, especially those involving age and gender issues. In fact, there is even an institution that carries its name, the *michere gilo*—whipping wand ritual. Baldambe (Aike Berinas, Father of the Dark Brown Cow) has described this ritual as follows:

> In these months when the herds graze close to the Hamar mountains the youngsters dance and dance. If they dance out in the bush, then the elders whip them with their whipping wands. They whip them and then they run to the homestead of a *gudili* or

jilo and dance in his cattle kraal where they will not be beaten. There might be a young man, a provocative one, who whips the girls even in the *gudili's* home. Then the *gudili* will get up: 'Why don't you kill him. He brings bad luck on us by whipping someone inside my homestead. In my homestead there must be no fighting, only play and dance. In an *ayo's* homestead there must be no quarrelling.' Hearing this talk some youngsters might say 'What is their whip? What are their rituals? What is the *bitta*?' And they start to dance in the bush, play with the girls and have intercourse with them. Then the elders rise up:

"*Ye!* Men!"

"*Yo.*"

"Have you seen this new talk? This means that we have to cut new whips."

Some important wealthy men tell some youngsters to bring them white body paint. To defy them, the youngsters will paint themselves first, saying:

"What is their bigness? Are they our fathers, or our grandfathers, or *barjo*?"

To provoke the elders they paint themselves white before the elders do, ridiculing them by this.

"*Ye*, please look, they make us into dogs!"

So the elders take their whips and they whip, they whip, they whip. That ends the dancing as all the youngsters flee into the bush. Hiding in the bush they don't eat any young sorghum, they can't dance, nor do they herd the goats. After the beating they have all fled. Their father's home, their mother's home, their older brother's home are all closed to them, so hunger dries them up. After some time they give in and enter the homestead of the *gudili*:

"We give in. Tell us what our fine will be."

Previously when they painted themselves they had said:

"You are not our fathers, you can't tell us anything."

Hadn't they? Now they have felt the pain of the whip, they say that they give in and want to give a goat as a fine. But the whip is not simply put down:

"So-and-so's son ran away. Let us whip him once."

"*Dauh!*"

"Stop, let the other one come."

"*Dauh!*"

So from the biggest to the smallest the youngsters get one stroke and then the elders take their goat and slaughter it.

"Now turn towards the rising sun: *pssss!* May your sickness go beyond Labuk, may it go before the setting sun. Little by little, little by little, little by little, grow up, grow up, grow up, grow up, grow up, grow up. Stay on the top of the mountains, grow slowly, and later on herd."

Like this they call forth *barjo* for the youngsters. (Op. Cit.: 119-121)

In olden days, that is before Hamar was conquered and incorporated into the Ethiopian Empire, an institutionalised form of whipping also occurred during the formation of new age sets (*anamo*). The *michere* emphasised what was being said and done, as Baldambe has explained:

To get its name a new age set collects goats and honey for its older brothers. They go down to a *barjo* creek where their spokesman offers a goat to the spokesman of the older brothers, who asks:

"From where do you have this goat?"

If it is from his older brother he will say so, for in the *barjo* creek you may not tell a lie.

"I, I got it from my older brother."

"*Yi*, you stole it from us? Thief!"

And *dauh! dauh! dauh!* they hit them with their whips and all the younger brothers run away. Slowly they return and the older brothers demand another goat as a fine for the theft of the first

goat. Then when honey is offered: "From whom did you take it?"
They are not allowed to tell a lie:

"I stole it from my younger brother."

"Thieves, we only want the things which belong to you!"

Dauh! dauh! dauh! again they whip them and the younger brothers
run away. The goats are slaughtered and roasted and the meat is
placed on fresh leaves. The honey is distributed in bowls. The
older brothers eat. Then the younger brothers pull off all their
decorations. They give their bracelets. They pull the feathers out
of their hair and remove their ear studs. They give all their
beads, everything. If one older brother has had a fight with a
younger brother, today he will demand the best piece from him.
All the decorations are put on a sheepskin cape and then the
distributor of the older brothers' shares out the wealth among
them. The older brothers with their whips stand upstream, the
younger brothers stand downstream.

"He, down there, should be one of ours. We hunted the lion
together, we hunted the leopard together."

They grab this one and pull him into their line. If the younger
brothers want him back they have to go and pull him out from
behind the line of the older brothers. If they dare do so the older
brothers whip them: *dauh! dauh!* and then they let them have
their age mate back. After this the older brothers tell the younger
brothers to stand together and look towards where the sun rises.
While they look upwards like this the older brothers bless them:

"Psssss", and give them their new name:

"Michemogori, psssss! Nyikorio, psssss!"

This is how the younger brothers got their name. (op. cit: 123-124)

In communication between men and women the *michere* has
similarly emphatic things to say. Let us again listen to
Baldambe as he tells how a young Hamar wife who has newly
joined her husband's homestead will provoke him until he takes
a *michere* in order to whip her:

Women have nothing else. Their way of fighting is by marriage. A man who fathers girls is said to be rich. When the girls get married, if the father previously had no cattle, then his cattle kraal will be filled. If he has no goats, his goat kraal will be filled up. If the father has no cattle then his girls will drive in cattle, drive in goats.

"Whose are these cattle?"

"They are girl-cattle."

"Whose are these?"

"They are so-and-so's girl-goats."

Thus he is rich. Honey is brought to him. Goats are driven to him. Grain is carried to him. Coffee is brought to him. Tobacco is brought to him. Thus it is.

Some girls are high spirited.

"I will not marry a man. *Yi!* That man is bad for me. He is a feeble man. His nose is pointed. His ears are big. His skin stinks."

Saying which:

"*Yi!* So-and-so!"

"*Woi!*"

"That girl of yours! Don't you have arms? Your mother, the mother-in-law, gave you the girl. Her father gave her to her father-in-law. Now that girl of yours refuses to give you water. Refuses to lie at your side. Refuses to give you her vagina. What do you say?"

So then he goes and cuts whipping wands, and cutting, cutting, cutting hides them in the bush. This is the case of the spirited girl, the one who refuses a man.

"Come with me, let's go and collect goats. Let's go down to our mother's brother's home and up to the home of my father's bond friend."

So he leads her away having cut the whips and left them in the bush yesterday. Now they go up to the place where the whips have been put.

"Those whips here are for you, they are what I bring you to."

And he grabs her. Yesterday he had also prepared some bindings from the *alkanti* cactus. With the *alkanti* bindings he ties up her legs, and her hands and beats her! When the fellow is sated his arm has come away from his shoulder. She then cries out:

"Babonas! Dear mother's child, born of my own mother, born of my own father, born of one man, sweet man, who tastes as sweet as honey, who is as good as butter! Now I say *nyarsh!* away with evil. Now I will no longer run away. Now *nyarsh!* away with my ways!"

When she says this:

"Slap your foot!"

"I won't run away."

"Slap it!"

"Pt!"

She spits on her hand and slaps the sole of her foot saying:

"May I bear only males for you."

She who speaks thus will bear male children. After this she doesn't run away. (Op. Cit.: 150-152).

This provocation of violence, which Baldambe has so vividly conjured up, begins already in early youth where it indicates that boys and girls have some stronger liking for each other. They don't show 'sweet and soft tenderness' to each other as we cultivate it in Western culture. Rather they express their love and attraction by laughter, showing their white teeth (the sign of beauty *par excellence*), fluttering their eyes and by the boy raising a *michere* high above the head, pretending a violent attack. One can hear such laughter and the whizzing sound of whipping wands at the evening dances where the girls provoke the young men to ever more exciting whipping escapades, fleeing from them and taking refuge in the bush only to return and get chased again to everyone's delight.

I find it difficult to understand the feelings of Hamar women, but they are certainly not weak, feeble, male-dominated creatures. To give a striking example, which is even well known outside Hamar: Part of the male initiation rites (where a youth has to leap over a row of cattle in order to become a fully grown man who may marry) is an episode where the women of the initiate's clan demand to get publicly whipped by the *maz*, other initiates who have already leapt over the cattle. This is how Baldambe has pictured the event:

> The people gather on the ridge and the girls dance around the cattle. The men keep the cattle from running away.
>
> "*Ukuli*, come and enter the cattle."
>
> So the *ukuli* comes and stands among the cattle, naked like a dead man. The cows bellow and the father's son stands there like a dead man and the father's cattle stand there as at a burial. 'The inventors of this ordeal are the *maz* let us kick them, let us punch them so that they may whip us' say the girls. They dance and sing:
>
> "The father of the spotted cow is standing up. This is our father's son's *kalma*."
>
> Singing they push the *maz* and the elders point out if they push the wrong *maz*.
>
> "*Eh, eh*! This *maz* is your relative, he should not hit you. The one who may hit you is this one, he is your *tsangaza*, the one whom you can marry."
>
> *Tsangaza* means the homestead into which our women marry. When our *ukuli* jumps, our girls are whipped by those *maz* whose girls we whipped before. This is the whipping of the girls by the *maz*. They whip, whip, whip. (Op. Cit.: 84-85)

Edmund Leach who saw this episode in Robert Gardner's Film *Rivers of Sand* interpreted the use of the *michere* as follows:

> A striking example of this point is provided by Rivers of Sand, a recent ethnographic film of the Hamar of Ethiopia made by Robert Gardner. The main theme of the film is the exaggerated economic subjection of married women to their husbands. The subjection is given symbolic expression when, on various ritual occasions, young men whip their potential wives with great

severity. The film gives examples of this whipping but it is quite evident that a strong sadomasochistic erotic element is involved. The girls visibly experience excitement in their docile submission to brutality. (Leach 1976: 48)

I don't know whether Hamar women and girls really have sadomasochistic, erotic emotions on this occasion, but it is clear that they are not docile, and that they don't submit to any 'brutality' which they do not themselves control, for it is they themselves who demand to be whipped, seemingly against the wish and inclination of the initiates. To substantiate this point let me relate some observations which I made at the time when I worked on the film *The Leap Across the Cattle* (Strecker 1979c):

4.2.1976. While the *maz* (neophytes) were painting their faces, girls like Dambaiti, Anti, Bargi, Kulizele and other women of the clan Karla came to them and violently demanded to be whipped. They sang the *goala* songs (praise songs) and then aggressively pushed their way into the group of slightly apprehensive *maz* searching among them for the right one to be whipped by (i.e. one who is not of their own marriage group), pulling him out into the open, dancing up and down in front of him, receiving one or two strokes from him, mainly over the shoulder which was covered with a skin cape. The two elders present and also the ritual assistant of the initiate drove them away, and later they appeared a second time, to be whipped and be driven away again. Later, when the neophytes came to the gateway of the home-stead, some women and girls who had been dancing and waiting for them there, selected their *maz* and got their whipping.

The real big scene developed when the *maz* had reached the front of the shade where most of the guests had settled. There in the cattle kraal a large group of Karla women were dancing the *goala*. Their desire to get whipped and their attacks on the *maz* reached a state of ecstasy which was enhanced by the angry attempts of the elders like Baldambe, Lomotor, Tsasi, Kapell etc. who tried to keep the women away from the *maz*. The *maz* used their whips a lot, and each time they had used a whip, they dropped it to the ground until the bundles of whips in their hands began to dwindle. When the *maz* had settled down for coffee in the shade the urge for more whipping slowed down. Only some female leaders like Gardu would still approach the *maz*, select one and get whipped. One of the typical features of the whipping is the fighting between women over a *maz*. I witnessed one such partly real and partly mock fight between Gardu and Bargi." (unpublished notebook 20: 140-142)

The gender relations underlying these ritual practices are hard to fathom. Does there really exist a one-sided domination of men over women, a one-sided submission of women under men, as Gardner and Leach have suggested? I have often thought about this and in the field kept my ears and eyes open to find answers to the question. Here is one entry from my notebook dated 24 October 1988:

Gaito, son of one of Berimba's daughters, tells me this morning that he will soon go to collect animals from his relatives together with his young wife. A special collar (*binyere*) will be made for her, and then they will go. Without our asking anything else he adds that he then will act very proudly. He will ask her to bring him tobacco—and then will let her wait, let her wait for a long time until he takes the tobacco. He emphasizes that he will not look at her while he keeps her waiting. He says he will also whip her, and indulgently he tells the old story of how he will take her to the bush, bind her hands and legs and then whip her. Only then will she smoke the milk containers well, grind sorghum well and cook good food. He adds that women are like goats. You have to herd them with the whip. If you let goats run freely they won't get well fed. You have to guide them with the whip to the places where they find good food, especially fallen leaves. Only if you guide them do their bellies get full.

Now, as the women know very well how to do things, the herding idiom can only express a delusion on the part of the men. Perhaps Gaito himself does not fully believe the story he tells. Women don't need to be guided, so what is happening here? Jean (Lydall) and I have often heard and sometimes seen the dominance display of men towards their wives. Or should one rather call it the semi-public humiliation of the wife; that is of the young wife? We have also heard of, and occasionally witnessed how men threatened to beat their wives. Also, we have seen women who had been beaten by their husbands. But in spite of this often it really does not look like the men being the real bosses. Rather it looks as if the men are provoked by the women to beat them. The women want the show of strength by their husbands. They don't want to make good food and drink for weaklings and men who have no determination and strong will. It is as if the division of labour has been sealed here by the symbol of the whip. Whipping is the essence of herding. A father hands a whipping wand to his son to herd goats. It makes good sense that this means of control of others should be transferred to the human domain. So if men and women want to 'speak' as it were with the whip, then the exaggerated story of the husband breaking one whip after another on the back of his wife fits very well. But it fits in a twisted way, for in the final analysis it is the wife who holds the reins. If a wife wants to make her husband believe that he has complete and final authority over her (and wants to make others think, that he has this authority and a strong will etc.) what better strategy could she use than to make him whip her? By whipping her he has almost publicly proclaimed: "I am in charge here", and by doing so he has assumed all responsibility. Also he is bound to believe that he controls his wife. But as I have said above, he does not control her. Instead she controls not only himself but also his feeling of controlling her." (unpublished notebook 39: 23-25)

By way of conclusion I now like to quote a further proverb about the *michere*. It explains why the Hamar prefer to use the whipping wand instead of the word in certain situations of social conflict. We, in Western culture, have developed a wholesome fear and disgust of any kind of physical violence against persons. But on the other side, we are naive about the use of words, thinking that they are harmless and believing the proverb, which says, "Sticks and stones can break my bones, but words can never hurt me". Here the Hamar are more sceptical and have, in fact, great fear of the power of words (*apho*, 'mouth', 'word', 'language'). They know from experience that words can cause good as well as evil, and that nothing is more dangerous than words uttered in anger.

Therefore, anyone who makes use of the *michere* chooses the less threatening, the less daunting means of conflict. "*Michere sa atap kolle*", says the proverb, "the whipping wand does not curse". With the *michere* one says, "I guide you", "I show you what is right", "I make you bend to my will." At times this may be, as we have seen, nothing but an illusion, but at other times the belief in the beneficial power of the *michere* may lead to misuse, even brutality. The misuse of the *michere*, however, does not differ much from the misuse of words with their potentially brutal effect on people.

It is certainly an exaggeration to say, as the Hamar do, that at the tip of the whip is honey and at its side butter, and the idea that, "Sticks and stones can break my bones, but words can never hurt me" is similarly hyperbolic. So both, Westerners and Hamar are wrong, but they are also right and could learn from each other, the latter by acknowledging the destructiveness of physical violence, and the former by recognizing more than before the potential harm inherent in the use of words.

Political discourse in an egalitarian society

The Hamar belong to those 'tribes without rulers' (Middleton and Tait 1958) which have non-centralized political systems and live without formal laws or punishments, without great distinctions of wealth, without social class, without nobility, chiefs or kings. My paper is aimed at contributing to our understanding of the way in which such egalitarian systems work.

The Hamar have hereditary ritual leaders (*bitta*). They also select political spokesmen (*ayo*), leaders for war (*djilo*), guardians for grazing land (*kogo*) and for cultivated land (*gudili*), but the basic agents of politics are the married men (*donza*). Conceptually they are likened to a grass, which has roots that spread like a web on the ground (*zarsi*).

Hamar politics is thus grass-root politics similar to the way people in contemporary democratic societies like to speak of and engage in grass-root politics. An important difference is, however, the fact that in Hamar the women are completely missing from public politics. They nevertheless exercise an important influence, which is hidden and difficult to fathom.

As some of the literature on the ethnography of speaking has shown, oratory plays an important role in traditional societies and its study leads us straight to the heart of politics (Bauman and Sherzer 1974, Bloch 1975, Brenneis and Myers 1984). The peoples of East Africa are known for their great competence in oratory. Among those who practice a significant amount of pastoralism, occasions of public oratory are often associated with the consumption of an animal or animals. In Hamar this institution, called *osh*, may be held at different levels of social inclusiveness. It may involve only a small neighbourhood, i.e., several adjacent settlement areas (*gurda*); it may involve a larger part or the whole of a territorial segment (*tsinti*); it may involve several territorial segments or parts of them; or it may even involve the whole of Hamar country (*Hamar pe*). But even though there will be differences in size, duration, general tenor, seriousness of matters etc., the general pattern of the *osh* remains largely the same, and it is this pattern which I explore in what follows below.

Hamar political discourse may be seen as a process that moves repeatedly through four related stages each of which has its own mode of communication.

The political process rotates in a never-ending spiral from informal conversation to divination to oratory to blessing and cursing.

When the usual routine of Hamar herding, farming, hunting, gathering etc., is threatened by sickness, drought, internal or external conflict etc., the political process sets into motion. First responses happen on an individual level. People ponder quietly over the seriousness of the affair and individually look for signs in nature, clouds, stars, sounds of animals and children etc., which help them to interpret what is happening. Also, during the early morning hours and in the evenings at the homesteads and the cattle camps, and during the day in the fields and at the water holes, people begin to exchange views about the problems at hand.

Once a problem has reached such proportions that the elders decide that public decisions are necessary, they call the married men (*donza*) of the locality to a public meeting (*osh*). Such a call is always preceded by the search for an animal, which will have to be slaughtered in order to feed the men who attend the meeting. Without such an animal (ox, sheep or goat) no public meeting can be held.

Once a man has been found who agrees to provide the animal, the elders will be informed about the appointed day and the place where the meeting will take place. When the men arrive, they first settle down in the shade of a tree, relax and then enter into informal conversations. This is how the proper political discourse begins. Such informal conversations are always part and parcel of a public meeting and are clearly a customarily proscribed form of action. The most manifest element of the informal conversations is the exchange of news, which allow for a better evaluation of the problem for which the men have been called to the *osh*. First the more junior men who are present will speak, especially when they have been witnesses to events and are well informed about details of the current problems. Later, when the facts have been told and discussed in detail, the more senior men, especially the spokesmen who have come, enter the conversation. Typically they will relate historical events, which have been in some way like the present situation and can act as precedents and models for how to cope with the current issues.

In a more hidden way the informal conversations provide a forum for social and cultural criticism, the articulation of social values and, most importantly, the formation of social consensus. Here at the informal conversations people speak their minds and argue with one another. Also they can speak at length for there is usually lots of time at hand and people are willing to listen to one another. A striking theme of the conversations is lamentation. Everyone complains about the fact that others will not listen to him, that things are going wrong because he has so little influence over others and the matter at hand, and that therefore he cannot be held responsible for all the disasters that surely will happen.

I have found that these lamentations follow the structural lines of Hamar society: junior men, for example, will complain about the senior men who will not listen to them, and senior spokesmen from one locality will complain that the spokesmen of other localities would not listen to them etc. That is, everyone complains towards the direction where he finds that his freedom of action and his influence is most severely impeded. It took me some time to understand the logic of such endemic lamentation. Now I think that lamentation goes very well with the egalitarian character of Hamar social organization and politics: everyone is checked by someone else. No one will ever enjoy complete political success. Complete success would lead to a concentration of power and influence once it was achieved repeatedly. Therefore, frustration must be a perpetual part of egalitarian politics. But the frustration is measured, and the very fact that people indulge in long and colourful lamentation rather than lapse into mute silence is an indication that their political spirit is alive and that their aspirations have only been frustrated but not killed.

If the problem, which is facing a particular locality of Hamar or Hamar country at large, is really threatening, a divination will be held. This happens when the informal conversations are finished. The men move to another shade tree where a diviner has settled down to throw sandals in order to ask questions related to the existing problem and how it may be solved. He asks his questions either directly or in form of propositions, which the sandals may either confirm or reject, depending on the way they fall to the ground. Thus he may say, "we move the herds and the rain will fall", and then the silent answer of the sandals will be "yes" or "no".

On the first and manifest level, Hamar divination acts as a means by which the elders focus on the most difficult aspects of their political decisions. While the diviner throws the sandals, the men sit around him, watch and ask him to pose the questions, which interest them. In this way the diviner does not act all on his own but is to a large extent the medium of others. In the last resort, however, neither he nor the other men matter. Only the sandals "speak" and provide information on which the elders will act. The political implication of this, I think, is obvious: through divination the *donza* achieve an absolution from their responsibility, because it is not they but a third party, the sandals that is deciding the matter.

The process of divination shares some characteristics with the informal conversations in that it provides an opportunity for the men to air their views and articulate social fears. In fact the latter is more prominent here, because the men may ask the diviner critically to examine the behaviour of others under the pretext that it may be the cause for the existing problem. Thus the divination does not only serve as a shield behind which one escapes responsibilities, it also acts as a way to find scapegoats and allows for accusations which are so indirect that the accusers need not fear any retribution by the accused.

While the conversations and the divination are going on, young men slaughter the animal or animals provided for the meeting and roast the meat over the fire. When the meat is ready, they call the men to come and sit down along a semicircle of branches with fresh green leaves that will serve as a table from which the men eat. They will slowly pick up the meat from the leaves while they listen to the speeches being made. Only selected men are allowed to speak at a public meeting. They are called *ayo*. The verb *ai'a* means 'do'. So the *ayo* are those who get things done, they are leaders, and they lead especially by what they say. An *ayo* is selected by his 'elder brothers' and 'fathers' (i.e. men of senior age groups) when, at a particular place and in a particular moment in time, there is need for a new spokesman. They bless him and install him by handing him a spear at a public meeting. But the privilege they offer is provisional and holds only as long as his leadership is good and fruitful. To give more colour to this important fact let me quote from a Hamar text:

> One boy is a goatherd, but tomorrow he is a warrior: "When you go that way, if you meet a leopard kill it. Kill the lion! Kill the ostrich with the feathers. Kill the giraffe and when you return in the evening bring the fillet." So the fellow draws forth service.

Such a man is an *ayo*. If those who go don't kill the giraffe, the buffalo, the lion, the ostrich, the leopard, but if they meet the enemy and one of them dies, it will be said: "His word is bad, his command is bad. Stop him." (Lydall and Strecker 1979b: 109)

At an *osh* the men sit in order of seniority, the oldest to the right, the youngest to the left, and the principle of seniority applies also to speaking, the older ones speak first, the younger speak later. When a man's turn has come to speak, he gets up from his place at the leaves, takes the spear and walks over to where the animal has been slaughtered and roasted. There he takes some of the chyme, which is the green and only partly digested stomach contents of the animal, and rubs it on to his spear, his forehead, his chest and often also his legs. Then he passes slowly back and forth along the semi-circle of listeners and begins to speak. Old and experienced speakers who know of the respect they command usually begin their speech with a noisy and stylized expression of anger. They reprimand the younger for failing to act properly, for neglecting their duties, for thinking of themselves and not being strong, reliable and courageous. From this intimidation the public meeting has its name, *osh*. *Oshimba* means to be intimidated, shy, in social fear, and the term *osh* implies this intimidation. But let us note that the listeners are not really intimidated, and that it is because of their proud rejection of authority that the spokesmen shout so vehemently and complain that people do not listen and do what they want.

After he has finished with his rhetorical anger, the speaker comes to the particular matter of the day. Typically, he places the current issue in a historical context and looks for parallels and precedents in the past. The older a speaker is, the further back his memories reach. After the first speaker follows a second, a third and so on depending on how important the issue is and how many spokesmen are present. No speaker is listened to in complete awe and silence. On the contrary, one often hears the younger *ayo* who are sitting in the audience call out to the others: "listen, be quiet", which attests to the inattentiveness of the others. Listeners sometimes also interrupt speakers, throw in their comments, tell them what to say, laugh and tease them and generally may begin to chatter with each other when a speech begins to bore them. Of course such a refusal to listen dismays the speakers immensely.

Also, when a meeting concerns matters of war and peace, and when the men are determined to fight even though the speakers urge them to be prudent, the men will begin to chant their war songs (*raega*) with which they indicate their willingness to fight and their rejection of any advice of prudence which might be interpreted as fearfulness by their adversaries. Thus in Hamar a public speaker may be "sung down" rather in the way in which at western political meetings a speaker may be "booed" or "whistled" down.

Usually, there is a limit to which people can continue a meeting. The sun will get hot and the herds will have to be watered etc. Therefore, if a matter cannot be finished at one public meeting, another meeting will be called where the debate can be continued. In a sense, no debate is ever really finished and Hamar political history can be viewed (and is told as) a long line of public meetings. At each *osh* preceding ones are remembered and future ones projected and anticipated.

I have called the *osh* a debate, but I must qualify this. We speak of a debate when people try to persuade each other by refuting the arguments of others and by showing the strength and validity of theirs. At a Hamar *osh* such features are surely present, but debate should not spoil the central aim of the *osh* which is to articulate consensus. The *osh* is not the place and time where people should sort out and debate things from scratch. We have seen already how the *osh* is preceded by informal conversations and divination. The debates should have been finished during these earlier stages, and ideally the public speeches should express similar views, and agree on the way, which would lead everyone out of the existing problem.

I now turn to the fourth mode of Hamar political discourse, the curse (*asha*) and the blessing (*barjo aela*). We have already seen how the first three processes have gradually moved from a very open mode (conversations) to a more stylized and closed mode of communication. The curse and the blessing are even more closed and focused than the preceding divination and oratory. In the act of cursing and blessing the will of the group is expressed most emphatically. Here the consensus is complete. There is no divergence, no debate, no doubt.

Cursing and blessing are closely related to speaking. Only the more senior spokesmen may do it, and they often place it at the end of their speeches. There are various ways in which a speaker may combine cursing and blessing with his speech. Sometimes, when for example a speaker is so upset by a problem that he wants to get rid of it as soon as possible, he may begin his speech with a curse and having thus unburdened himself (and his audience) he moves on to speak.

There are also occasions where after the *osh* the men move to another place where the *ayo* then raises his spear and calls the evil to leave and the good to come forth.

Here is an example of a blessing (Lydall/Strecker 1979b: 14). The speaker is standing in front of the men and lifting the blade of his spear up into the air while he calls, he makes rhythmic gestures of pulling or drawing the desired thing (state of affairs) towards himself, and the men, who are imitating his movements with their hands, answer in refrain.

Leader:	Chorus:
Eh-eh!	
My herds are at Mello,	
which are in the open grass lands,	
may my herds come lowing, ...	come
grazing the grass may they come, ...	come
having eaten may the calves come, ...	come
leading their kids may the goats come...	come...

When a spokesman curses, that is when he "hides away" (*asha*) the undesired, he turns his spear around and jabs with the sharp metal point on the end of his spear in the direction towards which the evil should disappear, usually westward, where it should "get lost with the setting sun".

Leader:	Chorus:
Eh-eh!	
The herds are carrying sickness,	
may the sickness go beyond Labur, ...	may it go
may the sickness go beyond Topos.	may it go
Cattle owners you have enemies,	
down there, the Korre,	
if he looks at your cattle, may he die, ...	die
may his eyes fail, ...	fail
may his heart get speared, ...	speared
may they disperse like doves, ...	disperse
and leave...	leave...

(Lydall and Strecker 1979b: 14)

As we can see, Hamar political discourse moves from an open form, in which differences, insecurities and alternatives are expressed and discussed, to more and more closed forms in which the differences are narrowed down and are funnelled as it were towards a consensus. Here lies the decisive difference that distinguishes egalitarian from centralized forms of political organization. In the egalitarian practice of the Hamar, the ordinary problems of everyday-life set the political process into motion. At the beginning, people's individual views differ and collide about the right ways of action, and only when the differences have been negotiated and consensus has been reached will joint action be taken. Egalitarian politics are here the exact opposite of centralized politics. The former begin with a multitude of wills, which come to a consensus while the latter begin with a single will, which imposes itself on a multitude of others. In centralized political systems, like for example ancient Egypt, all politics emanate from an apex, from the divine ruler whose voice commands downwards reaching each and everyone in the social pyramid. In Hamar things are different. There is no single will which imposes itself on others, but rather many different wills which first diverge and then move towards each other, find consensus and act together. Such agreement never lasts because things change, new problems arise and the political process is set into motion again. Egalitarian political discourse converges from difference of view to consensus.

Besides the funnelling of opinion, several shifts towards seeming "irrationality" characterize Hamar political discourse. The two most important shifts occur when the Hamar move from conversation to divination and then again from oratory to blessing/ cursing. How are we to interpret these shifts? Returning to a point I have made above, the shift towards divination may be explained as a way of reducing the social danger involved in decision making. The divination reduces the threat inherent in answers, suggestions, commands, advice, etc. separating, as it were, speaking from will. The men express their views and offer their advice freely and without disguise during the informal conversations when nothing they say has any claim of authority. However, when they move towards the formulation of binding decisions, they hide behind the shield of divination. Following the terminology of politeness theory, one can say that they employ a strategy by which they soften the face-threatening act (FTA) involved in proposing decisions affecting others (Brown and Levinson 1978, 1987; Strecker 1988). Not all decisions are equally problematic. It is when decisions are socially threatening and difficult to justify that one should expect divination to be practiced.

What about the shift from oratory to blessing/cursing? Here we find the reverse of what happens in divination. All politics moves constantly between acts of commitment and acts of non-commitment, of saying 'yes' and saying 'no'. While divination embodies a strategy of non-commitment, of saying "no, I have nothing to do with it", blessing and cursing constitute acts of strong commitment and affirmation. They say, "Yes, we want things definitely to become like this or that". But they seem irrational in so far as they express wishes that are beyond human control. In this way, Hamar political discourse moves towards a kind of magical action. But it is important to note that this magical element is intrinsic to all expressions of emotional emphasis, rhetoric hyperbole, mimesis etc., and that it can be found in all human communication. That is, whenever people attempt to move others by indirect means of persuasion they enter the realm of magic. The persuasive magic of the Hamar *osh* aims at influencing the future in a kind of prophetic way, and one is reminded of certain Dinka ceremonies led by the "master of the fishing spear" of which Lienhardt writes, "Like prophecies, the ceremony eventually represents as already accomplished what the community, and those who can traditionally speak for them, collectively intend" (Lienhardt 1961: 251).

To share or not to share:
Notes about authority and anarchy

Introduction

In his Malinowski Memorial Lecture entitled "Egalitarian Societies" given on 5 May 1981 James Woodburn criticized Malinowski's view that "authority is the very essence of social organisation". His fieldwork among the Hadza as well as the ethnographies of other hunting and gathering societies like the Mbuti Pygmies, the !Kung San, the Pandaran, the Paliyan and the Batok who all have subsistence economies based on immediate-return practices had shown him that indeed there are societies with a "closest approximation to equality" and a lack of "elaborate instituted hierarchy" (1982: 431-32). Among these hunting and gathering societies "equalities of power, equalities of wealth and equalities of prestige or rank are not merely sought but are, with certain limited exceptions, genuinely realized"(1982: 432).

The key to this genuine realization of social equality is the maxim of sharing. What the maxim of sharing does "is to disengage people from property, from the potentiality in property rights for creating dependency" (1982: 445). In the hunting and gathering way of life the maxim of sharing can be most successfully asserted, but as soon as other elements such as agriculture and pastoralism come in, sharing becomes more problematic, the egalitarian ideal less attainable and Malinowki's hydra of authority makes its appearance. The aim of the present paper is to elucidate this problematic of sharing and authority in societies which are neither exclusively based on hunting and gathering, nor on agriculture, nor on pastoralism but combine these three sources of livelihood, often with apiculture in addition.

My analysis is based on texts from *The Hamar of Southern Ethiopia, Vol. I-III* (Lydall and Strecker 1979a, 1979b; Strecker 1979a). From *Baldambe Explains* I take the normative and idealized account of the Hamar ethos of sharing. From *Conversations in Dambaiti* I draw episodes which reveal the limited adherence to the norms of sharing, and from the *Work Journal* I select those passages which are best suited to show how I discovered not only the limits of sharing but also the role of hiding in Hamar culture, and how I battled to understand the egalitarian, individualistic and even anarchic character of Hamar social life.

The ideal of generosity and sharing

In his account of the beginning of Hamar culture, Baldambe addresses the theme of hierarchy and equality and shows how sharing is essential for social life. This is what he says:

> Long ago, in the times of the ancestors, the Hamar had two *bitta*. One was Banki Maro, one was Elto. The first ancestor of Banki Maro came from Aari and settled in Hamar in the mountains. He, the *bitta*, made fire, and seeing this fire the people came... The *bitta* was the first to make fire in Hamar and he said:
>
> "I am the *bitta*, the owner of the land am I, the first to take hold of the land. Now you may become my subjects, may you be my subjects, may you be my dependents, may you be the ones I command."
>
> "Good, for us you are our *bitta*..."

[Baldambe enumerates many of the clans who came from various regions in the vicinity of Hamar and asked the *bitta* for land]

> "Take hold of the land! Share out the land!" ...

[Baldambe now turns from the land to the herds]

> "*Bitta*!"
>
> "*Woi*!"
>
> "We don't have any cattle, only a few clans have cattle, only a

few men have some. What shall we do?"

"You have no cows?"

"We have no cows."

"You have no goats?"

"Only one or two men have goats. Most of us are poor."

"If you are poor collect loan cattle and cultivate your fields so you can bring sorghum to those who own cattle. Herding these cows, drink their milk." ...

So then the people began to collect cattle. One man bought cows for goats. The people said to each other:

"The poor should not go down to the waterhole with nothing. The *bitta* told us that those who have cattle should share some of them, calling those to whom they give cattle *bel* [bond-friend]."

"Whose cattle are these?"

"These are the cattle of so-and-so."

"And yours?"

"I have a cow from a *bel*, an arrow from which I drink."

A cow from a *bel* is called 'arrow' because one take a blood-letting arrow to draw blood from the jugular vein of a cow, and mixing four cups of blood with one cup of fresh milk, one feeds the children."

(Lydall and Strecker 1979b: 4-5)

[Baldambe now turns towards marriage payment]

When cattle had been collected in this way the elders called upon the *bitta*:

"*Bitta!*"

"*Woi!*"

"The people are all poor they have no cows, they have no goats. It would be bad if one had to give much to get married. Tell us what to do."

"Do you ask me as the *bitta*?"

"We have asked you."

"*Eh-eh*. My country has mountains only [is dry, poor]... Give twenty-eight goats plus one male goat and one female goat."

"Good. What about the cattle?"

The *bitta* said:

"Both rich and poor should give the same: eighteen head of cattle, plus one 'stone cow' and one 'cloth bull', which makes twenty altogether" (Lydall and Strecker 1979b: 5-6).

[Then Baldambe expresses the ethos of sharing and mutual assistance by evoking the picture of a poor man struggling to prepare for his marriage and obtain a wife]

So the *bitta* told this, and now he told them to take the *boko* stick [a short ritual staff with a round head].

"Take this *boko*, become an *ukuli* [initiate] and jump over the cattle."

"The boy is poor, he has no cattle, what shall he do?"

"He should give gourds to the people and they should fill them with milk for him."

So the *ukuli* gave gourds to the local people who filled them for him.

"Now he has no girls [sisters, cousins]. What shall he do?"

"Call the girls of the people to collect the gourds of the cattle camps."

They came and he fed them and then they went and brought full gourds to his homestead. Then the boy said:

"I have no mother. Who will grind my sorghum?"

"*Ye!* It does not matter whether you have a mother or not. The *bitta* said the women of the people should grind your sorghum."

"The *bitta* said so?"

"Yes, he said so."

So he called the women of the local people. All the women came and grind-grind-grinding made the beer for him.

"I have no father, I have no older brother."

"Call the elders to build a shade."

So the elders built a shade.

"*Eh*, now I have jumped over the cattle but I have no wife. What shall I do?"

"Ask an elder whom you call 'father' to be your marriage-go-

between. Tell him to take a staff of *baraza* [Grewia mollis] which is a *barjo* tree [tree bringing good fortune], and go to ask for a girl."
So the boy did so:
"Father!"
"*Woi!*"
"Go and ask for that man's daughter for me."
Off he goes and *kurr* [ideophone], he arrives:
 "*Misso* [hunting friend]! I bring you a staff on behalf of a poor man."
"*Eh-eh!*"
"I bring you *bodi* [fat, richness, fertility]."
"Why do you bring *bodi*?"
"I come on behalf of so-and-so's son. He says he is herding cattle, and after a while, when he has grown up, and has collected cattle for you, he will drive them to you as marriage payment. Give him your daughter. The *bitta* has said it should be so."
"*Eh-eh!* Did he say so?"
"He said so" (Lydall and Strecker 1979b: 2-10).

To share one's wealth and to assist others is an achievement that will be celebrated and recounted at a person's funeral. This is how Baldambe has described what happens:

So all his achievements are enumerated: the beehives he has made, the fields he has prepared, the lions he has killed, the herds he has collected, the children he has begotten, the speeches he has given. All his achievements are recounted... Then comes the stage in the funeral when all the wealth of the dead man is shown. Some people are rich, others have no cattle and some have distributed all their wealth among their bond-friends. Before a rich man dies, he demands:

"The cattle that I have given to people, the cattle that are now dispersed in the bush, the ones I have given to the poor so that they may herd them, so that they may have enough to eat, let them be seen when I have died."

So the cattle are driven to his homestead from ... [all over Hamar]. When the bond-friend comes to the homestead he carries with him a cow's horn filled with butter. Arriving at the entrance of the cattle kraal he rubs the foreheads of each of the dead man's sons and then the throats of each of his wives and daughters. After this, he then anoints the throat of each of the women who have come with him. Having anointed the living, they turn to the dead. First the oldest son takes butter from the bond-friend and mixes it with butter from a cow's horn of his own homestead. Four times he rubs the butter on to the forehead of his dead father asking him to herd the cows like he used to do when he was alive. Then the bond-friend mixes his butter with the butter of the dead man's homestead and also rubs the dead man's forehead and calls to him to herd and bless the cattle. Now the oldest son goes and pulls off two branches from a *baraza* tree. He places them in the cow dung so that they are damp and full of cow dung. Then he touches the backs of the cattle that the bond-friend has brought and blessing in this way, he hands them over to the bond-friend. The bond-friend will give some cattle and goats and honey to the dead man's sons (Lydall and Strecker 1979b: 39-41).

This, then, is how people should respect and care for each other and by doing so to enhance their self-esteem and their name and fame. But everything they collect and share comes ultimately from *barjo*, from luck, good fortune, creation. At the beginning of this account where Baldambe tells how the *bitta* formulated the first lore of the Hamar, this dependence on *barjo* is expressed as follows:

"Dig fields. When you have done that, here is sorghum. *Barjo* has given us sorghum. Sorghum is man's grass. As cows eat grass so shall man eat sorghum. *Barjo* gave us the meat and milk of cattle and goats long ago, saying:

Drink the milk of cattle and goats and eat their meat. Cattle and goats shall chew leaves from the bushes and cattle shall graze grass. Put fences around your homesteads so that the hyenas, jackals and hunting dogs can not enter. The one who enters is man.

You have hands. Dig fields and when the sorghum is ripe bring some to the cattle owners, your bel, bring some to the goat owners, your goat *bel*. Make beehives taking the bark of the *donkala* tree binding the *arra* grass around it with the *kalle* creeper and smearing the inside with cow dung. Place the beehives well in the forks of trees. The bees will come to you from Ari country...."

[Baldambe tells of all the places from where the bees will come]

"When the bees have come the honey will ripen. When it is ripe, bring honey to the *bitta* so that he may call forth the *barjo* of your cattle and the *barjo* of your goats and that he may get rid of sickness for you. The elders should come to build my house and erect my cattle gateway." (Lydall and Strecker 1979b: 7-8).

Thus *barjo* shares out what is most essential for existence: grass for goats and cattle and 'grass' (in the form of sorghum) for human beings. The bees in turn provide the honey from which honey wine can be made which then is used to call forth '*barjo*', the source of all well-being.

The limits of generosity and sharing

The picture, which Baldambe has provided of the Hamar sharing their goats and cattle in order to ensure each other's well-being, speaks of a cultural dream and ideal. The dream exists because the reality is all too often quite different. Generosity and sharing have their limits, for the vicissitudes of goat herding lead to many temptations and provide ample opportunities for enriching oneself at the expense of others. The problem begins already at home, that is, in the composite herds of a homestead, where it is not always easy to distinguish the different goats and unambiguously identify their owners. Here is a conversation that exemplifies what I mean. It was one early night when women and children were sitting outside, next to the cattle and goat enclosures, relaxing and drinking coffee after a long day of exhausting work in the fields:

"Anti [a girl]: Why are the herds so noisy today? They sound as if they have been moving camp.

Gino [Anti's older brother, addressing his younger brother]:
Lomoluk, go and see whose kids are making such a noise.
Anti: They have just been milked.
Bargi [her mother]: Most of the kids are drinking from their
mothers now, there are only a few goats to milk…
Gino [to Lomoluk]: Please go over there and find out, which kids
are calling.
Bargi: The kids which are calling, whose kids may they be? Are
they the offspring of the thin goats? Look at them and come back.
If they have drunk and are still hungry, they should be driven
where there is more grass and a camp should be made for them
there.
Lomoluk [from inside the goat enclosure]: The kid…
Bargi [signalling him that she is listening]: *Yo!*
Lomoluk: It is the kid of the old goat with black spots.
Anti: And the others?
Lomoluk: The others, wait, they are calling down here! [from
inside the enclosure like before] One goat.
Gino [answering Lomoluk]: Hm.
Lomoluk: It is one of the yellow goats,… it is the kid of the yellow
blind goat.
Gino: *Hm*, that kid has become very thin.
Lomoluk [calling]: Mother!
Bargi: *Yo!*
Lomoluk: The kid that made such noise…
Bargi: Yes!
Lomoluk: Down there, the freckled goat which we have herded
for a long time already, see, it is its kid…
Bargi: Yes?
Lomoluk: It is the one that makes such noise.
Bargi: So milk the mother and then let the kid drink. [the
conversation now moves on to other topics and Lomoluk returns
from the goat enclosure, then Gino picks up the theme of the goats
again]
Gino: During the day she can go with the kids, why do you keep
the old goat in the enclosure?

Bargi: She goes with the kids.

Gino: *Hm*.

Aikenda [Gino's father's younger brother's wife]: He doesn't know that we don't keep her in the enclosure.

Anti: The day before yesterday she went up there.

Gino: The girls don't understand anything about goats, they might easily think the old one is small and leave her with the youngest kid in the enclosure throughout the day... You let the grown-up kids stay together with the very small ones inside the enclosure throughout the day, that's why I asked whether you also left the old one inside.

Anti: *Ye*, which grown-up kid?

Gino: The kid of the goat with the small black spots.

Anti: Gino, leave such talk, we will let this one graze.

Lomoluk: The kid of the freckled sick goat that cried this morning?

Gino: Yes, the one that made such a noise just now.

Anti: It is my father Baldambe's goat.

Bargi: *Ye*! Which one is Baldambe's goat?

Anti: Before we used to say it was Baldambe's goat, and then it was said it was Shalombe's goat, Shalombe's.

Bargi [reprimandingly]: Ach! You always say 'so-and-so's goat, so-and-so's goat!'

Gadi [Gino's father's younger brother's wife]: When I asked Gino before he said it was Shalombe's goat...

Anti: *Ye*!

Gadi: And when I asked Gino again he said it was Baldambe's goat.

Anti [laughs]: *Haha*!

Gardu [Gino's classificatory sister]: Your lies, they really are something bad.

Bargi: I have also never heard people beat the names of the owners of a goat so much.

Gardu [addressing Gadi]: *Uto*, they have said this about the goat...

Gadi: *Hm*.

Gardu: They take just this, just that and say it, saying that
Shalombe has bought the goat...
Bargi: The children just talk like this without thinking.
Anti: Let our grandfather tell you [Shalombe, Anti's
classificatory 'grandfather' who has been listening quietly].
Bargi: Whose goat is it then? [to Shalombe] Now Shalombe, why
don't you tell us about the goat?
Maiza [Baldambe's sister]: In this homestead I have never heard
anyone distinguish between owners of goats like this before.
Aikenda: *Ye*, isn't it customary to separate the goats from each
other and call them by their different owners? Since when does
one put goats of different owners together just so?
Shalombe: The goat is the offspring of the goat given by Tsaina's
son. It has ears that are cut differently.
Bargi: That was truly said.
Shalombe: How come you all ask about the sick goat? Let this be
the concern only of its owner.
Aikenda: *Hm*. We did not mean this.
Gardu: Yes, right.
Bargi: *Hahaha*" (Strecker 1979a: 121-129).

The need to identify goats correctly and allocate rights and
duties accordingly goes, of course, beyond the domain of a
single homestead, for it may easily happen that a goat goes
astray and is absorbed by another herd. Then it takes much
honesty to return the animal to its proper owner. But if honesty
prevails, this is much applauded like in the following example:

Baldambe: "Isn't Hamar something good? Look at this goat which
once got lost... Our herding boys said, just so: 'The fox has eaten it.'
At that time the sorghum was ripe. 'Gino, look for the goat.' 'I
have searched for it at Basho, I have searched for it at Singera, I
have searched for it aaall... over the country.' Recently an age-
mate of Lomoluk said: 'Lomoluk.' *'Woi.'* 'Look at his goat, it has
the ear-cut of your goats, the goats of Berinas' homestead. Take it,
it has already been a long while with us.' Now the goat has
grown up... When it got lost, it was small and thin, now it has

become big and fat. See, this is Africa, Hamar" (Strecker 1979a: 37).

The temptation to take from the property of others whenever an opportunity avails itself is an experience which most of the Hamar share. They are keenly aware of the fact that it is all too easy to let other people's animals, especially goats and sheep, run with one's own herds and eventually to keep them, together with their offspring. This is why they speak of mystical retribution, which will follow such dishonest behaviour, like in the following example:

Choke (with a calm, low and quiet voice): "The son of Tini's father, Muga had driven his goats from here to Pali and then again had moved his camp to Korta. At that time many men from Mirsha kept their cattle in the area. Now, aren't we talking about lost goats?"

Baldambe: "About lost goats."

Choke: "He moved from Pali to Korta. When the men of Mirsha had moved away, three thin sheep of theirs were left behind. These three sheep joined his goats. Hadn't the owners of the sheep returned to their own country? So they stayed, stayed, stayed, got healthy. But the owners were not told of this. Didn't Muga have his camp on his own, away from other people? So the sheep lambed, lambed. They did not die and they did not get sick. The sheep lambed. They multiplied, became young castrated sheep, became big, grown-up castrated sheep, became rams. While the sheep multiplied like this, Muga fell sick and could not speak anymore."

Aulebais: "Where was that?"

Choke: "Down at Laetan. Weren't you there yourself when Haila (a diviner) was throwing the sandals? That was when Haila's wife had died down in the fields. He threw the sandals, threw them, threw and watched them: 'Kubu (reciprocal term of address for two men married to women from the same lineage). Kubu. You have come to death, but you won't die. These sheep, what kind of sheep are they? They come and look at you. Or are these cattle?

No, no cattle.' He continued throwing the sandals and they kept coming back to the same, coming back, coming back. 'What sheep are these?' He continued throwing. 'First it looked as if the sheep had come on one path to you, but then – I see that you did not drag them by a rope fastened around their necks. It looks as if they have come on two paths – no, on one – not on one, on two.' He kept throwing the sandals. 'In the bush.' He, Haila, was a different man (very special)."

Aulebais: "*Nyarsh*, he was very sharp."

Choke: "This Haila, this Haila, he was a different man."

Aulebais: "Wasn't it Haila who pulled me away from death and made me sit up again?"

Choke: "He threw, threw, threw: 'What sheep are these?' He asked and listened, but Muga kept silent. 'Now if you don't tell me about these sheep, your father's goats and you will not walk this soil for much longer. Why don't you die then? If you talk about these sheep you will not die. What is killing you now are these sheep.'"

Baldambe: "As his sandals tell the truth he has grown to be disliked by people. They say: 'He always spoils our goats.'"

Choke: "Yes, that's why people are angry. They ask him to help them survive...."

Baldambe: "... and they hide the stolen goats that are killing them..."

Choke: "... are killing them. So they kill themselves. Haila threw the sandals again: 'Now, what are you doing? Here it is again! It is saying 'take me away from my kraal, let me be slaughtered in the open'."

Baldambe: "The sheep."

Choke: "A castrated sheep, so fat, fat, fat, fat that it struck anyone who looked at his herd. When you saw his herd from behind you would see this sheep, when you saw the herd from in front you would see it."

Baldambe: "Is he an offspring of those lost sheep?"

Choke: "My father's son, three were lost and they multiplied so much that they became a whole herd."

Maiza: "They were like sand."

Choke: "Like sand, they multiplied so much. It's they who brought the sickness. Then he began telling the truth: 'When the sheep first came to me they were three. They stayed with my son's goats and no one came asking for them. They stayed with me and they multiplied the most out of all of my goats and sheep. What shall I do?' 'Why don't you separate one of them from the others? Slaughter it out in the open for the people and leave the others with your herd.'"

Baldambe: "Yes, long ago the master, your father Berinas, told me: 'If any goats that get lost come to you, hand them on and let them run with the herds of someone else.'"

Choke: "Let them graze far away from you."

Baldambe: "Far away. If stray animals multiply inside your kraal they will bring sickness."

Choke: "...he was right."

Baldambe: "They kill the people."

Choke: "They kill."

Baldambe: "'Let stray animals be herded by others.' Today people speak differently. They say: 'Leave them, let them multiply and when they have grown old, give them to the people, the scavengers, to eat'."

Choke: "To eat."

Baldambe: "That's how they steal today. That's what they want."

Choke: "See what they want today! Then Muga brought out one castrated sheep and it was slaughtered. The people ate it. They were full and still there was some meat left. Later again at his father's funeral he killed another big sheep... He got rid of them at funerals, he got rid of them by giving them to those who asked him for animals..."

Baldambe: "So now he possesses only those that are truly his own?"

Choke: "Yes, which are his own, which belong to his head (like the hair which is part of the head)."

Baldambe: "Don't say that, say: 'those which are his whipping wands' (given to him by his father together with whipping wands)."

Choke and Baldambe: (laughing quietly together, delighting in their understanding of the intricacies of Hamar customs) (Strecker 1979a: 40-43).

If generosity and sharing have their limits already in times of plenty, and if people are ever ready to steal each other's goats, this is even more so in times of crisis, when the rains have failed and starvation is imminent. This is the picture which my *misso* (hunting-friend) Banko painted at a time when a severe drought was hitting Hamar and the surrounding regions:

Usually, about the time the Ethiopian police celebrate Easter, the first sorghum ripens and small children 'steal' from it and survive. But look at the fields today. They are empty, a desert! Where can we go to exchange our goats for grain? There is no more grain in Banna, nor in Tsamai, nor in Aari. The doors to Galeba and to Arbore are closed and there is hunger there anyway. We are now slaughtering our goats and those who have none take them by force. Soon we will run out of animals and then we shall kill each other over them: 'why don't you let me have one of your cows?' and we shall take up spears and kill each other. Soon there will be nothing but turmoil (Lydall and Strecker 1979a: 102).

Well, luckily Banko's scenario was exaggerated. What we witnessed was no real turmoil but an increase of demands by the poorer members of Hamar society to share the resources of those who were more affluent. Strong confrontations developed especially between affines who in meagre times always remember first those to whom they have given their daughters and sisters and whom they remind of the fact that they still owe them some marriage payment, like in the following two cases:

> The affine of Dube (Baldambe's brother) is at the gateway once again, demanding marriage payment in a provocative manner. Baldambe argues that he should get together with the girl's father to work out what may be due to him. The boy rejects this idea and a violent argument ensues, bringing to light the precarious relationship between affines. Once again the everyday life of Hamar seems to be on the verge of anarchy. The argument is laced with threats. The boy threatens to take what he wants by force. Not today and not here in the homestead but at some future date he will take a cow or two from the herds of the sons of Berinas, he will take them when the herds are out in the bush. Baldambe on the other hand, implies that his family is strong and ruthless and would not mind killing an affine who dares to provoke them. In the end when Wadu (a friend of Baldambe) has severely admonished him, the boy gives in and, intimidated, he sits among the men who settle down to drink their morning coffee. (Lydall and Strecker 1979a: 214-215).

Yesterday two women of Baldambe's clan Karla arrived at Dambaiti asking Baldambe to help them claim payment for some of their daughters. For the first time I see clan solidarity in a different light. To date the most impressive expression of this solidarity that I have witnessed has been the way in which clan members use the marriage of one of their women to blackmail the family of the husband into giving them goats and cattle. Today, I am seeing this solidarity from a different angle: a woman's classificatory brothers are the main allies of her family should the latter receive no adequate payment for her marriage. Clan members try to keep out of such matters, leaving all the appropriate economic transactions to the families directly involved. But if a woman's family is slow in making the legitimate demands, then the other members of her clan come into the picture. I have the feeling that if members of the woman's clan detect a weakness in the husband's family, they later exploit this weakness to their own advantage, blackmailing the other side into unnecessary payments. In this way, in-laws can become a real threat. This threat operates dialectically in everyday life: relations between affines are generally good precisely because this relationship is potentially bad. If a potentially bad relationship is turned into a good one, this is considered a true social achievement. Baldambe turned his affines, Hailu and Wadu, into his best friends. This is probably a general feature of social life: friendship and alliance can produce very close relationships when they bridge potentially dangerous gaps such as those between social classes, castes, colour bars... (Lydall and Strecker 1979a: 242).

In times of need, next to the affines it is the bond-friends from whom one demands a share of their wealth. For example, on the very day when Baldambe refused to give way to the demands of the affine who had come to his gate-way, he sent his younger brother Kairambe to collect animals from a bond-friend in order to pay a trader to whom he was indebted. My comment at the time was as follows:

This is yet another example of how the system of bond-friendship is a form of capital, which one lays up against unwelcome surprises. Whenever Baldambe is suddenly in need of 'cash', he starts thinking of his bond-friends. Many of them he has inherited from his father. Calculating, which of them he has left in peace for longest and which may have a cow at his disposal, he decides which bond-friend to bother on any specific occasion. Over the course of time, in this system you can receive an infinite number of cattle as a return on an original investment of a single cow. (Lydall and Strecker 1979a: 215).

To give one's cattle away as 'loan cattle' (*banne wak*) is not only a useful form of investment, but also a way of hiding them and making one's true wealth invisible. This is how Baldambe told me about it:

"As we chew our *muna* [sorghum rolls], I reflect on my attempt to work during the morning. I sigh and tell Baldambe that if I were a

proper anthropologist, I would be writing from now on, writing
without respite, so that the books would grow fat whilst I myself
grew thin. My youth would go into the books and my eyes would
darken, I would need glasses, my hair would grow white and with
a whisper I would talk to my students. I imitate the speech
mannerism of an old professor talking Hamar: '*Nanato, kami
wodimate...*" I relate what I would say about Hamar and when I
reach the institution of bond-friendship, pointing out that it is in
this way that a young man builds up his capital, Baldambe
suddenly interrupts my imaginary lecture. 'And by giving his
cattle away to his bond-friends, he makes sure that none of his
relatives and affines comes and takes them away from him
unexpectedly.' I had always thought that this 'hiding' was one of
the most important reasons for the institution but I had never
heard a Hamar state this clearly. 'Thank you, *misso*
Ogotemmeli!'"(Lydall and Strecker 1979a: 221)

The distribution of wealth and social influence

As the drought continued and people kept increasing their
demands on each other's wealth, I began to ask them about the
way in which they perceived the difference of wealth in Hamar.
This is how I described the attempt:

> I have developed a graphic scale for measuring wealth. It consists
> of showing five circles of different sizes. I ask Choke to identify
> all the individual men of the villages he knows best with one of
> these circles, the rich with the large circles, the poor with the
> small circles. My aim is to discover how certain structural features
> of Hamar society are perceived by the actors. The way that
> Choke carries out the task shows that he perceives Hamar as
> rather egalitarian. He enumerates as many poor as rich. (Lydall
> and Strecker 1979a: 235).

As I continued my research into wealth difference in Hamar, I
noted down the following observations and reflections:

> Raised voices in Aikenda's house wake me before sunrise. The
> abbreviations, the pauses, the pace, the quick echoing responses,

the varying levels of tone – all these tell me that great speakers
have arrived. I can also tell where they come from, only the men
of southern Hamar speak so powerfully. So I am not surprised to
find Arbala Lomotor [a good friend and in-law of Baldambe]
sitting next to the coffee pot. He, however, does not talk; he
leaves the word to an old, grey haired man. The old man, like
many of those who I have met from the south, has a strength and
confidence and ruthlessness, which I attribute to the environment
of the wide, open spaces of the south and their proximity to
hostile neighbours. The south seems to select for strong and rich
people. The south offers a regal way of life: large herds, especially herds of goats, periodically exchanged for grain from Banna,
Kara, Tsamai. In the south no poor man can survive. That is why
the census shows more people the further one moves north. In
Hamar terms, 'poor' means lacking herds of cattle and goats. In
some ways, wealth and oral competence go together, or more
exactly, oral competence and the ownership of herds! A remark of
Choke comes to my mind: he said that in the south everybody
talks at public meetings. He implies that this is bad, because it
prohibits clear decision making, 'Look at Assile, Wungabaino,
Mirsha, the men of those places never stop fighting and raiding.
Everybody does what he wants, nobody is listened to. Look at
Angude and Kadja, those men only allow a small number of
selected people to speak, and they stick to the decisions of those
speakers'. I wonder whether I will ever be able to answer the
question concerning the relationship between speaking and wealth
and I start thinking about wealth in general: how has the
distribution of wealth in Hamar developed over time? It may
well have changed considerably during the past generations. The
Hamar theory is that wealth used to be concentrated in the hands
of only a couple of families just two, or even one generation ago.
All the other people used to herd cattle they had been given by
the wealthy within a bond-friend relationship. It is said that
when the wealthy brought cattle to the waterhole, no one else
would approach. But doesn't the indigenous account always tend
to simplify the past? Just as a large number of ancestors are edited

out of the account, so too are most wealthy men and all past wealth is said to have been concentrated in the hands of only a few. The Marxist model of progressive concentration of wealth in only a few hands is the exact opposite of the Hamar model... Why do the Hamar see wealth as moving from concentration to dispersion rather than vice versa? Because this is how the wealthy individual's life cycle operates? Because the old people who have the greatest command over wealth always lose their hold when they die? Or does the theory refer to the time when the Hamar were recuperating economically from Menelik's invasion? At that time warriors such as Berimba accumulated a great deal of wealth in their hands after successful raids on the Borana, Gabare etc... (Lydall and Strecker 1979a: 236-237)

On the relationship between wealth, speaking and the life cycle I had noted a day earlier:

People may be allowed to speak publicly because their fathers were once wealthy. Could it be that the herds of wealthy fathers provide the sons with a good economic basis for exercising social influence? The son of a rich man is the one who supervises the herds and for this reason, quite frequently initiates actions like moving camp, watering, scouting etc. If his leadership comes to be recognised in this way, he becomes a 'speaker'. But as a 'speaker' he has to be generous, and gradually he is divested of his wealth as he tries to keep his supporters. Lomale, the most important 'speaker' of western Hamar, is the son of a rich father. So is old Bume, who has almost the same prestige as Lomale and who is said to have been rich in cattle and goats in times gone by. Today Choke counts them the poorest of Hamar. (Lydall and Strecker 1979a: 235- 236).

Reflections on authority and anarchy

From all the examples I have given so far one can see how under varying circumstances both inequality and equality are characteristic features of Hamar culture. The acceptance of authority and the 'premise of inequality' to use Maquet's

famous title (1961), lies at the back of the social constitution of
Hamar as attributed to the *bitta*, but in everyday life, any
outright assumption of authority is rejected and equality is
constantly asserted. During fieldwork I was puzzled by these
seemingly contradictory strains in Hamar culture, and again
and again I came back to the questions of hierarchy and
egalitarianism, order and anarchy. Let me provide two examples. The first concerns the nexus between individualized
knowledge and individualized social life:

> In the morning we have coffee in Aikenda's house. Baldambe is
> absent, but there are guests like Choke's friend Wualle Lokarimoi
> and Kula the 'black'. They say that the position of the stars
> indicates hard times ahead. While listening to the conversation
> it strikes me... how individualized all astronomical knowledge is.
> Everyone has particular observations to make. Each man puts
> them forward with much force and mystique, yet no one attempts
> any systematic account of the various astral phenomena. For me,
> this reflects the social structure. Knowledge is generally indiv-
> idualized and specific. Hiding and mystique cloud the channels of
> information so that no unified body of social knowledge can be
> acquired and maintained. The same individualization seems to
> affect ritual and almost all levels of social organization. Is
> 'individualization' the right word? What I mean is free indiv-
> idual choice in the application of general principles. As for
> example in intermarriage: there are clans but no segmentary
> structures nor obvious marriage patterns. There are distinctions of
> age, but no operational age-set system; there is leadership but no
> clearly defined office; there are differences in wealth, but these
> are drastically levelled through the institution of bond-
> friendship... I think the census will show in the end that there is
> a large degree of 'randomness' in the application of general
> principles. But once this is shown, the 'randomness' will no longer
> be random but rather a typical feature of individualistic Hamar
> social organisation in which everyone works towards a
> maximization of choices in any particular social situation.
> Because of the strong rejection of authority amongst the Hamar, I

have been referring to Hamar society as 'anarchic', but I propose
to use the term 'individualization' for the time being. (Lydall and
Strecker 1979a: 228-228).

The second example comes from the Hamar cattle camps and
is about the acceptance of past and the rejection of present
authority:

At night while Bali (Baldambe's younger brother) speaks to us
sitting on our cowhides, more and more young men join us and listen
with quiet intensity... An audience materializes almost in-
audibly, making the speaker feel that he is saying something
they value highly. And then slowly the members of the audience
sitting in darkness start to speak themselves. Their speeches are
long and are listened to by the assembled company. They
constantly invoke the 'old', the 'fathers', the 'older brothers' and
refer to the 'precedents' of which I have talked above. There is a
confidence and trust in the old and the established, which has
never seemed to me quite so marked before (although I realise now
that it has always been there). I suddenly realise that here may
lie one of the keys to understanding Hamar 'conservatism' and
(paradoxically?) its 'anarchy'. The cattle camps play a big part
in the socialization of the young men. Here, to a large extent, they
are free from the strict domination of the elders. Here they have
to make their own decisions, and these decisions are made on the
basis of precedents, by referring to what 'the great men of the past
would have done in such-and-such a situation. By invoking a
precedent the speaker almost becomes the historical person
himself, so by invoking historical authority they reject the
present authority of others. One might argue that Hamar anarchy
is a result of the fact that everybody rejects a living person's
decision if it is based on purely individual and contemporary
judgement. Outright individual cleverness and power are taboo
and no one may openly aspire to them. Instead one must make a
precedent of an incident in the historic past, which will be
acknowledged by others as offering the appropriate answer to a
specific problem in the present. (Lydall/Strecker 1979a: 249-250).

Conclusion

What I have tried to do in this small homage to James Woodburn, is to let the reader accompany me on my journey into what Baldambe used to call the 'thicket' of Hamar social life, and explore themes which always have been close to James Woodburn's heart, themes of sharing, the 'rhetoric of property'—as Carol M. Rose (1994) would call it—, immediate and delayed exchange, authority and, above all, the question of egalitarianism.

At the outset of his lecture on 'Egalitarian Societies' from which I have quoted already in the introduction, James Woodburn stressed that, "although very many societies are in some sense egalitarian, those in which inequalities are at their minimum depend on hunting and gathering for their sub-sistence... But there is, of course, no question of the equality being a simple product of the hunting and gathering way of life. Many hunter-gatherers have social systems in which there is very marked inequality of one sort or another, sometimes far more marked than the inequalities in certain simple agricultural or nomadic pastoral societies" (1982:432). And at the end of his lecture, he returned briefly to these agricultural or pastoral societies often called in anthropological parlance 'acephalous societies', 'tribes without rulers', 'societies without formal political offices'. Equality between household heads, he argued, are here only a starting-point, a qualification to compete in a strenuous competition for wealth, power and prestige" (1982: 446).

As the notes, which I have presented here have shown, the social life of the Hamar of Southern Ethiopia has a similarly strenuous character. It is torn between hierarchy and anarchy, equality and inequality, individualism and sociality, and the existing tensions are mirrored in the patterns of sharing.

Lomotor's talk, or the imperial gerund

In this paper I take a closer look at part of a conversation that I had in July 1973 with my friend Lomotor, brother-in-law of Baldambe (see Lydall and Strecker 1979a; Strecker 1998). Our theme was the background of current feuds between the Hamar and some of their neighbours, and at one point Lomotor related to me what was said at a meeting, which had recently been held between the Hamar and the Galeba (Dassanech). This passage, included in the ethnographic album *Music of the Hamar* (Strecker 1979), is especially moving and worth listening to for its own sake. It has even inspired artists—first Tilman Künzel and later Carmen Eder—to accompany it with music that emphasizes its prosody, its rhythms, its modes and tones of feeling. But here I examine this extraordinarily powerful instance of Hamar oratory partly to demonstrate a culture specific style of speaking, partly to highlight a particular aesthetic, but above all to make the more general point that *tension phenomena* are worth our attention, for tension is inherent in nature, inherent in life, inherent in human experience, and therefore also inherent in the use of language.

As the dictionary tells us, 'tension' involves a state of being stretched, strained and filled with excitement, like the stress by which a bar or a string is pulled. This relates to the verb and adjective 'tense' meaning "(of cord, membrane, or figuratively of nerve, mind, emotion) stretched tight, strained to stiffness, causing tenseness (a tense moment)" (The Oxford Concise Dictionary).

One of the most effective ways to create tension in discourse is to use gerund clause structures, which carry the hidden message that just as the author masters the complex structure of the sentence, he or she is able to grasp difficult issues, and above all, is able to master people. This is why one can speak of the 'imperial' gerund.

Lomotor's speech begins with a gerund, which is supported by a short ejection and a chuckle that are repeated:

Maxulo d'abais

Maxulo having risen (Maxulo: a spokesman of the Galeba)

Ye, Maxulo! Eh.

Oh yes, Maxulo! (Lomotor imitates the inviting character of the meeting and laughs because of his satisfying memories)

Maxulo d'abais

Maxulo having risen [...]

Then Lomotor imitates Maxulo and other speakers with a series of directly quoted utterances until, in the end, Lomotor finishes saying:

Amais tau won dalkono

Having said which, wasn't it, what we talked about." (Strecker 1979b: 22).

Tellingly, the use of the gerund is here associated with the physical act of rising, and taking a spear. This amplifies what we already know from the handbooks both of grammar and of rhetoric: gerunds have a projective, tension-raising property. They 'raise matters', analogous to the way in which Maxulo raises himself physically and takes a spear into his right hand in order to address the audience and make it the target of his rhetorical will. In 1973 I recorded a public meeting that took place at the Hamar cattle camps. The description I provided for the resulting record gives a picture of such a speechmaking situation:

In the grazing areas of the Lower Omo where the territory of the Hamar borders those of the Galeba and Bume, the young Hamar men have slaughtered an ox. The meat has been roasted over a fire and served on freshly cut bunches of green leaves which are placed on the ground in a wide semicircle. About one hundred Hamar men sit down and begin to eat the meat.

At first, while they eat, everyone is silent. Then after a while, one of the oldest and most influential men present rises. He takes a special spear, which is a symbol for his privilege to speak in a public meeting. He removes the leather cover that protects the sharp blade of the spear and walks over to the centre of the semicircle. Here he takes some of the contents of the ox's stomach—the partly digested green substance consists of grasses, herbs and leaves, and symbolises health and fertility—and rubs it on his forehead, chest and knees. Then, according to his personal temperament and the content of his speech, he passes repeatedly in front of the semicircle of sitting men with a fast or slow stride. First he does not say a word and one only hears his steps on the ground. The stillness and tension grows until eventually he breaks it with the loud cry: "*Hai!* Hamar, listen to me!" Then he begins his speech. At first he scolds the men and intimidates them. In particular, he addresses himself to the younger men and says that only they should speak from now on, as it is they who are interested only in evil and not in good. He accuses them of having brought bad luck, saying that war, sickness, drought and all other suffering are ultimately the outcome of their bad social behaviour and their careless enactment of the rites for the dead.

After his vehement introduction the speaker turns to the special problems of the immediate situation. On the day of the recording (June 1, 1973) the war with the Bume was at issue. The first speaker and then the one who follows him admonish the men and tell them to leave the Bume in peace so that they can concentrate on the defence against the Galeba who are by far the more dangerous. However, the men are eager to fight. They want to settle old debts with the Bume, the sooner the better. Therefore they raise their voices and chant war songs, which are led by a solo singer. The speakers ask them to stop

and continue to speak for peace. But the singers don't stop. In
their songs they ridicule the enemy. Sometimes they get on their
feet, individually or in groups, and while they call out the
names of their dance oxen they trample on the ground and
point with their weapons in the direction of the enemy. In this
way the public meeting changes into a dynamic opposition
between individual speakers and the singing collective. The
process continues until a decision has been reached. If those
who want peace succeed (as in fact happened on this day) the
final speaker lifts both his arms and calls for rain, bees, health,
fat ... If those who want to fight succeed the speaker points his
spear towards the enemy" (Strecker 1979b: 23-24).

It was a public meeting like this one, which Lomotor witnessed and reproduced for my favour, and which I will now give in
full. Lomotor's account is energized by a wide-spanning gerund
that acts as a bow of tension with which the speaker shoots off
rhetorical arrows. These are indicated on the right side of the
text and summarized in a diagram that follows below.

Lomotor's account of Maxulo's speech

1. *Maxulo d'abais*
   Maxulo having risen,

2. *"Ye! Maxulo!" "Eh."*   Protasis/Gerund
   "Oh, Maxulo!" "Yes."

3. *Maxulo d'abais:*
   Maxulo having risen (said):

                              ...

4. *Edi ogoro – kutsona atadau?*
   Are these people fathered for vultures?

5. *Guderina atadau?*   Indignant Question
   Fathered for hyenas?

6. *Ai ai aina atadau?*
   Fathered for the sun, sun, sun?

                              ...

7. *Edi edina ko atade.*
   (No,) people are fathered for people.

8. *Angi ataise wakider ki gutade.*
   Fathering a son, so that he may go with the cows.

9. *K'ulider ki gutade.*
   That he may go with the goats.

10. *Amider ki gutade.*
    That he may go to the fields.   AFFIRMATIVE ANSWER

11. *Otoder ki gutade.*
    That he may go with the calves.

12. *Ankasider ki gutade.*
    That he may go with the lambs.

13. *"Goba, sa ainexal yir tio" amaise erga ki yitade.*
    That he may be sent on errands saying: "Run over there
    and get me something from him!"
                                        ...

14. *Ae a atan – kutso.*
    He whom you fathered –
    vulture (eaten by vultures).

15. *Ae a atan – kutso.*
    He whom you fathered – vulture.

17. *Ae a atan – kutso.*
    He whom you fathered – vulture.   LAMENTATION

18. *Ae a atan – kutso.*
    He whom you fathered – vulture.

19. *Ogoro hamo ko da'ai?*
    Where does this lead to?   LAMENTING QUESTION
                                        ...

20. *"Shada daidu?"*
    Is Shada (Hamar spokesman) there?

21. *"Daidi."*
    He is.

22. *"Ariangule daidu, Boia?"*
    Is Araingule there, Boia?

23. *"Daidi."*
    He is.

24. *"Lomotor daidu?"*
    Is Lomotor there?   SELF POSITIONING

25. *"Daidi."*
    He is.

26. *"Korre daidu?"*
    Is Korre there?

27. *"Daidi."*
  He is.

28. *"Baido daidu?"*
    Is Baido there?

29. *"Daidi."*
    He is.

                                        ...

30. *"Ye! Aena igira arna oisai?"*
    Ye! Why do you ask about these men?

31. *Anama inna ne.*
    They are my age-mates.

32. *Ayona ne.*
      They are leaders.

33. *Dalkaina ne.*
    They are speakers.   EMPHATIC POSITIONING

34. *Donzana ne.*
    They are adult men.

35. *Na imbet bankin tiate 'hai!' amaise dalkana."*
    The ones who yesterday taking the spear
    together with me, calling 'hey!' spoke.

36. *"Eh, eh. Aena igira niekinie. Yeria i dalke."*
    Eh, eh. They shall come. Man, let me speak.

                              * * * *

37. *Amakisaxa yeria inta niab,*
    When he (Maxulo) said this,
    man (then) I came   INTERLUDE

38. *woxa ukab, kulla lamma, woxaxa makan.*
    slaughtered an ox, two goats,
    together with the ox, three.

39. *Yeria ukab.*
    Man, these I slaughtered.

                            * * * *

40. *"Lomotor, dorka.*
    Lomotor, sit down (Maxulo says).

41. *Nyangole, dorka.*
    Nyangole, sit down.

42. *Shada, dorka.*
    Shada, sit down.   SINCERE INVITATION

43. *Korre, dorka.*
    Korre, sit down.

44. *Nana sherkana kira yedi pen kaisaina, kira,*
    You young boys who
    destroy the country,

45. *kira edi binna dalke.*   SARCASTIC INVITATION
    only you should speak.

                           ...

46. *Wunga amba wunga yisa nokon payan wuchaina,*
    The cattle of your father who drink the good water,

47. *woxa kamara yin paxaisaxa, yeria muden kataina,*
    having knocked the horns of
    the dance-ox, you the ones
    who put a decorative collar
    on its neck   WOUNDING QUESTIONS

48. *whu-whu ama.*
    the one who goes 'whu-whu' (expells air).

49. *"ka yin paida imba woxau?" pura intau?*
 "He who looks so good is my father's ox?"
 is it not I who sings like this?

50. *"Durpha kisaxa imba ki ise."*
 "Let him grow fat so that my father may eat."

51. *Woxa zia shudin isaino goabais ,eh-eh-eh' amais*
 The bull grazes, having shown his splendour,
 grunts 'eh-eh-eh'

52. *Gama kisaxa* (snaps fingers)   Sᴀʀᴄᴀsᴛɪᴄ Eᴠᴏᴄᴀᴛɪᴏɴs
 and mounts the cow   ᴏғ ᴛʜᴇ Dᴇsɪʀᴀʙʟᴇ

53. *Da'aise...*
 Having existed... (time passes, the cow calves)

54. *Ran tsadais:*
 Having milked the cow,

55. *"Akano ko ran, ikano ko ran kume" amae.*
 The one who said: "May your little sister,
 may my little sister drink milk."

56. *"Wunga imba wunga ki shudin isais ki tsotse", amae.*
 Who said: "My father's cattle,
 may they eat grass and multiply."

57. *"K'ulla imba kulla ki shudin isais ki tsotse", amae.*
 Who says: "My father's goats, having eaten
 grass may they multiply."

58. *Aena kira yedi ne, yedi binna dalke.*
 The ones who talked like this   Eᴠᴏᴋɪɴɢ ᴛʜᴇ Iᴍᴘᴏssɪʙʟᴇ
 were you. Only you should speak now.
                               ...

59. *Aena kiran dalkin ye enna garidine.*
 The things people used to say
 you abandoned long ago.

60. *Aena kiran dalkino ana sia ne.*
 The things people used to say, you don't like.

61. *Aena kiran dalkin ana sia ne.*
 The things people used to say, you don't like.

62. *Aena kiran dalkin ana sia ne.*
    The things people used to say,
    you don't like.   ACCUSATION

63. *"Peno ko nagaia de!" ana sia ne.*
    "The country should be well!" you don't like.

64. *"Wunga ki paya shudin dede!" ambaino ana sia ne.*
    "The cattle should graze well!" you don't like.

65. *"Nana ki shuphont dorke faya!" ambaina ana sia ne.*
    "The children should sit safely in the shade!"
    you don't like.

                                    ...

66. *Payano: Galeta nasa cho adain,*
    kutso isaino ana fayano.
    What you like is if the son of a Galeba
    born down there (at Lake Turkana)
    is eaten by vultures,   CHIASM

67. *Hamarta nasa kot adaino*
    ana kutso isaino fayano.
    A Hamar boy, born here, eaten by vultures,
    that's what you like.

                                    ...

68. *Mengist dalkin garata?*
    Haven't you abandoned the talk
    of the Government?

69. *"Ya! Mengisto ainu!" a amata?*
    "Ya! The Government, who is that?"
    Didn't you say this?

70. *Pogamonka asa. Har aia, ya?*
    That's your falseness.   THREAT
    What have you achieved?

71. *Ta mengist gon dalkab. Bairo mengist.*
    Now the Government has spoken truly.
    Bairo (luck, fortune) is the government.

                                    ...

72. *Ogoen garata?*
    Didn't you leave all this?

73. *"Hai! Wunga anna gishima*   LAMENTATION
    k'ulla anna gishima,
    amin annun koi'ma,"
    "Hey! Herd your cattle, herd your goats,
    dig your field",

74. *in amen garata?*   LAMENTING QUESTION
    when I said this, didn't you reject it?
                              ...

75. *Ana faya: Rana kumo, iinka rana bao,*
    What you like is to drink milk
    and carry it in your belly,

76. *gobo, gobo, gobo, chober Galata*
    daeso kutsona imo!
    run, run, run, kill a Galeba down   SARCASTIC ACCUSATION
    there and give him to the vultures.

77. *Gobo, gobo, gobo, gobo, gobo Hamartal*
    kote daeso kutsona imo.
    Run, run, run, run, run, kill a Hamar
    here and give him to the vultures.

78. *Ana yin tei, ana fayano?*
    Isn't this so,   CONCILIATORY QUESTION
    what's good for you?

79. *Wunga enna dibadana, ki kaie.*
    The cattle which were stolen before,
    let them get lost.

80. *Murrana pent bankin utono ko kaie.*
    The rifles that came into the   CONCILIATORY INVITATION
    country with the war,   (retrospective)
    let them get lost.

81. *Nana enna diana ki kaie.*
    The children who have died, let them get lost.

82. *Nasa ta iinka badana,*
    For the boy who is now carried in the belly,

83. *nasa ta wunga gishaena.*
    for the boy who now herds the cattle,

84. *k'ulla taki imba kulla diana ki kaie!*
    now let my father's goats
    which have died, get lost!

85. *Ta k'ullin donna, wungen ta donna,*
    for the goats which exist now,   CONCILIATORY INVITATION
    for the cattle which exist now,   (prospective)

86. *shuphoa paya ka taki in dorkana,*
    bunna dorkaise in wuchaina,
    for the good shade in which I sit now,
    for the coffee which, having sat down, I drink,

87. *wo dalke!"*
    let us talk!
                                          ...

88. *Amais tau won dalkano.*
    Having said which, isn't it,   APODOSIS/GERUND
    what we talked about.

                                          *

The diagram that follows below is meant to bring out the over-all structure of Lomotor's speech more clearly. It concentrates on a single instance of Hamar speech competence –the imperial gerund. A host of questions remain if one wants to understand the many rhetorical strategies employed by Lomotor. The use of central figures of speech such as hyperbole, irony, sarcasm, chiasmus, metonymy, synecdoche, metaphor, as well as strategies of politeness (Brown and Levinson 1987) or rather strategies of domination (Strecker 1988) would be of prime interest here. But these, as well as other instances of Hamar rhetoric, will have to be dealt with elsewhere and at some other time.

Diagram: **The Gerundial Bow of Tension**

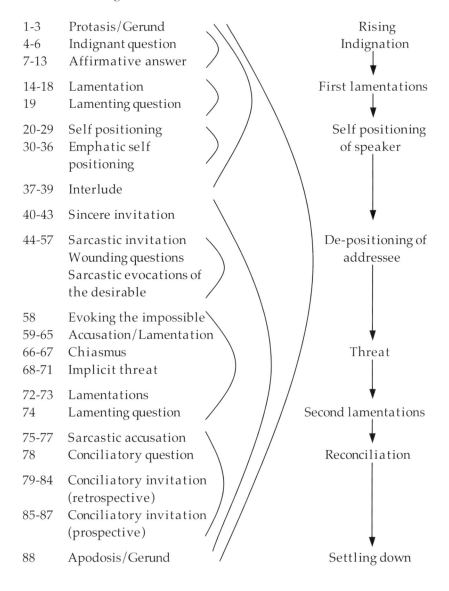

1-3	Protasis/Gerund	Rising
4-6	Indignant question	Indignation
7-13	Affirmative answer	
14-18	Lamentation	First lamentations
19	Lamenting question	
20-29	Self positioning	Self positioning
30-36	Emphatic self positioning	of speaker
37-39	Interlude	
40-43	Sincere invitation	
44-57	Sarcastic invitation Wounding questions Sarcastic evocations of the desirable	De-positioning of addressee
58	Evoking the impossible	
59-65	Accusation/Lamentation	
66-67	Chiasmus	Threat
68-71	Implicit threat	
72-73	Lamentations	
74	Lamenting question	Second lamentations
75-77	Sarcastic accusation	
78	Conciliatory question	Reconciliation
79-84	Conciliatory invitation (retrospective)	
85-87	Conciliatory invitation (prospective)	
88	Apodosis/Gerund	Settling down

Predicaments of war and peace

Initially, I wanted to deal in this paper mainly with the ethnography of war and peace in southern Ethiopia, and I intended to keep theoretical debate to a minimum. But, as armed conflict has recently been mounting both abroad and here in Ethiopia, and as we are trying to hold our eleventh International Conference of Ethiopian Studies (1991) amidst a world of warfare and trouble, I find it necessary to tackle some more general questions, which urgently need to be answered.

The topic still relates to war and peace, but the focus is on theory and method in the anthropological study of warfare, and I will critically examine some of the work done in this field during the past. My point of departure is that engaging in armed conflict and writing about it are not separable activities because theory and practice influence each other and constitute a causal whole. Because it is so basic, let me repeat the point: fighting and writing are not separable because knowledge influences action and vice versa. This is why we must work towards a critical theory of warfare. A critical theory helps to undermine the practice of armed conflict instead of legitimating and thus perpetuating it like many of the existing theories of warfare tend to do. In my paper I want to expand on this point by examining Katseyoshu Fukui's essay *Cattle Colour Symbolism and inter-tribal Homicide among the Bodi* (1979).

The use of 'and' in the title makes one wonder what kind of relationship may exist between the unlikely pair of cattle colour and homicide, and at close inspection it turns out that Fukui says nothing about the primary function of perceiving, knowing, caring for and speaking about individual cattle by means of their colour patterns, but, following Berlin and Kay, he gives a nice outline of Bodi colour classification and the way in which colours are used to name favourite cattle. He also shows how the Bodi, like so many other pastoralists in East Africa, ritually link people to particular animals and name them after them.

Fukui sees in this linkage an act of identification and mentions that persons identify themselves with their favourite animals by receiving their names after them, by wearing necklaces signifying the animals, by singing about them and so on (Fukui 1979: 163, 170). He sums up this identification with the statement that "It is no exaggeration to say that a man regards life without his *morare* (favourite animal) as hardly worth living (Op. Cit.: 170). As Bodi men identify themselves with their favourite animals, they are distressed when these animals get sick. Therefore they perform an animal sacrifice or go and kill a member of a neighbouring group in order to help their favourite animal to recover. They go also to commit homicide when the *morare* has grown old and has died a natural death or has been ritually slaughtered and eaten by the age-mates of the owner. As Fukui says, "Sometime after this ceremony, the man who has lost his *morare* will take a few age-mates with him on an expedition to kill a member of a neighbouring group" (Op. Cit.: 170). When he returns, the killer is ritually cleansed, and later receives scarifications on one of his arms, which signify that he has slain an enemy.

Fukui gives four cases of such homicide and then ends his paper with a short paragraph entitled "Continuing inter-tribal homicide." Here he says,

> It has now been established that the death (or sometimes illness) of a man's favourite animal (mostly an ox) is a primary factor in the killing of members of neighbouring groups. As the Bodi put it (...) 'When a *morare* dies, I become resentful and go to kill a Mursi or highlander'. For the Bodi, cattle do not belong to the animal world (...) but to that of mankind (...). The *morare* institution is the most striking illustration of this belief. If his *morare* is ill a man

will sacrifice another animal to aid its recovery, as though he wished himself to recover from an illness (Op. Cit.: 175-176).

I will return to this passage presently, but before I do this let me quote Fukui's final statements:

Thus, while cattle continue to die, there will, of course, be no lack of occasions [sic, I.S.] for men to go on *lufa* [raiding, I.S.] expeditions against neighbouring peoples... When I asked the Bodi, "Will there be an end to killing and warfare if you get many cattle and abundant pasture?", they replied "No; they will go on for ever" (Op. Cit.: 176).

Now, there are a number of points in Fukui's paper, which ask for criticism. I go through them one by one: The most general is that Fukui suggests that the Bodi will go on killing others forever. They will never stop killing because they hold certain beliefs about the identity of man and beast and think that they can only rescue their beasts and themselves by killing innocent others.

This sounds mad and exotic and may be what people expect to hear from anthropologists, but to me it is an expression of the alienated stance of the anthropologist, and I dare say that if Fukui had asked the Bodi a more sensible question and had discussed with them the reasons for warfare more deeply, the Bodi would have given him quite a different answer.

Instead of giving us detailed documents of Bodi speech and action, Fukui provides us mainly with stereotypes. Take for example to the following: "So interested are the Bodi in cattle that their daily conversations seemed to be about nothing else" (Op. Cit.: 150). Anyone who is familiar with the pastoralists of East Africa knows that here Fukui has grossly distorted the character of their discourse. True, cattle feature prominently in the daily concerns of pastoralist—and how could it be otherwise—but people's daily conversations are, like in all other societies, an integral part of their social life and revolve around politics, economics, kinship and marriage, rituals and beliefs, song and dance, warfare and the like. It would be the task of the ethnographer to listen closely to these "daily conversations" rather than reduce them to "talk about cattle".

This leads me to Fukui's thesis that the death of a man's favourite animal is a "primary factor in the killing of members of neighbouring groups". This is a shallow analysis. Are we really meant to agree that certain fancy beliefs can be primary factors for action? From all we know about the production of "fancy beliefs", we have to expect that they are based on rational practices and have a persuasive and rhetorical character. In other words, beliefs are never "primary factors", and should not be mistaken as such.

A primary factor among the Bodi (as among so many other pastoralists) is the desire to create in the members of their society a strong commitment to their herds. Herding cattle, goats and sheep is often a lonely and extremely trying activity. It involves hardships of various kinds, including the protection of the herds from dangerous animals and their defence against raiders from neighbouring groups. One way of strengthening the commitment of the herdsmen is the institution of the favourite animal, usually an ox or castrated he-goat.

The institution has a persuasive function and its form is poetic. In the technical language of rhetoric the choice of the favourite animal is that of synecdoche: a significant part is chosen to represent a whole. The favourite animal stands for the whole herd. Thus people focus on a specific and clearly perceptible part (the ox) rather than an unspecific and amorphous whole (the herd).

The exaggerated way in which the favourite animal is decorated, praised in song, ritually slaughtered and psychologically invested with feelings may in turn be described by the rhetorical form of hyperbole.

In order to understand the kind of commitment created by the favourite ox, it may be useful to recall a custom, which

Fukui does not mention but which used to be common to most of the pastoral groups of southern Ethiopia and northern Kenya. When they were threatened by others, the warriors would drive their favourite oxen towards the enemy, singing the praise of these animals and showing that they were ready to die for them if the enemy would dare to touch them. Nobody knows who invented this custom, but it is certainly a good strategy for committing the individual herdsmen to the herds and even risk death in the defence of them.

Seen in this light, the rituals and beliefs associated with a man's favourite animal are not primary factors for his action but rather secondary or derived ones. In other words, they have no independent grounding but depend on other factors such as the need for commitment and devotion to the herds.

I think that the defensive practice, outlined above, will find approval by everyone, including the Bodi, Mursi, Nyangatom, Hamar, Maasai, and, for that matter, their anthropologists. But I doubt that the treacherous homicide for the favourite ox which, according to Fukui is practised by the Bodi, will ever find general approval, and I am also convinced that the Bodi themselves would condemn the practice if we were to engage in a meaningful conversation with them about this mater.

In fact, I even doubt that the Bodi would agree with Fukui's analysis. They would probably tell us that no Bodi really has to kill anyone because of the illness or death of his favourite ox. Here it would have been extremely important to have accurate data, covering a certain span of time, which would show on the one side how many Bodi committed homicide when their, favourite animals got sick or died, and on the other side how many refrained from killing, and the reasons why they did so. But Fukui provides only the very general statement that "the man who has lost his *morare* will take a few age-mates with him on an expedition to kill a member of a neighbouring group." In this form, the statement is certainly false and misleading and exemplifies the alienated and positivist position of the anthropologist. True, some Bodi will go and kill, but others will not, and this difference is crucial for a critical understanding of what is happening, and of how things could be changed.

I have said above that the beliefs and rituals associated with the favourite animal cannot be primary but only secondary or derived factors for homicide. But, interestingly, the empirical cases of Bodi homicide given by Fukui only partly support such a refined thesis.

True, there are cases where men go on expeditions with the only intent of killing others and bringing home their trophies, but there are also cases where the sickness or death of a favourite animal are not real driving motives but are simply used as convenient excuses for raiding. To illustrate this point I quote Fukui here at some length:

> A man's animal had become senile and was slaughtered by his age-mates in the normal fashion. Ten months later he went on a *lufa* expedition, accompanied by 25 young men... His aim was to kill and not steal cattle but his companions, from the start, were only interested in taking cattle. Not being able to find any, however, they killed four Dime... (Op. Cit.: 172).

A further case shows that Bodi homicide, rather than being motivated by favourite animals may be an undisguised expression of aggression and expansion. A Bodi's favourite animal had died:

> Several days after its death, he shot a woman in an area called Fardi in the northern highlands, her death being witnessed by some of his age-mates. In the same month many Bodi raided the northern highlands, together with the Tishana, taking more than one thousand cattle and killing hundreds of people (Op. Cit.: 175).

What has gone wrong in Fukui's paper is that he has pictured the Bodi as prisoners of some irrational beliefs and concludes that their homicide will go on forever. In this way he has created a hopeless situation, which is worse than the horrific reality itself, for how can there ever be a way out of it?

This leads me to my final criticism. I have already quoted the sentence where Fukui says: "For the Bodi, cattle do not belong to the animal world (...) but to that of mankind". Here the ethnographer has created mysticism, which is alien to the Bodi and other East African pastoralist.

It is complete nonsense to say that for the Bodi cattle do not belong to the animal world. They certainly belong to the domain of the animal world. This is the ground from where they are then metaphorically likened to human beings. As in the metaphor "George is a lion", the expression "cattle are human" brings two separate domains into focus so that the attention oscillates between two separate domains, the domain of animals and the domain of humans.

This metaphorical likening of man and beast creates lively thoughts and feelings, but there is nothing irrational in it. When we hear "George is a lion", we think about the way in which George may be like a lion, with a tail, a roar, a mane and claws and all, how he may be king of humans like the lion is 'king' of the animals, how he is brave as a lion etc. Wouldn't it be hilarious and would we not laugh if one day an anthropologist came from Mars and after much intensive fieldwork would publish his (or her) finding that: "For the English (or Germans, French, Italians etc). George does not belong to mankind but to the animal world?"

We would laugh, but we would also be disturbed, for the misunderstanding would signal how alienated the observer and the observed have been from one another, and we would say to each other, "lets talk to him (or her) and see to it that he gets things right, because as long as he confuses metaphorical with literal meanings he will misrepresent us and make us look silly and irrational".

In other words, the likening of ox and man that underlies the institution of the favourite animal must not be taken literally but should be interpreted as metaphor. If we interpret the likening in terms of the theory of metaphor, the seeming irrationalities vanish and we realise that the Bodi are not imprisoned by immutable beliefs. They themselves have created and are creating the beliefs as part and parcel of their ongoing rhetorical strategies and to the same extent that they make their beliefs they can also modify and change them.

My point in all the criticism which I have voiced so far is that if we turn to the subject of warfare, we do not only face empirical but also theoretical and methodological problems. The difficulties are not easily mastered, but the least we can do is to acknowledge the fact that people make their own history, and that cultural forms are not immutable.

Fukui has pictured the Bodi as prisoners of conventional beliefs, but there is a critical difference between convention and performance. To paraphrase Stephen Tyler, social life is neither anarchic nor determined but a process emerging from the intentional acts of wilful egos constrained by convention (Tyler 1978: 135). It is this difference between convention and performance on which we have to focus when we want to study warfare. Let me explain this by means of cases form the Hamar who live not far from the Bodi is South Omo.

Case 1

In March 1973 my friend Bali was staying at the cattle camps in the valley of the Lower Omo. One day he and a number of his Hamar age-mates went scouting because they were at war with the Galeba (Dassanech) and their relationship with the Bume (Nyangatom) was also full of tension.

At noon they reached an area which was rich with certain trees that carried edible fruits. As they were resting in the shade chewing the fruits, a group of hungry Bume turned up which had come also to have a share of the abundant harvest.

Bali, who told me the story a few days later, heard some of the Hamar talk to each other but did not quite understand what they said. Then, suddenly a Hamar jumped up and killed one of the Bume visitors. The other Hamar followed suit killing the Bume one by one. Only Bali acted differently. He allowed the Bume elder with whom he had been sitting and talking in the shade to hide behind his back, and he held his rifle ready to shoot anyone who would dare to harm his guest. His age-mates respected him and allowed Bali to accompany the Bume elder back to the Omo river and thus lead him into safety.

Case 2

Some late evening in June 1973 when the sun had already gone down, my friend Baldambe and I were sitting in the cattle kraal of our homestead in Dambaiti. This is one of the places where men retreat when they want to talk in quiet to one another, for there, among the cattle, no one will disturb them at this hour. Baldambe had been speaking to me for a while when suddenly we heard the song of a man approaching the homestead. The man came singing, praising Baldambe, who was his mother's brother, and telling in his song that he had just killed someone from a neighbouring tribe. According to custom, Baldambe should have risen now and should have received the killer at the gateway of the cattle kraal, welcoming him with elaborate ritual. But Baldambe did not move until eventually the singing stopped somewhere not far from us in the dark of the night. Then he whispered to me: "He comes and calls me with endearing names and thinks I will praise him for the homicide he has committed. But he went and killed an innocent Bume (Nyangatom). We are at peace with the Bume, why does he think he can show his bravery by killing one of them? I will not welcome him, I will keep silent, no matter what he and others may think and say of me...".

Case 3

The third case is mentioned almost in passing in my diary on July 1st, 1973:

There are many groups of people and herds passing through Dambaiti these days. They are on their way north in search of grass because the pastures are exhausted in the south. The girls carry milk containers, cow hides and water calabashes on their backs, the men drive the cattle and the goats. The leader of one such group is an age-mate of Baldambe, and Baldambe tells him where the best pastures, the waterholes, ridges to camp on are around here. I join them to listen and learn that this man is Aira Allamba, the man who saved the only surviving Galeba down in southern Hamar recently. Aira seems to be a strong, tough person. Heavy scarification on his chest tell of his past killings and when I ask him why he saved the Galeba, he merely says: "My homestead is not one of liars". Later I discover that in the past he himself had once been saved by his Galeba bond-friend when the peace between the Galeba and the Hamar suddenly came to an end overnight (Lydall/Strecker 1979a: 149).

I think these cases speak for themselves and prove that not all the Hamar follow conventions of killing. As among the Bodi, so among the Hamar, killers are celebrated. They are given special names, receive scarification on the chest and the like. But thoughtful men like Bali and Aira do not kill in order to be celebrated, and responsible men like Baldambe do not celebrate thoughtless killers. Rather, these men base their actions on general and universally acceptable principles which have little to do with the "quest for honour" or any other such motive. They may get celebrated and respected because they have killed, but their killings will have been motivated only by the defence of themselves or others, and not by the wish to win social esteem, vent their anger about the loss of a favourite animal or the like.

In principle Bali, Baldambe, Aira... are opposed to every form of aggression, and they have a keen eye for the deception which is going on when people try to legitimate their blatant aggression against others (raiding for cattle and other forms of robbery) by insisting that they have to prove their manhood.

Baldambe has often pointed out this perversion to me, and I have often heard him say: "Yes, you should prove your manhood, but you do this by watching the gate of your father's cattle kraal and defending it against anyone who may attack it". In his text *Baldambe Explains*, Baldambe has given a good outline of how the Hamar and Bume made peace with one another more than half a century ago. On that occasion the Bume came to Hamar country singing:

> Let us forget our fighting,
> let our stomach become one,
> let us forget our fighting,
> let our stomach become one,
> let our talk become one,
> let us be brothers,
> let us be in-laws,
> let us be friends....
> (Lydall and Strecker 1979b: 33).

The will expressed in this song was sincere, and in spite of many problems, which had to be overcome, this peace has lasted until today. There have been occasional killings (see for example cases 1 and 2 above) which were motivated by beliefs and values very similar to those of the Bodi, and I think that it would not be difficult to find some mindless Hamar who would say: "this killing will go on for ever" (compare the Bodi statement quoted by Fukui 1979:176). But in fact there is no good reason why the killing should go on forever. The reduction of fighting which the peace treaty between the Bume and Hamar brought about is a convincing proof of this.

Temptations of war and the struggle for peace

Historical setting

The Hamar who live in the southernmost part of Ethiopia stress that in olden days they were lucky and escaped the worst effects of war and drought, which throughout history have plagued the Horn of Africa.

The late Hamar spokesman, Balambaras Aike Berinas, also known as Baldambe (Father of the Brown Cow), has characterised this original safety of Hamar with the following fable:

> Hamar country is dry, its people are rooks, they are tough. Living between the rocks, and drying up, they dig fields and make beehives. That's Hamar. The *maz* (initiates) used to strum the lyre together with the elders:
>
> "Our father's land,
> *Bitta* (ritual leader), Banki Maro's land,
> When the rain will fail it is not told.
> Our father's land has no enemy,
> Only the *wombo* tree (Ficus sp.) is our enemy."
>
> So the lyre used to be strummed '*kurr, kurr, kurr*'! The sorghum may get lost, but the Borana don't climb up the mountains, the Korre don't climb up into the mountains. The Korre kill men at Sambala, they kill down at the Kaeske. The Maale kill men in the open plains... No one climbs into the mountains to kill. In the mountains, however, there is a tree called *wombo*, which has a trunk, which reaches high up. When the fruits ripen at the top, when one's stomach is grabbed with hunger, then one climbs up the ripe tree. Having climbed up one eats, eats, eats, eats, eats, eats, until one is swollen with food, and one's arms and legs are

shortened. The way down is lost. So one sits in the branches and sleeps, and as one sleeps one falls—*wurp! dosh!*—one is dead.

"Our fathers' land, you have no enemies,
only the *wombo* tree is your enemy."

For us Hamar the *wombo* is our enemy. In our father's land, rain never used to fail. Our *'bitta'* never told of its failure. Our grandfathers did not tell, our forefathers did not tell. There was rain. (Lydall and Strecker 1979b: 157-58)

However, in recent times the situation has changed. The rains have become unpredictable and during periods of drought people will be driven crazy because they don't know anymore where to find food:

Nowadays the months when you (the rain) fail are many. In the month of *kile kila* you left us dry, in the month of *dalba* you left us dry, in the two months of *mingi* you left us dry, in the two months of *shulal* you left us dry. Altogether that's seven months when you left us dry. Then in *barre* you made us crazy and drove men to Galeba (Dassanech), and drove men to Aari, and drove men to Ulde (Arbore). *Barre* means being crazy. Men getting crazy are lost. (Op. Cit.: 158).

Despite their relative safety the Hamar were affected by a number of large-scale conflicts, which extended into their territory during the past three centuries. First, some time during the eighteenth century, there was an invasion from the East when the Borana tried to expand into the Woito valley. Hamar oral tradition tells of prolonged fighting in the valley which only ended when the ritual leader of the Hamar (the *'bitta'*) sent an army of stinging bees and other biting insects against the intruders who fled, it is said, in horror and confusion.

In the nineteenth century came a second invasion, this time from the South. First the Samburu whom the Hamar call Korre arrived, and then the Turkana followed who in the middle of the nineteenth century swept around the southern end of Lake Rudolf looting and decimating the people they found on their way. But the incursion was only short, and because the Turkana weakened the Korre with whom the Hamar and Arbore previously had competed for the rich and healthy pastures between Lake Stefanie and Lake Rudolf, the Turkana campaign is remembered until today as a blessing, and oral tradition has given it a kind of mystical dimension.

The third invasion came from the North and had a devastating and lasting effect. At the very end of the nineteenth century, during the "scramble for Africa", the Ethiopian Emperor Menelik II sent his troops as far south as possible in order to counter the territorial ambitions of the English who then were trying to extend Kenya to the North.

During the first phase of the conquest many lives were lost, people enslaved and livestock taken. But later, when the Emperor had assigned his warlords as governors to the region, they often tried to get on better terms with the impoverished populations. In fact, they provided them with arms so that they could jointly embark on raids into Kenya. In this way, the firearms, which initially caused the destruction of the people of southern Ethiopia, later helped them to recover and replenish their herds. Oral tradition is rich with stories and songs about these raids into Northern Kenya. I quote here an episode, which shows how at first the Hamar would use the firearms not to kill but only to intimidate people. According to Baldambe, his father Berinas was one of the first to acquire a rifle from the Amhara. He used it to raid cattle from the Korre who by then had retreated deep into Kenya:

> Berinas fired just one bullet into the air and this was enough to put the Korre into flight. After he had taken the cattle, he sent the Korre woman (who he had captured) to follow her own people... In olden days it was forbidden to kill women and children. The one who was carrying a weapon would kill the one who was carrying a weapon too. They also sent some Nyeringa women back home whom they had captured on their way, and then they returned with the raided herds. (Op. Cit.: 14-15).

The fourth invasion was the Italian occupation, which reached southern Ethiopia both from the North and the East and lasted from 1937 to 1941. The occupation had two particularly negative effects for it enhanced existing divisions and animosities between different local groups and in addition brought an unprecedented number of rifles into the area which the estranged groups could use to fight each other once the Italians had gone. This is how, for example, Baldambe has described the war of revenge, which the Hamar then waged on the Arbore:

> As soon as the Italians had left the country, we began to raid each other. We raided the Maale, we raided the Ulde (the Hamar often refer to the Arbore by one of their segments, that is Ulde or Marle), and the Galeba came and raided us Hamar at Turmi. How can I describe the fighting that arose here? First we attacked the Maale and wiped them out. Then Berinas said: "We should attack the Arbore because they, together with the Italians have treated us so badly." Were we, the Arbore and Hamar, not people from the same country? But still they sided with the Italians although they had come from far away, and together with them they turned against us. Now, as the Italians had disappeared and had left the Ulde on their own, my father Berinas said: "We have some rifles of the Italians, and we still have some of our old rifles left which we hid from the Italians. Let us go and wipe out the Ulde. After we have wiped out the Ulde, in their country only the gazelle and the ostrich shall move, and their land will be empty."
>
> This is how Berinas spoke. He called men to assemble at Barto, and from there the war party left for Ulde. But at that time some of the Hamar lived among the Ulde as their servants. They worked for them in the fields and were also friends of the Ulde. The leader of the Arbore was at that time Arkulo, another was Wuyi, another was Agare Oto, and there was another whose name I have forgotten. They were four in all. Those four had guns of the Italians in their hands, and only a few young men were with them

who also were armed. Thus there were only a few rifles in the settlement of the Ulde, just a few, but we, the Hamar, we all ran away once these rifles began to fire, and we returned back to our own country. (Op. Cit.: 38).

While the Italian occupation strengthened existing animosities, it also strengthened existing ties of friendship like those which existed between the Hamar and the Bume (Nyangatom) as Baldambe recalled:

> The Bume and we were at that time good friends. The Bume had ammunition and rifles, but they had not forgotten the peace talk, which they had with my father Gino (Berinas; for an analysis of this peace talk see below). They gave ammunition to the Hamar and sold them the rifles saying: "The Hamar are our friends. Now the Italians have left. Let us go hunting together. In earlier days we have already made fields together at Bulkai (lower Omo) and have hunted together. Let us be friends." The friendship of the Bume is true. (Op. Cit.: 39).

A fifth large scale conflict which had and still has an impact on the people living in southern Ethiopia was the Somali war which began as a conflict between Somalia and Ethiopia in the 1970s and then turned into an internal Somali war which even today has not yet fully ended. The war brought many modern firearms not only to Somalia but also to southern Ethiopia and the Hamar and their neighbours.

Traditional patterns of warfare

The traditional patterns of warfare between the Hamar and their neighbours may be described as follows:

First there is a kind of 'forced exchange' where the raiders do not want to kill anyone but are only concerned to bring home, as the Hamar say, "the butter milk cow for the mother", a cow which enriches the herd and produces so much milk that not all of it needs to be consumed immediately, i.e., freshly, but can be used to make butter. Baldambe, has described this 'forced exchange' in an almost playful fashion:

When we have lost our cattle, our mothers' brothers and our fathers call out:

"Hey, children!"

"*Yo!*"

"Have you lost your cattle?"

"We have lost them"

"Do you see the mountains over there? Do you see the Borana mountains? Those are no clouds, those are cattle. If you go there you will collect cattle."

The Borana on their side:

"Children!"

"*Yo!*"

"Do you see the clouds over Hamar?"

"We see them."

"Those are cattle, those are cattle."

If cattle have been lost in Borana a father will say to his son:

"There over Hamar those are not clouds those are cattle.

Go and get them." (Lydall and Strecker 1979b: 23)

Ideally no killing was involved in such cases, and, as the following conversation shows, at times the raiders even took special care not to harm the other party. This is what my friend Choke told me:

Choke: "Afterwards some Hamar went on a raid again, they were two together. They went to the Kirya waterholes. The girls they found among the goats were how many?" (shows two fingers).

Ethnographer: "Two."

Cho: "They took them together with the goats they led them, led them. *Misso* (hunting friend), that day the Hamar were good, they would not kill. They led the girls, the Gabare girls, till they reached the edge of the mountain. There they slaughtered a goat for them, roasted the meat for them, filled the empty stomach with water and showed them their footprints: 'Look at the footprints and follow them till you reach your home'. That's how they sent them home..."

Eth: "They took them with them so that they could not call people?"

Cho: "Yes. '*Yi*, the girls will come with the goats later, they will come later. Yi! What has happened to the girls, the sun is going down and they have not returned!'. That's how they wanted to cross the Kenya border before the other discovered that the herds had gone."

Eth: "I like this story." (Strecker 1979a: 72-73)

But even though a theft may involve no violence, thievery is prone to lead eventually to armed conflict and once violence has been used both in defence and in the attempt to retrieve the stolen herds, there is the danger of even further escalation where ruthless leaders urge their men not just to go and steal cattle but kill the owners as well. Choke has described this development, accusing his own people, the people of a region called Angude, for starting the atrocities:

Choke: "On this raid they started the killing. Four Gabare died. They did not send them away with a sign of their hand. My friend, those who started the killing are our people."

Ethnographer: "Of Angude."

Cho: "Of Angude only. Before they used to chase the owners of the herds away with their hands, they would not kill."

Omalleinda (a neighbour): "Run, run!"

Cho: "'Run, run!' and then they would take the cattle."

Eth:" On that day they killed without reason?"

Cho: "They shot at the owner of the cattle just so, *'dull-dull'* (imitates sound of gun) and they fell dead, dead, they had no guns. Then again Loirambe's raiding party rose. On that day I was there, my friend, they killed many, they wiped out a whole settlement... Loirambe got up and said: 'Kill people, kill them all off, people, people, people (knocks on the ground to emphasise the power of the speech, then he pauses), kill the people all off, kill the people all off'. That was a very big meeting. My friend, your friend Kairambe was there, on that raid he killed two people, he killed two people. I didn't kill. We did not come to the settlement in time as we had run in a different direction thinking the settlement was there. When we heard the firing and arrived everyone was already dead." (Strecker 1979a: 75-77)

Traditionally, those who have killed an enemy sing in praise of themselves on their way home and are ritually greeted and honoured at the gateway of their father's homestead. Baldambe has described this as follows:

> If they encounter the enemies and kill them, the killers return singing. If someone kills a Borana he sings:

> "Father's home, so-and-so's father's home,
> He is the debtor of the father's home,
> He is a man from the mountains,
> He is a man from the cliffs..."

> The women greet the killer:
> "*Elelelelelelelelelele*... !"

This means: good, good, good, good. At the cattle kraal gateway the father gives a goat to his son and son's *misso* (companion). Its throat is cut and blood is spilled over the killer's shoulders. His father greets him by lifting his right hand in which he holds the gun and the genitals of the slain enemy. He puts these up at the gateway and then decorates the killer with a garland of *naja* (Kedrostis pseudogijef). Now the women decorate the killer with their beads and belts. The goat is roasted and eaten inside the cattle kraal and the men sit down together and sing:

> "*Yo-woi-yo, hamodjilea*,
> he is the friend of the girls,
> *hamodjilea*,
> semen separated from his backside,
> *hamodjilea*,
> he is a youth from Mt. Marme,
> *hamodjilea*,
> he is a youth from the mountains." (Lydall/Strecker 1979b: 112-4).

The song shows how one indulges in exposing the loss and the pain one has inflicted on the other. But note that the ritual at the gateway also speaks of a bad conscience and fear of mystical retribution, for the blood, which is spilled over the killer's shoulder, is meant to wash away his guilt of having slain a human being.

The traditional patterns of conflict also involve peace making, alliances between different groups and, of course, a host of double-dealings, betrayals and the like. Most famous for their dubious manoeuvres are the Arbore and Kara whom the Hamar call 'snakes' for the following reason: Both groups are small, but they are nevertheless very powerful because they live near the River Omo and the River Woito respectively. Here they own cultivation sites which produce harvests at a time when other groups who depend on rain fed agriculture tend to have run out of grain and need a share of the crops harvested at Kara and Arbore in order to survive.

In fact, for a certain period of the year, the 'poor' Hamar, that is those who own no substantial herds, tend to become 'serfs' of the Arbore while the Bume become 'serfs' of the Kara. In our conversation Choke and Omalleinda have expressed this clearly:

> Choke: "All our poor people were then among them (the Arbore), harvesting the crops for them, stacking the sorghum, *ahm* – all the work in the field was done by the Hamar. They didn't know how to grind, those who ground for them were (Omalleinda joins in), the Hamar. (Together with Omalle-inda) Those who fetched water for them were the Hamar."
>
> Ethnographer: "Was that slavery?"
>
> Cho: "The Hamar said to himself: 'Let me be clever, serve them here and carry home the sorghum to my mountain – work well for them down there, up here make your own field. Then go down to them and work for them in the harvest while they just sit and rest.' It is the same as with the Bume and Kara."
>
> Eth: "It's the Kara who sit and rest."

Choke: "While the Bume work for them. He, the Marle (Arbore), sits down while the Hamar works for him." (Strecker 1979a: 71)

Sitting in this way on their rich cultivation sites, the Arbore and Kara would receive visitors from all the surrounding groups who came to share in the harvest.

Later, when it rained again in the mountains, the Arbore and Kara would in turn visit their neighbours. In this way they would get to know many details about where and how their neighbours lived, where they had their homesteads, fields, pastures, water holes and the like. In short, they would acquire knowledge, which they then passed on to others.

This is why the Hamar call the Arbore and Kara 'snakes'. They accuse them for pretending to be one's friend while at the same time telling one's enemy how best to rob one's cattle and kill one's people. Thus the Kara are said to habitually help the Galeba to attack the Hamar, the Banna to attack the Bume, and the Bume to attack the Mursi. Of the Arbore it is said that sometimes they help the Borana to attack the Hamar while little later they act the other way round, helping the Hamar to fight the Borana like in the following account:

Choke: They (the Marle, i.e., Arbore) told the Hamar: "Look here, the Borana raiding party is coming. Be clever! Send your women away from your camps." So the Hamar sent them away and lay in ambush... Then at night the war party arrived. The Marle led them and then they returned. Hadn't they said before: "We will lead them?" That's why the Hamar waited for a while, so the Marle could return safely. "Let them just shoot at the fires in the camps!" That's how they waited. They saw them as they approached the camps in a long line... So then they shot at the fires in the camps, *durrr – durrr – durrr – kuk-kuk-kuk-kuk –* (imitates the sound of the guns)... (but) no one was there. They all were in the bush. As the Borana were driving off the herds, the Hamar attacked them on the way. They chased them, chased, chased...then, my friend, there aren't any Borana anymore. There aren't any Borana anymore my friend (knocks on the ground to indicate how they were beaten). Holding on to them the Hamar finished them off. The guns, which they took may well have been as many as this (shows seven fingers).

Ethnographer: "They truly prepared a trap for them?"

Cho: "They truly did. Didn't they say, 'We are all one, all friends'?"

Eth: "*Hm*. Those who led them to you were the Marle, …"

Cho: "… and who shot at them were the Marle."

Eth: "Unbelievable."

Cho: "*Ha-ha-ha*" (laughs quietly, Strecker 1979a: 69-71).

Theoretical considerations

Ever since 1970 when Jean Lydall and I began fieldwork among the Hamar, we have witnessed warfare in the region and together with our host and teacher Baldambe as well as other friends from Hamar, Bashada, Kara, Arbore, Tsamai, Dassanech and Nyangatom, we have discussed the reasons for the conflicts and at times also have tried to do something about them (see for example Lydall/Strecker 1979a). Also, we described some of these conflicts (Lydall/Strecker 1979a), recorded people's accounts of them (Strecker 1979b) and devoted a whole book to the documentation of one of the major wars, which occurred between the Hamar and Arbore in 1974 (Strecker 1979a).

But I did not venture any theoretical view on the matter until 1991 when I gave a paper at the Eleventh Conference of Ethiopian Studies entitled "The predicaments of war and peace in South Omo" (Strecker 1994). In it I criticized the approach of Fukui and Turton's study of *Warfare among East African Herders* (1979). In particular I took issue with Fukui who had suggested that killing and warfare would necessarily go on forever between the Bodi and their neighbours because their cultural conventions offered no alternatives. Bodi men, so Fukui, feel resentment whenever their favourite ox dies and therefore go to vent their anger by killing members of neighbouring groups.

Thus, because of their cultural attachment to cattle, whom they metaphorically liken to human beings, warfare is destined to go on forever between the Bodi and their neighbours.

I objected to this, saying that Fukui had pictured the Bodi as prisoners of conventional beliefs and had not taken account of the critical difference between convention and performance. In order to strengthen this argument I quoted Stephen Tyler, who had said that social life is neither anarchic nor determined but a process emerging from the "intentional acts of wilful egos constrained by convention" (Tyler 1978: 135). Generally, I insisted, we must focus on the difference between convention and performance when we study warfare (Strecker 1994: 306).

In order to illustrate what I meant, I provided three examples which showed that at least among the Hamar, who live near the Bodi, not all men follow the conventions of killing. There was Bali who defended and saved a visitor from Nyangatom when all others were cruelly killed by the Hamar. There was Baldambe who refused to bless a nephew who had come to his gateway after killing an innocent Nyangatom. And there was Aira, who saved his bond-friend's family when war suddenly broke out between the Hamar and Dassanech (Strecker 1994: 306-307). These were thoughtful men who would not kill in order to be celebrated, or to vent their anger because of the loss of a favourite ox, or for any other superficial reason. They only subscribed to killing in defence.

If one looked closely, I suggested, one would find that among the Bodi things would be similar. Some men would go and kill for 'conventional' reasons while others would not, would in fact object to the injustice of such killings. This difference, I insisted, was crucial to see how things could change and how killings need not necessarily go on forever, not among the Bodi, not among the Hamar, not anywhere.

In a spirited comment Abbink scolded these "over-optimistic assumptions". "The Bodi", he wrote, "and other small-scale tribal groups living 'in the kinship mode' can be said to have a 'positional' idea of personhood, not an individual one" (Abbink 1994: 6). This was why men like Bali, Baldambe and Aira must be viewed as freaks whose refusal of violence was destined to be ultimately futile given the "larger socio-cultural whole in which they are socially and economically embedded" (Op.Cit.p.6). What counts, according to Abbink, are only "hard underlying reasons" like "resource competition", "real engrained cultural differences", "long-term adaptive behaviour... in the political ecological system" and the like (Op. Cit.: 4-5).

I fully agree with Jon Abbink, Taddesse Berisso (1994) and others who say that we must try to understand the "hard underlying reasons" which tend to tempt people to go to war, but I also insist that it is equally important to abandon the determinism to which, following Tyler, I objected in 1991 (see above). Although I had not read him yet, I subscribed to the view of Michael Bakhtin, who, in his celebrated essay on Fjodor Dostoyewski and the hero in the polyphonic novel, had written that it would be wrong to limit anyone to what she or he had done earlier, for people could always refute whatever might have been said and thought about them in the past by acting differently in the future, and as long as they were alive they could morally and ethically grow and change and transcend their previous limitations (Bakhtin 1985). Bakhtin's ideas apply particularly to peace making, for peace making can only proceed if people are not intent on defining, reifying or judging each other but rather are ready and willing to believe in each other's hidden potentials and in the fruitfulness of providing each other with an opportunity for a new start.

As I found out later, my attempt to develop a new approach to the theory and practice of peace making partly followed and partly preceded similar efforts made by other anthropologists at that time, first in Europe and then in the United States. I am referring in particular to *Societies at Peace: Anthropological Perspectives* (Howell and Willis, eds. 1989) and *The Anthropology of Peace and Nonviolence* (Sponsel and Gregor, eds. 1994). Each of these two volumes was the result of a major collective effort, and in each we find theoretical and ethnographic contributions, which examine peace as part of the "construction of moral and semantic universes" (Howell and Willis 1989: 3).

A forerunner of these new anthropological studies of peace was *Learning Non-Aggression: The Experience of Non-Literate Societies* for which Ashley Montague had invited a number of anthropologists to contribute (Montague 1978). In this volume Montague had argued vehemently against the determinism of "hereditarians" and "environmentalists" and had emphasised the social roots of peace and aggression, but later he took an even more radical stance.

That is, in his 1994 foreword to Sponsel and Gregor's collection of essays, he squarely asserted that there is no other barrier to peace except wilful ignorance, and he quoted Spinoza who in 1670 remarked that "Peace is not an absence of war, it is a virtue, a state of mind, a disposition for benevolence, confidence, justice" (Sponsel and Gregor 1994: X). The virtue of peace depends, as Montague says, on mutually shared hope, which acts as a driving force and constitutes the possibility for the fulfilment of peace (Op. Cit.: X). This, of course, supports what I tried to say in my paper on the "Predicaments of War and Peace in South Omo" which Abbink criticised for its "over-optimistic assumptions".

The premise of contemporary anthropology that war is not a necessary concomitant of human existence is, of course, not new. In fact the view is already thousands of years old and has been expressed in fables and stories the whole world over. Let me provide the example of Pyrrhus, who was one of the most skilled generals of antiquity and over time has become a figure around whom legends and myths have been woven which are of interest here because in one way or another they tell us of the thoughts and feelings which the ancients held about war and peace. In Western thought the name Pyrrhus evokes above all the idea of useless victory. That is, Pyrrhus is the prototype of a victor who turns out to be the looser. This goes back to 279 BCE when at Asculum the Greek and Roman armies fought a particularly bloody battle. Pyrrhus was afterwards congratulated by a friend on his victory but he answered, "One more victory like that over the Romans will destroy us completely!" (Plutarch 1973: 409). This candid reply has been remembered (or was invented to be remembered!) to the present day, so that we speak of a 'Pyrrhic victory' whenever we mean a victory gained at too great a cost and whenever we want to remind each other of the fact that 'victories' are not necessarily what they appear to be, and that possibly and even very likely they may be nothing but a first step to defeat.

However, Plutarch has also related another story, which reads like an ancient fable about the needlessness and folly of war. The story says that, yes, Pyrrhus was a great general, but his victories were useless, senseless, unnecessary because fortune had given him already, as Plutarch says, "the opportunity to enjoy his possessions without interference, and to live at peace ruling over his own subjects" (Op. Cit.: 397). But when the citizens of Tarentum invited him to be their leader in a war on Rome, Pyrrhus accepted. Then Cineas, a great Greek orator, tried to persuade Pyrrhus of the futility of his plans:

> "Pyrrhus," he said, "everyone tells me that the Romans are good soldiers and that they rule over many warlike nations. Now if the gods allow us to defeat them, how shall we use our victory?" "The answer is obvious," Pyrrhus told him, "if we can conquer the Romans, there is no other Greek or barbarian city which is a match for us. We shall straight away become masters of the whole of Italy..." There was a moment's pause before Cineas went on. "Then, sire after we have conquered Italy, what shall we do next?" Pyrrhus did not yet see where the argument was leading. "After Italy, Sicily, of course," he said..." "No doubt what you say is true," Cineas answered, "but is our campaign to end with the capture of Sicily?" "If the gods grant us victory and success in this campaign," Pyrrhus told him, "we can make it the spring board for

much greater enterprises. How could we resist making an attempt upon Lybia and Cartharge...?" (Cineas replied) "But after all these countries are in our power, what shall we do then?" Pyrrhus smiled benevolently and replied. "Why, then we shall relax. We shall drink, my dear fellow, every day, and talk and amuse one another to our hearts' content". Now that he had brought Pyrrhus to this point, Cineas had only to ask him, "Then what prevents us from relaxing and drinking and entertaining each other now? We have the means to do that all around us. So the very prizes we propose to win with all this bloodshed and toil and danger and all the suffering inflicted on other people and ourselves, we could enjoy without taking another step.'"(Plutarch 1973: 399-400).

This dreadful story, so delightfully told by Plutarch, shows how the futility of war was known already in antiquity. But one might also add that the same knowledge existed probably even earlier, that is ever since people first raised arms against each other. There will always have been a Pyrrhus who would want to go to war, and always a Cineas who would argue against it.

Witnessing the struggle for peace and the temptations of war

In 1973-74 I found myself in the midst of ever increasing armed conflicts between the Hamar and their neighbours, and in order to show the dynamic and complex nature of the situation and allow the reader to understand both the Hamar who struggled to keep peace and those who followed the temptations to go to war, I draw here at length on my diary and the conversations I had with Baldambe and my other friends in Dambaiti (Lydall/Strecker 1979a; Strecker 1979a).

Everything began in the morning of 29 April 1973 in the mountains of Hamar at Baldambe's homestead in Dambaiti where one of our neighbours had put on a pot of coffee. That morning the following grim talk developed:

Usually, about the time that the Ethiopian police celebrate Easter, the first sorghum ripens and the small children 'steal' from it and survive. But look at the fields today. They are empty, a desert! Where can we go to exchange our goats for grain? There is no more grain in Banna, nor in Tsamai, nor in Aari. The doors to Galeba and to Arbore are closed (because of war) and there is hunger anyway. We are now slaughtering our goats and those who have none take them by force.

Soon we will run out of animals and then we shall kill each other over them: 'why don't you let me have one of your cows?' and we shall take up spears and kill each other. Soon there will be nothing but turmoil. There are no fruits in the bush ripe enough to eat, there is nothing but salad. Times have never been as hard as this before (Lydall and Strecker 1979a: 102-3).

My friend Banko who had conjured this dismal picture then added that the lot of the neighbouring Bume (Nyangatom) was even worse than that of the Hamar.

Driven by hunger they came to visit the Hamar at the cattle camps where the people of the territorial segment called Kadja who were loyal to Baldambe would welcome and feed them, while the people from Angude killed them:

To illustrate the desperation of the Bume, he (Banko) tells me the following story which once again reveals the divisions amongst the Hamar..: One night about a week ago, the Kadja men who have a cattle camp close to the Omo found a young Bume boy among their goats. He had been driven there by starvation and the Hamar fed him with milk and blood. They even slaughtered a small goat for him and the led him back to the Omo (i.e. back home). A few days later some Angude men shot a deer close to the Omo and while they were eating it, a half-dead Bume approached them asking for food. A young Angude man got up and speared him to death (Op. Cit.: 103).

I think that these entries in my diary clearly show how in spite of an objective threat of hunger there was still no objective need for the Hamar to kill, and that any theory which would attribute the killing of the Bume who came to share the meal in the forest to some 'hard underlying reasons' rather than to an 'absence of virtue' (see the theoretical discussion above) would be utterly misleading. A few weeks later, the Kara accompanied by some Banna and Hamar attacked and destroyed two Bume villages at Aiba on the west bank of the Omo River. In fact, the villages were inhabited mainly by descendents of the legendary Murle of the Lower Omo, a branch of a group which otherwise lives mainly in the southern Sudan. Baldambe was very disturbed upon hearing the news and commented that those who fought the Bume were digging their own graves:

> (4.7.1973) A young man from Kara and one from Mogudji are our guests this morning and they give us the details of the raid on the two Murle villages. We hear all about the massacre and the rituals the Kara performed before the raid and about the participation of Hamar... Baldambe remarks that all those who fight with the Bume are digging their own graves and goes on to say that in olden times the men would have whipped all the 'thieves' who joined the raid and would have killed any youngster who spoilt a peace agreement without permission. Killing was only allowed in defence of cattle and land and, of course, during raids that were ritually licensed by the elders and war magicians. Those who had raided and killed without permission would hide from public social control by living with the stolen herds in the bush for a long time. Today, Baldambe says, people praise any killer without distinction. Cynically, he imitates the call with which the women welcome the killer home: 'Elelelele!' (Op. Cit.: 149-50; see also Tornay 1979 for an account of the Kara attack on the two villages).

Against all odds, Baldambe kept working for peace between the Hamar and Bume, castigating everyone who turned against the Bume and refusing to honour anyone who was involved in the killing. By the middle of November Baldambe and the men of Kadja had averted the most immediate crisis and I made the following entry in my diary:

> (15.11.1973) A Bume boy came into Hamar territory, driven by hunger. He was picked up by some young men who brought him to

an elder. The elder called all the young men of the neighbouring area together and said to them: 'Kill him!' This was his way of emphasizing the taboo on killing him, for hadn't the speaker of Kadja just explicitly forbidden the killing? Baldambe stresses the point that at the recent meetings only the Kadja men 'had the word' and they insisted that Kizo (a grazing area near the Omo river and close to Bume territory) was Kadja territory. The men of Angude, Mirsha, Wungabaino and so on (i.e. other territorial segments of Hamar) were allowed to keep their herds there but they were not allowed to act against Kadja's interest, which includes, among other things, keeping peace with the Bume." (Op. Cit.: 183-84)

As we have seen, Baldambe and the men of Kadja were eventually able to secure peace with the Bume. But—in the safety of their mountains—they soon began to hear news of fierce fighting between the Galeba and the Bume. Interestingly, in these conflicts also the Kara and Arbore were involved:

(2.1.1974) In the evening, as we drink coffee in front of Ginonda's house, Banko emerges from the dark. He leans on his spear and stands and waits... Everyone knows that his stance constitutes a powerful command, so a cowhide is brought and coffee is served to him with speed and respect. He gives me the 'talk of the country': fighting between the Galeba and Bume has been heavy. The Galeba attacked the Bume at Nakua and drove away three herds of cattle. As the fighting continued, the Ethiopian police arrived on the scene and requested that the Galeba withdraw. But the Galeba replied by firing on the police, killing two of them. Just as last year, the Bume overtook the Galeba and collected at the waterholes where they waited for them, guns in hand. It is said that many Galeba died and that the Bume pursued them all the way into Galeba country, where they retrieved their own cattle and took some of the Galeba's as well. Some fifteen Kara men and, even more interestingly, some Arbore joined in the Galeba raid. So that's where those two 'snakes' the Kara and the Arbore, meet— in Galeba! This makes me think of an interesting parallel between

these two small river peoples and their two large antagonistic
neighbours. Like the Hamar and the Arbore, the Kara and the
Bume have been fighting over the crops that grow by the river.
The Bume's successful self-defence action makes the Kara uneasy
and they now expect the Bume to attack them any time,
especially since the Omo is running low and it is easy to cross by
foot. The Kara have been buying as much ammunition as possible;
they even buy some from the Hamar with sorghum. At night the
Kara and their Hamar guests watch the ford close to the Kara
settlement where the Bume can cross the river. The crops are
ripening now and the Kara cut any ripe grain quickly, remove it
from the fields and hide it in the bush. Everyone believes that
the Bume meant what they said when they came to the river once
to announce that they would soon come on a 'visit' after which
they would not be concerned about the survivors for there would
not be many (Op. Cit.: 229-30).

Not only the situation between the Bume and Kara but also
between the Hamar and Arbore began to deteriorate at that
time. First there were a number of clashes like the following:

(3.6.1973) Baldambe tells me he has heard about new fighting, not
with the Galeba but with the Arbore: a few days ago they
clashed at Assilebaino. After the Arbore had raided them at
Karabaino, the Hamar had pulled their herds back into the
impenetrable mountains. But as it had recently rained on the
lowland plains there was an abundance of grass and water and the
Hamar could not resist driving their herds into this fertile area.
The Arbore had expected this and had sent a party of raiders into
Hamar territory. But the Hamar too were on the alert and their
scouts spotted the raiders, who had arrived during the night. As
it was early in the morning, the Hamar had not yet driven their
herds away from their enclosures and they had time to organise
themselves. They encircled the Arbore and attacked them. Two
Arbore were killed and two wounded. The Arbore retreated in
order to carry their wounded to safety. Then they returned and the

fighting continued. Two Hamar received light wounds (Op. Cit.: 142).

As these clashes continued, the Hamar began to plan a full-scale war against the Arbore. They were to 'exterminate' the Arbore just like the Bume said they would 'wipe out' the Kara in retribution for the losses they had inflicted on them. I was staying at the Hamar cattle camps when I first heard of this. The impending raid put me in a difficult position. What should I do? Was there any meaningful way for me to act? I thought about this and then decided that the best thing for me to do was to return to Dambaiti and witness what happened there:

> (19.1.1974) A couple of days ago, when I first heard of the planned raid I thought for a moment of interfering, but then I realised that I didn't even really know what it was that I was thinking of interfering with. How big was the raid to be? Was it really going to happen? If I tried to stop the raid, if I tried to interfere I would only make my powerlessness obvious. On the other hand, to pretend that I was not against the raid and rush to Assile in order just to try and see what was happening would be to make a fool of myself. One can not study warfare in the way one studies 'harmless' customs and counts cattle. So it seems to me that the best thing to do would be to return to Dambaiti quickly, set up my recording gear next to the coffee pot and listen (Op. Cit.: 260).

This is how we returned to Dambaiti:

> On our way up to the Hamar mountain-plain we did not meet a single man... Moreover, last night a few drops of rain fell, extinguishing old footprints—but there were hardly any new ones: 'Nobody has been here today, everybody has left, and tomorrow we will hear the firing of guns from the other side of the Hamar mountain'... When we drive into Dambaiti, only the smallest children, those born during our period of fieldwork, welcome us by standing on a little ant-hill and waving their hands... Anti serves us coffee in Aikenda's house. When we have finished, Baldambe arrives and we all sit outside on the *boaka* (open space) and exchange our first 'talk of the country'. Baldambe evokes an

insane picture of himself walking home, meeting countless people going in the opposite direction to join the raid: here our Ogotemmeli (an old blind hunter who introduced the French anthropologist Marcel Griaule to the intricacies of Dogon culture), anthropologist, intellectual, son of a great leader and warrior, walking alone against the stream of his people who pass him by on their way to fighting: madness and confusion! In the villages he passes, he meets only three old men who do not join the rush to the war. Women call out to him, 'Where are you going?' Baldambe answers them, 'Well, someone has to make the fire while all the other bulls have gone.' 'Oh, yes, make fire, make fire!' To 'make fire' is an euphemism for 'to fuck'. Tears run from Baldambe's eyes as he tells us this (Op. Cit.: 261-62).

In *Conversations in Dambaiti* (Strecker 1979a) I have documented the social drama which unfolded in Dambaiti when the raiders were away, and when they returned, beaten, humiliated and full of regret. Here I provide only a few excerpts of these conversations.

During the first days of suspense, when no one knew when and how exactly the raid on Arbore would happen, Baldambe and his friends in Dambaiti worried and gloomily forecast the defeat of the Hamar. Like so often before when they attacked the Arbore the Hamar would take to their heels and run:

Baldambe (addressing his old friend Walle, Lokarimoi): "Bond-friend, how often have we run away? Didn't we run away from the Ulde first when Arkulu was their leader? Say 'one'."

Walle: "One."

Bal: "Didn't we run the day when Anyero died?"

Wal: "We ran after we attacked Maetzan (east of Arbore)."

Bal: "And didn't we run when Sinka died?"

Wal: "That makes three."

Bal: "Doesn't it? Then recently, when so many of us died, didn't we run away? So we Hamar have already run away five times." (Strecker 1979a: 91)

I had heard Baldambe say that this time the Hamar would be defeated like before because once again they had gone not really to fight but to get cattle. I broached this question to Walle, and the following conversation ensued:

Ethnographer: "My friend was angry yesterday with Hamar."

Baldambe: "Who?"

Eth: "The one who is called Baldambe, Ogotemmeli. He said: 'The Hamar have run to Ulde for cattle and that will turn out badly for them'."

Bal: "*Hahahaha.*"

Eth: "They should go and show the Ulde their strength instead. But now even children have joined the raid and they have become so many that they are incapable of fighting and will only run away. What do you think, is that right?"

Bal: "Lokarimoi."

Walle: "*Hmm.*"

Bal: "He says: What my friend Baldambe said angrily last night was: 'The Hamar went to Ulde for cattle, but there are the owners of the cattle. Their fathers had instructed them: Here, your cattle, look after them well. Here, your father's goats, look after them well. With their father's cattle they bought guns, bought bullets. The owner of the cattle is standing up like a man, the Hamar will not break him'."

Wal: "*Hmm.*"

Bal: "Now the Hamar have gone for cattle. Had they talked together before: 'Kill the owner of the cattle first, the owner of the goats, kill him. Kill the father of the children, the husband of the wives. Eradicate the owners first like this and then take the cattle slowly,' this would turn out well and would allow the Hamar to survive. In this way the Ulde would..."

Wal: "... see our strength."

Bal: "But now they have taken their guns. The men from Assile want to take cattle, Kadja wants to take cattle, Mirsha wants to take cattle, Shanko wants to take cattle, Bonkale wants to take

cattle... man, there are the owners of the cattle and our men will
return dropping their shit. That's what I have said and he asks
you whether you agree with this or not."

Wal: (emphatically) "True, True!" (Op. Cit.: 87-88).

The raid was ill-fated as forecast already by Baldambe, and
when the raiders returned, Anombe, Baldambe's brother-in-law
gave us a long account which showed in every detail how right
Baldambe had been. I quote Anombe here at length because this
allows us to see how he experienced the raid.

As the Hamar had decided to attack not the western but the
eastern Arbore (i.e., not the Ulde but the Marle), they had to
wade for many hours through the reeds of the delta north of
Lake Stefanie. Here a sharp piece of wood growing in the water
cut Anombe's foot and incapacitated him right from the
beginning. When we visited Anombe the day after he had
returned home, Baldambe first asked about Anombe's foot:

Anombe: (to his wife) "Spread out the cowhide so that they may
enter and sit down."

Baldambe: (after having settled down, to Anombe) "How is your
foot?"

Ano: "Look at it, it is something one does not speak about (that is,
it is really bad and really hurts)."

Bal: "What kind of wood cut it?"

Ano: "How could I see it? It was under water... As we were crossing
to the other side it pierced my foot, just like a knife. '*Yi!*' I felt the
cut but walked on through the water. When we reached the dry
land on the other side, the flesh had torn open, one part hung
down and the other was bent upwards. 'You have come looking for
it, so don't complain.'... Who knew the way over there? There was
only the way through the reeds and the water. And in it there
were holes so that the water reached your knees, reached your
thighs, reached your stomach... and as we continued walking the
sun went down. None of us knew how long we would walk through
the reeds. Those men of Assile mountain, accustomed as they are,

who of them did really know the way? Have they ever sent anyone into the sky saying there was a way? I wonder who has ever crossed this before... we walked all afternoon in water and reeds. We only reached the other side at about the time when the cattle here are milked and when those who have only a few cows have already gone to sleep. It was dark, people could not see each other. You had to bend down and peer closely:

'Who is this?'

'It is I.'

That is how we looked for each other. We were scattered all over the place, like goats.

'The settlements are close by!'

Not at all, they were far away at the foot of the mountains.

They said:

'The settlements are close by, don't you hear the dogs bark, the cow bells ring?'

But none of them had ever gone and really looked at the country. (short pause, Anombe reflecting) The Marle must have made true sacrifices to the ancestors so that the Hamar went mad. He knew we would be coming.

'Lie down and rest!' (one of the leaders said)

Baldambe, haven't you seen it before? When the Hamar step on the Marle land they go crazy. Instead of lying down and resting quietly: *dyan-dyan-dyan* (imitates chaotic talk), 'let's go and kill people'. So I called my younger brother and said to him: 'Boy, I can't walk with this foot. We have come together with everyone from our country for what we looked for. We wouldn't have come if it concerned only our own homestead, but now they made us join this raid. Let those who want to go and kill go ahead. Leave it, sit here with me, and let us go tomorrow when the clear light has come.'"

Baldambe: "Who was with you?"

Anombe: "Your hunting-friend Uri (Anombe's brother), and Lukusse (Baldambe's brother). We were stopping our people from

going on in the night. Lukusse and Tsasi (another brother of
Baldambe) had already sent back the young ones of your
homestead... The young men Dube and Makonen (Baldambe's
brothers) were over there with us. They sat with us there in the
night like birds. We who had seen too much of war before, asked
them to sit with us like birds and wait for the morning light.
Others had left during the night and had gone on. It is they who
met death. I don't know what was driving them there. All the
time Lukusse's men and we were together. The man from over there
who has now died (Gaito, one of Baldambe's best friends), we
were first together with him, but then he left us and we didn't
hear of his death until much later. The other boy of the
homestead up there (another man from Dambaiti who was killed
in the raid) he just went mad and left his older brother to go on his
own way. He went looking, looking, looking, I wonder what he
was looking for! I think that some were really killed by
something, which had made them lose their senses. It was
madness, which killed them.

On our side we went ahead and when we arrived the cattle had
already been taken: 'Help drive the cattle!'

So we turned back towards the water. As we turned we thought
there were others of us on the other side of the herds, but there
weren't. We were driving the cattle and not a single shot was
fired by us. We continued driving the cattle till we came to the
area where you, brother-in-law, once made a raid. There the
Marle overtook us and were waiting for us. 'Who is driving the
cattle on the other side?' we asked ourselves and we kept hearing
the shooting at the foot of the mountains. Some were killed, our
men, as they attacked. That is what is said but we did not see it.
As we reached that place the bullets were coming. We were (so
many that) a bullet flying high over my head would still hit one
of us. Then everyone began to run. Upon this: 'Uri,.. don't return to
the fighting...We have nothing which we can bring to our wives,
come this way'... Lukusse was then still with us all the time. The
fighting happened to our left but we were down by the water and

didn't see it. We went on and as we were about to enter the reeds they came."

Baldambe: "The owners of the cattle."

Anombe: "The owners... Uri fired one shot at them there and that was all. We returned. As we walked through the water... I saw Lokolil Korre's younger brother who was hit by a bullet in the arm and I also saw Nukimba's son's son who had a wound in the leg. We all returned the long way through the water and the reeds and after we had reached dry land I didn't meet others until I had reached the foot of the Hamar mountains where I met with Lukusse again. He, like us, had run away when the Marle began claiming back their cattle." (Op. Cit.: 175-78).

Later Baldambe asked Anombe and Goiti, a man from Dambaiti who also had taken part in the raid, what the spokesmen had said at the public meetings, which preceded the raid. Sarcastically Anombe and Goiti imitated the spokesmen as follows:

Anombe: (imitates the speaker) "I have called you."

Goiti: "I truly have called you."

Ano: "I truly have called you. Today none of them will survive. He is s woman. I will pick him, he is soft like the *mulaza* plant (unidentified, has soft roots and is easily pulled out)."

Goi: "His gun won't fire."

Ano: "His gun won't fire. Man, I have everything well prepared. Man, I have truly killed him. Go over there and kill him. Just fetch him, while he is weak like *mulaza*. I have poured water into his gun."

Goi: "Man, never before have I liked it as much as this time!"

Ano: "Man, never before have I liked it as much as this time!"

Goi: "Even old limping men will kill today." (Op. Cit.: 185-86).

While some spokesmen belittled the enemy in this way, others belittled the Hamar, calling them weaklings and in this way tried to provoke them into action:

Anombe: "This is what Oitamba's son said. He spoke at the end of the speeches and provoked the men:

'I am the last to speak, now you will not talk anymore.'

He provoked, provoked. Hadn't he taken his spear?"

Baldambe: "Taken."

Ano: "Provoking, provoking us: 'Today I have gone on my way having prepared all the rituals well. I have gone on my way with babies; I have gone on my way with the blind. Hm. Now you, whom I have brought up, rise and sing the war song. If anyone asks you who you are, say 'I am the son of so-and-so'." (Op. Cit.: 187).

Now, to ask someone to say that he is the son of so-and-so means to remind him that in order not to spoil the name of his father he must not be a coward, must not be concerned with his own safety, must be a 'bull' who ruthlessly attacks the enemy. Therefore, if a man gets up at one of the meetings, which precede the raid and publicly identifies himself with his father, this is like an oath, a public announcement that one is ready to die. According to Anombe, Baldambe's hunting-friend Gaito was driven to his death because he was provoked and forced to commit himself in this way:

Anombe: (addressing Baldambe) "Upon this (after he was provoked by Oitamba) your hunting-friend at first did not get up, he kept on sitting and only pointed his gun towards the enemy. Only slowly he got up and said: 'My father's name is Kala, I am the son of he who was called Kala'." (Op. Cit.: 187).

Also Lukusse, Baldambe's brother was provoked in a similar manner but was wise enough not to respond to the provocation:

Anombe: "One man—it is said he was from Assile, I don't know his name, but I heard what he said."

Baldambe: "Tell us."

Anombe: "He called Lukusse and said: 'Don't the Marle owe your father's homestead a debt?' (the Marle had killed one of Lukusse's brothers some time ago)... They were singing war songs but Lukusse would not join them and trample (trampling is a strong sign of a commitment to fight), he just got up and pointed his gun towards the enemy: 'Here, my gun is black and the owner of the cattle is mine. Man, the left wing of the fight is mine!' That is what I heard him say. When that man from Assile asked: 'What about the debt of your father's homestead?' Lukusse did not answer. It is this kind of spokesman who drives the brave ones to their deaths." (Op. Cit.: 191).

But people are not only driven to their deaths by others, it is also because they have lost their '*barjo*', their luck or good fortune. Thus Anombe and Baldambe were convinced that Gaito died in the raid because something had killed him already at home:

Anombe: "Gaito himself died before he could kill anyone. Not a single bullet had left the mouth of his gun. (pause) If something has killed you here already, how can you survive over there? That was his misfortune..."

Baldambe: "He who consults the intestines and sees for himself the death of someone from his homestead, how can he go on a raid? ... *Ach*, friends, that which extinguished him, it hunted him to his death."

Ano: "Say: 'It closed his ears so that he would not listen to his age-mates'."

Bal: "It hunted him to his death."

Ano: (moved with a high voice) "Hunted him. *Ye-ye*! I have seen this with your brother-in-law, and now... (again). If you try to hold them they just go mad. *Ye*! ..."

Bal: (recalls his last conversations with Gaito and remembers how he had wanted to warn him) "Had he come on his way back from his older brother I would have told him that if he went it would mean his death. I would have told him to stay put here like an owl. Hadn't the diviner seen in the intestines those who die in war? Hadn't he seen the ox slaughtered at the funeral and the coffee pot which is put on at the funeral? He went on the raid. Knowing that there was death through war within his homestead. I was going to tell him that the diviner was hiding the truth from him, that when he talked of some one already dead he really meant the death of someone living, but then I myself was afraid to tell him."

Goiti: "Yes, so it is."

Bal: "*Hm.*"

Ano: "Brother-in-law, he had even sent word to us: 'Alma, Kula, Banko, I won't join the raid of which the news has reached me. I have some other important matter to settle, I don't think I will be able to join you.' But when we all arrived over there I saw him. His father's sister's son who was with us had been saying all along that he would come and join us after all."

Goi: "That is what his father's sister's son said."

Ano: "'He won't stay behind.' When I saw him over there, I said to someone: 'Tell him he should not go'... 'Why don't you tell him?' 'How can you send him into the fight although you have seen his death?' Didn't I tell them? ... I liked him very much. Did I ever dislike him? Hasn't his death made me very sad?... Had I told him he would have survived."

Baldambe: He would not have survived. Only the raid as a whole would have survived. – Wait! He would not have survived. When he went over there, didn't many die?

Ano: "*Hm.*"

Bal: "That was caused by his misfortune as revealed in the intestines. Wasn't it he who killed the others? Had they said: 'You whose bad luck was forecast by the intestines, return,' he would have turned back, but no one said: 'You go ahead alone, all we others will return.' This would have been his medicine! But no one said this. *Ach* – let it get lost! ..."

Ano: "I said to the others:... Are you leading Gaito to his death?... So take him with you, but I will be very surprised if he returns. Aren't you going to talk to him? Go ahead, if you don't do it I will do it.' After I had said this (his voice gets suddenly very quiet) they said I should not talk like this and hold my mouth... (raises his voice) *Yi*! And then I just could not look at Gaito without feeling bad. I saw him last when he had arrived at the other side and we were trying to stop our men from attacking before the night was over."

Goi: "Gaito looked bad, not like a human being."

Ano: "Hadn't he lost his shadow?"

Goi: "He had lost his shadow."

Ano: (vehemently) "He had no shadow anymore. His shadow had been taken away. The shadow with which you walk, you know what I mean—it wasn't there anymore. We said, let us keep a good watch on him, but when the bullets began flying something chased him away from our side."

Goi: "Something chased him ahead."

Ano: "He reached that very small homestead with only two cattle. The owner of the cattle had hidden in a hole in the earth. He aimed his gun at him whom the ancestors had taken hold of and from behind the bullet hit him in the back. The first we heard was: 'Gaito has died.'

'*Hm*'. 'That is what you have always wanted.' 'Do you let people knowingly walk into their death?' That is what I had said. That is their madness, the madness I had seen already at my older brother's death. (raises his voice) He who has been taken hold of (whom the ancestors have destined to die), he won't listen to you if you try to talk to him... Gaito, wasn't he bright before? But when his heart had been taken away how could he have listened to us, he would not have turned back. Wasn't his shadow put down over there a long time ago? Hadn't his shadow been fastened over there? That's how it is. (pause, then Anombe continues quietly) Our meeting ground of Kadja has never seen something like this before."

Bal: (sighs) "Let it get lost!" (Op. Cit.: 192-98).

The men argue that not only the warriors live or die according to their individual destinies, also the raid as a whole is destined to succeed or fail for reasons which only divination can reveal. Or, to put it differently, that it is the diviner who exercises the greatest influence over people. It is he who induces them to fight, saying that the drought will end and rain will fall if they go to war and so on. Baldambe sarcastically points this out to Anombe and Goiti, implying that the raid on Arbore ultimately was the product of the diviner's mind:

> Baldambe: "He who has consulted the sandal oracle is Djagi Bacho. He threw the sandals by himself after he had dreamt that he should do so.' Wasn't it like this?"
>
> Goiti & Anombe: "Yes, so it was."
>
> Bal: "Some of it was his dream, some his sandals: 'This day, this day, if you now go down to the river and no rain falls immediately then I have not consulted my sandals, then I have not dreamt.' Wasn't it like this?"
>
> Goi&Ano: "Yes."
>
> Bal: "'Man, if you don't get up this month and finish him, then it's your end, then all the country will belong to him.' The one who said this was the son of Bacho and the one who brought the news was Nyetigul's son Darsha. (sighs) Let it get lost!" (Op. Cit.: 190).

As Baldambe, Anombe and Goiti were talking in this way about the causes, especially the different kinds of 'madness', which had led to the disastrous raid and the death of Gaito as well as many others, a guest entered and, implying that the raid was not that mad after all, said the Hamar could very well have brought home cattle had they only acted quickly enough. Upon this, Baldambe let loose the following tirade:

> Stop getting rich with empty words. While you have to carry the burden of the hard time (the present drought) you are brave only in your talk. In fact you are the cause of the misery of others. Have you considered the tears which these hard times have brought to the women? Look, your mother is hungry, your father's cattle are hungry, your father's goats are hungry, the kids are hungry, your children are hungry. Where will you survive? Will you survive in the country of the Bume, or? Will you survive in the country of the Aari, or? Will you survive in the country of the

Marle, or? Or where will you survive? Are you the only one who has a voice? You have spilt it. (pauses in his emphatic speech) Now look! Should you cry about the dead or should you try to find something to fill your stomachs? Haven't you gone mad?" (Op. Cit.: 199-200).

Madness as the ultimate cause of war

From the conversations which I have quoted above we have learnt that the Hamar attribute war to madness. Here I want to explore this important point more fully. Also, I want to show that the Ancients also held similar ideas, and that even today we ourselves draw connections between madness and war although we are not always aware of this.

The Hamar, like other groups in Ethiopia, attribute great significance to the great toe and hold the idea that it manifests the well-being, good luck and good fortune of a person. Interestingly, the idea that the great toe embodies the fate and good fortune of a person was also found in antiquity. Thus Pyrrhus whom we have met already above, had, according to Plutarch, a magically powerful right foot with which he would heal patients from diseases: "While the patient lay flat on his back, he would gently press upon the region of the spleen with his right foot. There was nobody so poor or obscure that Pyrrhus would refuse him his healing touch, if he were asked for it" (Plutarch 1975: 386). Furthermore, "the great toe of his right foot was also said to possess a divine power, so that when the rest of his body was burned after his death, this was found unharmed and untouched by the fire" (Op. Cit.: 386-387).

When it comes to war, however, the Hamar do not speak so much of the great toe and victory as of the feet and defeat. Running feet are their metaphor for combat like in the following example where my friends Baldambe and Choke examine the sky one morning after the Hamar have left for an attack on the Arbore (also called Ulde):

Baldambe: "Well, if the raiders were still meeting and talking, there would be a black cloud. A black cloud, dark like a rain cloud. Now they have got up and are already on their way."

Ethnographer: "Why?"

Bal: "Look at the brightness, '*misso*'. At the clearness. That is dust, dust only. The white over there that is dust. That is the men running, the cattle that are running. Over there, the white."

Eth: "It means that cattle are running?"

Bal: "It means that the people are running (...). The white ones (white clouds) are the ones who run (...)."

Choke: "And when the raiders are on their way, the clouds show us their footprints: *ba-ta-ta-ta-ta-ta-ta*, white and spreading out like my hand (points towards Ulde, spreading his fingers). That's how the clouds form (...)."

Bal: "Look at all the whiteness which flashes like metal, those are their footprints. The white over there that is dust. That is the men running, the cattle that are running" (Strecker 1979a: 32-33).

The running, which Baldambe and Choke see in the clouds is, as I have said, more likely to lead to defeat than to victory, for in the eyes of the Hamar all excited running is dangerous. People should not run but walk like baboons who move with natural ease, rarely hurt themselves and also have the strange capacity to know what lies ahead of them. Their instinctive knowledge and ease of motion make them safe. Thus Baldambe blessed the men who had gone to attack the Arbore by wishing they would walk like baboons:

"Let the people walk their different ways as baboons do.
The people of Kadja, let them walk their ways as baboons do.
The people of Bana, let them walk their different ways as
baboons do..." (Op. Cit.: 3).

But the wish that people may walk like baboons is not only uttered in the context of war, it is also often used in blessing to emphasize the wish that one's fellow human beings should be well and sane and know what they are doing. Many people stumble from one mistake to the other, run into trouble, get thrown off their feet and loose their way in the struggles of everyday life. This is why one wishes them to walk like baboons and to have a green right great toe.

Furthermore, erratic running and walking are associated with lack of orientation, loss of sound judgement and madness. Thus at the height of the dry season there is a month which the Hamar call the "mad month" (*barrae*) because at this time people tend to get crazy searching desperately in all directions for water, pasture and grain (see also Baldambe's fable at the beginning of the chapter).

According to the Hamar, this craziness lies at the back of war. In their eyes, people mostly fight because they have gone mad, are out of their minds, have lost their self-control and power of reasoning. A grown-up married man is called a *donza*, someone who can control himself (*donsha*) and does not get mad, fly into a rage and fight even when he has been wronged. The term *donza* implies that as a responsible person you will encounter and suffer injustice, but this should not disturb and blind you. Rather, you should "put a stone in your heart" (so that it does not shake like a gourd filled with water) and think and act calmly, for everyone who does not have this mental and emotional power of self-control is a danger to society and his actions are prone to cause conflict and war.

In Anombe's account (see above) he repeatedly drew a connection between running, madness and defeat: Gaito died because "something chased him away from our side", because "something chased him ahead", because "that which extinguished him, it hunted him to his death." Others "were really killed by something which had made them lose their senses. It was madness which killed them…" When Anombe urged some of the men to sit with him "in the night like birds" and be safe in this way, they did not listen, and "it is they who met death. I don't know what was driving them there".

The latter was, of course, a rhetorical remark, for Anombe, Goiti and Baldambe later agreed with each other that it is the spirits of the dead who drive people crazy so that they go to war and die. Gaito died after the diviner had already seen his death in the intestines of a sacrificial animal. Let me again quote the particularly telling passage where Anombe tells how Gaito had gone mad, would not listen and was doomed to die: "That is their madness, the madness I had seen already at my older brother's death. He who has been taken hold of, he won't listen to you if you try to talk to him... Gaito, wasn't he bright before? But when his heart had been taken away how could he have listened to us, he would not have turned back. Wasn't his shadow put down over there a long time ago? Hadn't his shadow been fastened over there?" ('Shadow' is used as a metaphor for soul or spirit.)

But not only your own dead forefathers cause you to go mad and die in war, also the dead forefathers of those who you attack may determine your fate. This is why Anombe said that the Marle "must have made true sacrifices to the ancestors so that the Hamar went mad", and that "when the Hamar step on the Marle land they go crazy".

Finally it is interesting to note that according to Anombe the war leaders tried to provoke the Hamar and wanted them to trample with their feet on the ground as a strong sign of their commitment to fight. Such trampling is associated in Hamar (as well as many other groups in East Africa) with ecstasy, loss of consciousness and possession. Therefore one can say that the war leaders wanted the men to get mad and loose their senses, and they were offended when Baldambe's brother Lukusse "just got up and pointed his gun towards the enemy" but otherwise remained sober and refused to trample.

Not only the Ancients and the Hamar have associated the movement of feet with madness. We ourselves, that is speakers of Indo-Germanic languages, have done the same. In German *irren* means to make a mental error while *irre*, means to be 'mad, crazy, deranged'. Kluge's etymological dictionary (1960) provides the additional information that the Latin *errare*, the English 'err' and the German *irren* have an old root '*ers*' from which the Old Indian *iirshyá* (jealousy) and *irasyáti* (he is angry), the Gothic *airzeis* (mad, seduced), the Old Anglo-Saxon *yirre* and the Old German *irri* (angry) derived. Like the Hamar *barri*, the German *irre* involves an uncontrolled movement of feet. When you are mad (*irre*) you do not only go wrong mentally (*irren*), you also loose your orientation and walk hectically in different directions (*irren*).

This aspect of bodily movement in the notion of error also comes out clearly in English where according to the Concise Oxford Dictionary 'erratic' means "uncertain in movement; irregular in conduct, habit, opinion" and where 'errant' means both someone who "errs, deviates from correct standard" and also someone "roaming in quest of adventure", especially a knight.

As we have seen above, the Hamar make the same connection between madness, error and war, and they think that from madness and error come the greatest social dangers and the most unpredictable threats to peaceful life. Those who are mad will stumble, fall and bring misfortune, while those who are sane will walk 'like baboons', and their 'green big toe' will bring good fortune, abundance and well-being.

The rhetoric and magic of ceremonial peace making

Although the Hamar think that war is ultimately caused by human madness (which in turn may be caused by the spirits of the dead, see above) they do not address this most fundamental cause directly when they engage in ceremonial peace making but focus on more immediate and intermediate causes instead. Let me illustrate this with the help of an account in which Baldambe has described a peace ceremony held between the Bume and Hamar two generations ago. First I provide Baldambe's text and then I attempt an interpretation:

When the Hamar and Bume were enemies, they said to each other: "Let us forget our quarrels, let us become one family again". The Bume *bitta* (ritual leader), who was called Loteng, called to my father who was then a spokesman:

"Berinas!"

"*Woi!*"

"Do you have a *bitta*?"

"I have a *bitta*."

Whereupon he brought out ten sacks of sorghum and gave them to my father to bring to *bitta* Elto. When my father had given Elto the sorghum, Elto got up and said:

"Bring a biiiiiiig pot of honey to the Bume *bitta*. Our country is full of honey. The Bume do not know how to make beehives. I have made beehives. Bring honey to the Bume *bitta* so that he will call *barjo* for us, the '*barjo* of the cattle, of the goats and of the children'."

So my father brought the honey to the Bume *bitta*... Then the Bume performed their peace ritual. Loteng took a big spear, which is used in calling for rain, and in sending away the sickness of the cattle, and called his people to come... They all came and an ox was slaughtered. Loteng then said:

"We Bume and the Hamar have been fighting. Now Berinas has offered us peace... The Hamar *bitta* has given us a big pot of honey. Berinas says that we should all become one family again, and that we should forget our fighting. That is good! Yesterday we killed Hamar and dressed our heads with ostrich feathers and we scarified our chests. Let us forget the scarifications, let us forget the feathers."

They brought two spears:

"We have used these spears to kill each other. Now Berinas should take one and use it to call forth rain. The *bitta* Elto should take the other and bury it in the earth."

Next, Berinas brought a white, white, white, white, white ox that had not a single colour other than white. All Bume, Kara and Hamar were called and my father said:

"Do you see this white ox?"

"We see it."

"My stomach is like this, completely white, neither black nor speckled, nor brown, nor yellow. My stomach is pure, it is only white. Eat this ox. May the stomach of the Bume and the stomach of the Hamar become one. May they become like this ox. May the stomach of the Bume only be white. May the stomach of the Hamar only be white."

Then my father slaughtered the ox. The elders gathered together and ate it. They called forth the end of all fighting:

"May the sickness of the cattle get lost,
may the sickness of the goats get lost,
may our spear that killed get lost."

Then the Bume took the rain-spear intended for Berinas and fastened a branch of the *dongo*-tree to it, and put an ostrich feather at the top. With this they went into Hamar country and when they came to Berinas' home they began to dance and sing:

"Let us forget our fighting,
let our stomach become one,
let us forget our fighting,
let our stomach become one,
let our talk become one,
let us be brothers,
let us be in-laws,
let us be friends,
let us be *misso*
let us be *bel*."

Singing and dancing they came to the house of my father. Again my father brought a white ox... He called the Hamar elders:

"The Bume elders have come. Hamar elders!"

"*Yo!*"

"Bume elders!"

"*Yo!*"

"Look at this ox. What colour does it have? White. Is there any black in it? No. Are there any speckles in it? No. Is there brown on it? No. Isn't its colour just white? It is white. My stomach is as white as this. I tell you the truth. Now you Bume, tell me the truth, the only truth."

Then the Bume *bitta* got up and answered:

"Berinas has told the truth. Bume, in your belly there is war. Do you see this spear? Do you see this big spear?"

"We see it."

"Its blade is big, isn't it?"

"It is big."

"If you should make war, if you should kill the women and children of Berinas, if you should steal his cattle, then this spear will turn back upon you and kill you. Like Berinas' stomach, my stomach has become one and is like the white ox. Now you and Berinas and his children shall become in-laws, friends, one family."

Then the ox was slaughtered and the other spear was brought up to *bitta* Elto who buried it in the earth. Isn't then the spear dead? Since the spear was buried the talk of Bume and Hamar has become one. If people start fighting:

"*Ai-ai-ai*! Stop it, stop it, stop it! *Bitta* Elto and spokesman Berinas have put magic into the spear. Fighting is bad."

So the fighting has now ended, because of the ostrich feather, the *dongo* branch and the spear of the Bume, our honey and our white ox. When we killed the white ox we rubbed our hands with chyme from its stomach, and rubbed the chyme on our bodies so that we might all become one, like the grass and the water and the plants in the ox's stomach. If the Bume should start a war we Hamar will get up and call out that they should die, and they will simply die. If we Hamar start a war and kill the Bume the Bume will call out that we should die, and we will simply die. This is the talk between Hamar and Bume." (Lydall and Strecker 1979b: 31-34).

Baldambe's account provides a vivid picture of the event and of the speakers' intentions: their will to respect one another and be one family again; their wish to forget all wrongs of the past and harbour no bad feelings in the future; their hope that all will adhere to their promises—and their threats that the spear will turn back on anyone who dares to break the peace.

What is stressed most repeatedly and at times almost violently is the stomach. Why such insistence on the stomach and on activities related to it? In my view, the explanation runs as follows: when the speakers at the peace ceremony ask the listeners to positively change their attitudes, they do not mention or even allude to madness, even though madness constitutes, as everyone knows, the most serious danger to peace. Yet it simply would not help to exhort others saying they should not be mad anymore. This would only upset them and generate the very madness, which needs to be averted.

With the stomach it is different because one has control over it. To understand this fully one must know that among people like the Hamar and Bume it is the pride of every man to control his stomach, to never ask for food if it is not offered freely, to never complain even if he has to starve days without end. I have witnessed this often in Hamar. During times of plenty it would be the men who would get served first, often even in public, so that everyone could see how richly they were feasting. But during periods of drought it would be the men who first would go without so that the children and guests could be fed.

So when the orator at a peace ceremony mentions the stomach and speaks of the need to purify it, make it white and rid it from war, everyone gets immediately reminded of his own well-developed power of self-control. This, as I see it, is the logic of reasoning here. To put it differently, when the Hamar focus on the control of the stomach they follow the maxim of, as we would say, 'mind over matter' and mean that just as people should be able to control parts of the body, they should also be able to control their social behaviour.

There are, of course, further reasons why the peacemaker draws attention to the stomach or belly. The most obvious is that, as the anthropological literature on witchcraft accusation has demonstrated, people almost universally experience the belly as a seat of particular kinds of anger, such as hate, malice, grudge, spite, envy and vengefulness. It is this 'anger in the stomach' to which most efforts at peace making is addressed. At least this is what we learn from Baldambe's account.

The orator first draws attention to his own stomach and says that it is not black (like 'dark' thoughts of vengeance), not speckled (like 'mixed' feelings), not brown or yellow (like bile, the fluid secreted by the liver which in English is figuratively used to express peevishness) but pure, completely white like the ox which was slaughtered to seal the peace. By eating together, so the orator continues, the men will become one because in their stomachs they will carry the same substance, the meat of the ox. Not only this, they will become one like the grass, the water and all the different kinds of plants in the ox's stomach. They will mix and become a new substance, which is healthy and protective like chyme. In addition, Baldambe says, that the first things the Bume and Hamar do in order to show their desire for peace, are activities also related to the stomach. That is, the Bume gave food (brought ten sacks of sorghum) to the Hamar, and the Hamar gave food (a biiiiiig pot of honey) to the Bume. The food was then used to prepare beer and honey wine with which the ritual leaders (*bitta*) blessed their former enemies and called forth their well-being: "Bring honey to the Bume *bitta*", said Baldambe's father Berinas, "so that he will call *barjo* for us, the *barjo* of the cattle, of the goats and of the children". Finally, and very importantly, Baldambe explains how the spear is used in peace making. Not a simple spear but a 'rain-spear' was involved in the ceremony, and it was adorned with a branch of the *dongo*-tree and an ostrich feather.

In order to grasp some of the meaning of this, one needs to know that *dongo* (Cordia ovalis) provides, together with *baraza* (Grewia mollis), the best whipping wands (*michere*) which the Hamar as well as their neighbours use both to herd animals, especially small stock, and to 'herd' (*gisha*) people, especially children, young men and women. The Hamar say that at the top of the *michere* there is butter and honey, meaning that the use of *michere* leads to abundance and well-being. In fact, *michere* are an extension of the human body and in many ways similar to the *dumai*, the right big toe. The *michere* of a person who has *barjo* (luck) will bring him good fortune, like the 'green big toe'. This is why elders often carry *michere*, especially the very long ones made from *dongo*, and this is why the *dongo* branch gives added magical power to the rain-spear.

Furthermore, from *dongo* come both the drilling sticks with which the Hamar ritually kindle new fires and the charcoal with which they smoke the milk containers. In both instances *dongo* is used for cleansing. Analogically, the *dongo* fastened to the rain-spear is meant to emphasize that the spear should cleanse people and rid the communities of their disease, that is war.

While *dongo* alludes to herding and the domestic sphere, the ostrich feather evokes hunting and the domain of nature. Also, it speaks of the exuberant dancing and feasting which follows the attainment of peace. To create peace always means to renew an embracing harmony with nature, which was spoilt when people killed each other and shed their blood on the ground. The spokesmen blessed the people, the herds and the country using a rain-spear charged with additional symbolic power. But at the same time they used the spear as an instrument to force peace upon the people. As Baldambe said, they put magic into the spear: "*Ai-ai-ai-ai*! Stop it, stop it, stop it! *Bitta* Elto and spokesman Berinas have put magic into the spear".

Here we can see how among the Hamar and their neighbours peace making at times involves something more than the social use of metaphor (Sapir and Crocker 1977), or the persuasive power of tropes (Fernandez 1991). The Bume *bitta* got up and said:

"Bume, in your belly there is war. Do you see this spear? Do you see this big spear?"

"We see it."

"It's blade is big, isn't it?"

"It is big."

"If you should make war, if you should kill the women and children of Berinas, if you should steal his cattle, then this spear will turn back upon you and kill you."

This is indeed a very massive threat and goes beyond the more symbolic images with which the spokesmen at other moments in the peace ceremony try to evoke the possibility of peace. The image of the spear, which can turn back upon you, is more than a simple simile. It evokes in the minds of the speakers and listeners that magic has been put into the spear; magic more powerful than words, for it will kill anyone who would dare to break the peace.

Belief in the magic of the spear is strengthened by experience. As we know, the Bume *bitta* brought two spears saying: "We have used these spears to kill each other. Now Berinas should take one and use it to call forth rain. The '*bitta*' Elto should take the other and bury it in the earth."

The spear given to Elto was buried in the mountains of Hamar where it has remained ever since, and the spear given to Berinas was inherited by his son Baldambe who kept it in his house at Dambaiti, in fact in the house which we used to share together (Lydall/Strecker 1979a). Often I witnessed how Baldambe took this spear in order to participate as a spokesman in public meetings where he eagerly spoke for peace with the Bume and cursed all those who would dare to begin a war with them.

As long as he lived, Baldambe's threat was effective and kept the Hamar and Bume apart. But in March 1995 Baldambe died and was buried in the mountains of Hamar near the grave of his father Berinas. For two more years the old peace between the Hamar and Bume continued, but then, in March 1997 the

Bume suddenly attacked the Hamar. The assault was huge and on a scale unprecedented in history. Here I give only the barest outline of what happened.

There had been a prolonged period of drought in 1996-1997. In fact, the drought had been so severe that almost all the water holes in the mountains of Hamar had dried up and most of the grass had perished. Therefore the Hamar had driven all their herds down to the Omo which used to be a large river but now had almost dried up, providing only a trickle of water for the many animals. The river was easy to ford now, and the large concentration of herds 'in grasping reach', as it were, was extremely tempting for the Bume. Also, they knew that Baldambe had died. Were he still alive, perhaps they would have refrained, but, as the spear was now without its master, they disregarded the magic that had been put into it.

I had just arrived in Hamar when the attack occurred. The drought had ended and there had been heavy rains over the previous days. At night a blanket of clouds covered the whole land in darkness, and it was this darkness, so the Hamar later said, which tempted the Bume to attack. They knew where the main cattle camps of the Hamar were located, they knew approximately how many men were tending the herds, they knew the terrain from hunting and earlier visits to the Hamar, and they knew how and where to ford the river even in the darkness of night.

The Hamar also knew that the Bume might be coming, for the Bume recently had made a minor raid in which they managed to drive away some cattle and had boasted that this was only the beginning, that they would return to 'visit' the Hamar again. Being aware of the danger, the Hamar left their cattle camps at night and hid in the cover of the bush.

Hundreds of Bume crossed the Omo river that night, maybe as many as two thousand, according to the Hamar. They split in to three groups, which were to encircle the Hamar cattle camps, take them by surprise and drive all the herds across the river. But as they were on the way to take their position, some Bume were detected by the Hamar who fired a few shots at them. This sparked off an exchange of fire, not, however, between Hamar and Bume but between the Bume themselves. The darkness of night, which they had thought would protect them, now turned against them and stopped them from realizing that they were shooting, not at the Hamar but at each other.

Armed with newly acquired Kalashnikovs and large amounts of ammunition, the Bume fought a most extraordinary battle amongst them selves through much of the night while the Hamar kept quiet in their hiding. At dawn, when the Hamar returned to their cattle camps and inspected the scene, they found that some of the Bume were dead, others were wounded and guns and ammunition were littering the ground.

At his homestead my friend Choke could hear the fighting all night and was one of the first to get the full news when his friends returned from the cattle camps next morning. Two days later, when Choke gave me an account of the event, he was full with exhilaration and his eyes gleamed, for he knew that I understood the significance of the event, that I knew without saying that here the magic of Baldambe's spear had been active and that the curse which Loteng uttered two generations ago had finally found its target.

By way of conclusion

The aim of this short essay has been to invite the reader to listen to the Hamar and witness their struggle for peace in the face of war. I began with Baldambe's fable of the original safety of Hamar country, a safety both from the threats of the natural world (drought) and the social sphere (war). Then I recalled the large-scale conflicts which in the past three centuries occurred in the Horn of Africa and in many ways also affected the Hamar. After this I outlined the traditional patterns of warfare and showed that in spite of the external incursions the Hamar have upheld much of their old sense of security even until today. It is from this vantage point of original safety that one can understand the various personal thoughts and feelings expressed in the sections 'Witnessing the struggle for peace and the temptations of war' and 'Madness as the ultimate cause of war'.

The final section dealt with an example of collective and ritualised peace making. I examined the rhetoric and magic involved and tried to show that the peace maker employs three strategies: Firstly he relegates the ultimate cause of war (the mind) to the realm of the unspeakable (see Tyler 1987); secondly he uses his rhetorical skills to address the intermediate cause of war (the body) and makes it the focus of persuasion; and thirdly he turns to the means of war (the weapon) and uses it for magic as the strongest shield against the madness of war.

Embedded in the presentation and interpretation of Hamar discourse was an attempt to articulate my own theoretical position. Following Tyler (1978) and Montague (1994) I argued against determinism and emphasized the need to study war not as a necessity caused by resource competition, cultural differences or other 'hard underlying reasons', but (to paraphrase Spinoza as quoted by Montague 1994: x) by people who wilfully have abandoned "virtue, benevolence, confidence and justice."

Rhetoric in the context of war

Introduction

In this paper I want to provide some glimpses of Hamar rhetoric in the context of war and in this way continue with, and build on, themes I have pursued in earlier papers and presentations at the International Conferences of Ethiopia Studies and elsewhere (see bibliography).

I have selected four cases from *Conversations in Dambaiti*, the third book of the trilogy *The Hamar of Southern Ethiopia*, which I published together with Jean Lydall way back in 1979. The *Conversations* document a social drama that ensued during the dry season of 1974 when the Hamar raided their neighbours, the Arbore (depending on circumstances also called Hor, Ulde or Marle) who live in the Woito Valley north of Chew Bahir (Lake Stefanie).

There is a further reason why I have chosen the topic of rhetoric. Like so many other post-postmodern anthropologists I have been searching for a new paradigm for the study of culture. Two great teachers and friends who have inspired me most in this, are Baldambe (Balambaras Aike Berinas) from Hamar and Steve (Professor Stephen Tyler) from Rice University, Houston, Texas. Both have pointed to the same direction—rhetoric. Rhetoric is the key to a new (and one can also say very old) theory of culture. In a number of workshops, seminars and informal meetings devoted to the theme of 'Rhetoric Culture' my colleagues and I have tried to fathom this idea.

Rhetoric culture theory says that culture emerges from and is sustained by rhetoric. This implies that we need to explore both, the culture of rhetoric and the rhetoric of culture. On the one hand we need to study the rhetorical competence of people in different cultures, and on the other hand we need to examine the way in which this rhetorical competence creates conventions, styles of life, patterns of culture. The present paper focuses on the first (the Hamar culture of rhetoric), but at the back of the analysis the latter (the rhetoric culture of Hamar) also lies.

As I wrote in the introduction to *Conversations in Dambaiti*:

> I was at the cattle camps in the lowlands of the Omo Valley when the Hamar in the mountains were preparing for the raid, and by the time I returned to Dambaiti the men had already left. Those who had stayed behind were the women and children, some old men, our host and teacher Baldambe and my friend Choke who had accompanied me on my journey to the cattle camps. The moment we arrived, I began to record all the main conversations in Dambaiti" (Strecker 1979a: vi; The *Conversations* begin late afternoon, January 1974).

Calling forth the safety of those who have gone to war

The men of Baldambe's family, of his settlement (Dambaiti), of his territorial segment (Kadja) and in fact from all over Hamar had left for war when Baldambe called forth *barjo* and invoked their well-being, even though he did not agree with their raid. In my diary I noted down how Baldambe dissociated himself from the Hamar who were on their way to war, as follows:

> Anti serves coffee in Aikenda's house. When we have finished, Baldambe arrives and we all sit outside... and exchange our first 'talk of the country'. Baldambe evokes an insane picture of himself walking home, meeting countless people going in the opposite direction to join the raid: here our Ogotemmeli (famous Dogon sage who described Dogon cosmology to Marcel Griaule), anthropologist, intellectual, son of a great leader and warrior, walking alone against the stream of his people who pass him by on their way to the fighting: madness and confusion! In the villages he passes, he meets only three old men who do not join the rush to the war. Women call out to him, "Where are you going?" Baldambe

answers them, "Well, someone has to make the fire while all the other bulls have gone." "Oh, yes, make fire, make fire!" To 'make fire' is an euphemism for 'to fuck'. Tears run from Baldambe's eyes as he tells us this. He always laughs so much that tears fall. The girls put on another pot of coffee for Baldambe. When it is ready Baldambe, Choke and I sit down and exchange our respective news in detail—and I record (Lydall and Strecker 1979a: 262-63).

Like usual, Baldambe blessed before the conversation began, but his *barjo aela*, his calling forth good fortune, was more intense and serious than usual. It seemed as if he tried his utmost to save his people from the dangers of war. He did this by projecting order into the impending chaos and by mustering support for his plea for safety. He referred to and called upon his ancestors and his father in order to back up the power of his blessing. His forefathers used to call *barjo*, and Baldambe mentioned this as precedent for the claim that his own voice will be equally effective. He invoked history and tradition to lend weight and authority to his call for well-being as in the following lines:

"The meeting ground of my ancestors,
the gateway of my father's herds:
let them be well, let them be well, let them be well.
My father used to call *barjo*,
my ancestors used to call *barjo*.
I inherited the word from my father,
I inherited the word from my ancestors.
Let *barjo* herd my father's cattle.
My father's goats, my father's children:
well, well, well, well, well.
Herd cattle, herd goats, herd people, herd children...
The father's gateway,
let it be well, let it be well, let it be well.
May he herd the cattle.
May he herd the goats.
May he herd the children.

Let the people go like baboons...
Let the people who walk down the path to Ulde,
let them go like baboons.
The people from Bilbemba,
let them go like baboons.
My father begged with his word for *barjo*.
I, let me call *barjo* using my father's words.
Barjo. Well, well, well, well!" (Strecker 1979a: 2-5).

The power of the *barjo aela* builds up gradually and heightens as Baldambe uses intensification ("herd goats, herd cattle, herd children"); repetition ("let it be well, let it be well, let it be well"); parallelism ("My father used to call *barjo*, my ancestors used to call *barjo*"). But it is a *barjo aela* without hyperbole and exuberance, which on other occasions are characteristic of blessing. In this case the mood is subdued, full of fear and the issue is not addressed openly but remains hidden behind ellipses and euphemisms like when Baldambe says: "Let the people who walk dawn the path to Ulde, let them go like baboons". The picture of people going like baboons is a marvellous example of rhetorical creativity and competence. It remains strange and cryptic, however, until we know, that the Hamar attribute superior knowledge to the baboons, especially an ability to sense danger from afar. As the Hamar say, a baboon is not prone to error like humans are, and—very tellingly—he never stumbles, he never falls. This is why it makes sense for Baldambe to call forth the well-being of his people by letting them walk 'like baboons'. I have never heard anyone else use this equation in blessing. Therefore it may well be that Baldambe has created a unique expression here. But if he has done so, the simile is still grounded in Hamar culture.

Part of Baldambe's attempt to create mental and emotional order and confidence is that he uses neither metaphor nor metonymy but prefers synecdoche instead. He repeatedly invokes the well-being of the gateway of his father's herds. This can be understood as a well-chosen synecdoche, where a significant part, the gateway, stands for the whole homestead and its inhabitants. The use of this synecdoche is, however, not idiosyncratic. On the contrary, it follows and emphasises a traditional pattern of Hamar thought and action.

For example, the 'father of the homestead' likes to sit close to the gateway and watch as the herds, and also the people, leave in the morning and return in the evening. Here, as the individuals pass one by one through the gateway, he can see how they are and notice if anyone is missing or someone is not well. Thus the gateway receives every day high practical attention. This in turn has its corollary in the realm of ritual where important acts are usually performed at the gateway, either at the gateway of the goat enclosure or the gateway of the cattle kraal.

A paragon of ritual performance at the gateway is the blessing provided by the *bitta* (ritual leader), described by Baldambe as follows:

> Goats are brought with the gourd to the *bitta*.
> 'May the master come forth from the house, may he come out.
> The gourd has come. Sweep the gateway.'
>
> Then the *bitta*'s wife puts on her head-dress,
> her goat skin cape and her cowry-shell belt,
> and sweeps the entrance to the cattle kraal.
> After this the *bitta* comes and stands by the gateway...
> (then) he begins to chant and the elders answer in refrain:
> *Eh-eh*!
> The herds are carrying sickness,
> may the sickness go, may it go,
> may my herds come lowing, come
> may the girls laugh, laugh
> may the women dance, dance! (Lydall and Strecker 1979b: 13-15).

Finally, we may note the rhetorical character of the notion of *barjo*. In a paper on the uses of *barjo* in Hamar I have already analysed it as follows:

The basic agents in Hamar politics are the *donza* (married men) of a settlement area who act collectively and are likened to a certain grass (*zarsi*), which spreads over the ground... According to the *donza* they carry their *barjo* with them wherever they go. Whenever it seems necessary to exercise some specific control over the world the *donza* get together and call *barjo*... If the term *barjo* sometimes seems to mean a substance which one shares, sometimes seems to refer to an immanent power to live, sometimes indicates simply a general state of well-being or the specific well-being which goes with a person, animal, plant or object, etc., then this lack of distinction and the openness of the concept go very well with the absence of any single locus and mode of social power in Hamar... The *barjo aela* is a brilliant rhetoric strategy because it does two important things at once: it allows the men to exercise control over others while inhibiting the control of others over themselves (Strecker 1988: 72-73).

Debating the signs of war in the sky

In my diary I described the situation where Baldambe and Choke debated the signs of war in the sky as follows:

Even before sunrise I am up and about armed with my tape recorder, for I know that Baldambe and Choke will be watching the early morning sky to decipher what it augurs about the raid. Baldambe points to the sky and asserts that the Hamar have attacked because the sky over Ulde is white and the clouds are dispersed. The raiding party would still be sitting talking if the clouds were dense and rounded. Such clouds indicate a public meeting. This is the sky that prompted Baldambe's interpretation (Lydall and Strecker 1979a: 264).

Baldambe and Choke had mixed feelings as they tried to read and interpret the signs in the early morning sky. Partly they wanted to see the Hamar win and successfully raid the Arbore, and partly they wished that the Arbore would teach the Hamar a lesson. Also, they were not sure how, when, or whether at all, the Hamar would attack. If Baldambe and Choke were calm during the blessing on the previous evening, if they spoke in unison and projected an image of order and harmony onto the world, this morning during their attempt at divination, they were excited, saw suffering and disturbance in the sky and began arguing with each other:

Ethnographer: "The sky, the sky, what does it say?"

Baldambe: "*Misso* (hunting-friend), see over there, the white which was lying there, the white which is lying across, across, across, across. Here above us it leads over there, it lies across. We don't know what it means. Here above us the clouds lead over there, and there they bar the way. *Misso, Misso* (he points excitedly towards the clouds) see the very small white cloud over there, which has slipped into the middle of the sky."

Eth: "*Hmm.*"

Bal: "You see. *Wooo*, that cloud bars our way. Again, see here the small straight one. It bars the way of all those who have not yet crossed beneath it. It stops all of us who have stayed behind. Look how the clouds have been put up as if to stop us. Later they will grow even bigger and bar the way more powerfully. Those that lie across–all across. Look at those over there who watch the cattle, the clouds nearby. They watch, they watch. Those over Maen, those that lie across Maen, they watch them over there."

Eth: "Do the clouds say that the raiders have attacked already?"

Bal: "Well, if the raiders were still meeting and talking, there would be a black cloud. A black cloud; dark like the rain cloud. Now they have got up and are already on their way."

Eth: "Why?"

Bal: "Look at the brightness, *misso*. At the clearness. That is dust; dust only. The white over there, this is dust. That is the men running, the cattle that are running. Over there, the white."

Eth: "It means that the cattle are running?"

Bal: "It means that the people are running, *dull-dull*. If the people were still meeting and talking, if they were all gathered together, there would be a black, round cloud, a black round cloud, a black, round cloud. It would stay there all day."

Choke: "And when the raiders are on their way, the clouds show us their footprints: *ta-ta-ta-ta-ta-ta-ta-ta*, white and spreading out like my hand (points towards Ulde, spreading his fingers). That's how the clouds form."

Bal: "Look how they spread here."

Eth: "What do the clouds mean over there?" (points at clouds)

Bal: "Father of Theo, those lying across the middle of the sky, that's the blockade. The small one that lies close to the mountains, it stops those who are here from following the others. Up, high above us, those are we who are at home, we who watch. We cannot follow those who have gone. The white ones are the ones who run."

Eth: "The ones who beat the soil with their feet."

Bal: "*Dull-dull, dull-dull*, the dust. Isn't it the dust? Today the sky shows only dust."

Eth: "*Misso*, have they attacked now or not?"

Bal: "Attacked, attacked! Today they have attacked. If they hadn't, there would be clouds."

Eth: "There would be black, round clouds."

Bal: "Yes, *misso*, I know all this. They have attacked; look at all this dust. Look at the red flashing light: *ra-ra-ra-ra-ra-ra – barcha-barcha-barcha-barcha.*"

Cho: (joining him) "*Ra-ra-ra-ra-ra-ra-ra.*"

Bal: "Look at all the whiteness which flashes like metal, those are their footprints. On the left up there that is Bura, Tsamai. They also are watching."

Cho: "Look, *misso*, the big ones which collect all together."

Eth/ Cho/ Bal: "...that is the country of Bura, Tsamai."

Bal: "They have attacked."

Cho: "They have attacked today. Before the sky did not look like this. (Baldambe joins in) *Ra-ra-ra-ra-ra-ra-ra.* Watch! Usually the sun does not look like this."

Eth: "I have not seen it like that."

Cho: "The people's blood."

Bal: "This, this, which looks red. It is the smoke of the guns."

Cho: "Isn't it all clearly revealed up there in the sky?"

Bal: "The *puk-puk*, the red *ra-ra-ra* wasn't there before."

Cho: "The sun has died over there, they have attacked."

Bal: "Didn't I say to my friend last night that if the guns had sounded today, the sky would be clear, there would be no clouds? If people were still talking, there would be clouds. Look here, they have attacked."

Cho: "They attacked a short while ago."

Bal: "No, now, just now!"

Cho: "When we entered to drink coffee."

Bal: "If the attack happened when we entered for coffee, then they would have survived."

Cho: "Would not have survived, not survived. They would survive now that the sun has risen. If they were attacked when we were drinking coffee, then they would have died. Wouldn't their bullet belts be lying on the ground then?"

Bal: "On the ground."

Cho: "Wouldn't they just run with their guns? Wouldn't a stupid person who has just bought himself a new gun throw it away and run for his life with only his bullet belt? They would be trapped. But if the sun had risen, they would have put on their bullet belts, would have stepped out to go to their fields and would have survived. If they attacked when we were drinking coffee, then they will have decorated their heads by now."

Bal: "Those who are up there in the mountains have heard the gun fire by now."

Cho: "Up there one can hear it closely."

Bal: "Look at the sky: see how it is clearly laid down."

Cho: "*Ra-ra-ra-ra-ra-ra-ra-ra-ra.*"

Bal: "Theo's father, look how the sky knows all this. How over there all are resting like a lake over Hamar country. See how the father of the raid sits and watches. See the blockade over there, there are no footprints of returning cattle and here the people sit close together and worry. Their hearts are full of worry, they sit and watch, look. Let all this get lost! Come, let's drink coffee."

Eth: "Yes, let's go inside."

Bal: (laughing) "Hey! Are you saying 'Africa's work stinks?' *Hahaha*."

Cho: (cynically with a high pitched voice) "Hey, people, listen, listen."

Bal: "*Hahahahahaha*."   (Strecker 1979a: 32-35).

One can see clearly how the excitement finds a lively and colourful expression in the use of ideophones, which are an essential part of Hamar rhetoric culture (compare Jean Lydall's contribution to the present ICES entitled "Having fun with ideophones in Hamar"). Here are the most prominent ideophones, which Choke and Baldambe use:

"People are running, *dull-dull*."
"The clouds show us their footprints, *ta-ta-ta-ta-ta-ta-ta-ta*."
"Look at the red flashing light: *ra-ra-ra-ra-ra-ra-ra – barcha-barcha-barcha-barcha*."

Also, off and on Baldambe and Choke express either their certainty or their uncertainty about the meanings in the sky, and in this way they add to the general excitement and mental and emotional involvement, like in the following examples:

"Here above us it leads over there, it lies across. We don't know what it means."
"Yes, *misso*, I know all this".
"Isn't it all clearly revealed up there in the sky?"
"Look at the sky: see how it is clearly laid down."
"Theo's father, look how the sky knows all this."

The frequent address of *misso* is yet another rhetorical element which heightens excitement and attention. In Brown and Levinson's terminology (1978) it embodies a 'positive politeness strategy', or, as I would say, 'rhetoric of positive politeness' which signals that a person wants to involve another. It acts as an appeal to the other's readiness to accept one's wish, that is in this case one's interpretation, one's attempt at self-persuasion and then, in turn, at persuasion of the other.

As Baldambe and Choke examined the sky, they constantly thought and spoke by means of metonymy. This trope moves from apparent effects to less apparent causes, as in the following example: When Baldambe said, "Look at the brightness... at the clearness. This is dust, dust only! The white over there, this is dust. That is the men running, the cattle that are running", what he did in rhetorical terms was to think and speak metonymically. He created the associative chain of 'brightness—dust—running'. He was clearly aware that the brightness was caused by some phenomenon in the sky, but in his divinatory mood he conjured the idea that the brightness was there in order to tell everyone that now the dust was rising, that now people and cattle were running, that now the battle had begun.

The rhetorical thrust of the expression is thus not metaphorical and does not lie in a likening of brightness, dust and battle but rather it is metonymical in that it implies a causal relationship: the brightness of the sky is seen as an effect of the fighting and proves that fighting has begun. In a similar vein Baldambe and Choke detect clouds which are "lying across the middle of the sky" and interpret them as a blockade, and they point out that the big black clouds over the Hamar mountains are the communities of Hamar where now, as the men have left for war "the people sit close together and worry". Here the clouds have a metonymic (rather than metaphoric) character in that they seem to emanate from people's worry. The dark thoughts of the people result in the dark clouds above them, their sitting close together leads the clouds to draw together. Or, perhaps, people and clouds are jointly affected by some third element. In terms of Hamar rhetoric culture this would be the *barjo*, the fate and good fortune of both the place and its people.

Anxiety and the talk of aggrieved women

Early in the morning of 23 January 1974 two shots woke me up and told me, as all my neighbours in Dambaiti, that the men had returned and had brought the bad news that some one had died on the raid. The shots were fired at my friend Kula's homestead. Together with Bargi (Ginonda, Baldambe's sister-in-law) I went to see what was happening, and we heard that Aike, Kula's younger brother, was killed. We also gathered the first scraps of information about the raid. The Hamar attacked the Arbore, drove away some of their cattle and then were overtaken by the Arbore who killed many Hamar. I noted down in my diary how, when Bargi and I returned to our homestead, the world around us lapsed back into an unnatural peacefulness, with children playing, the bells of cattle and goats sounding:

> The tears of Ginonda, Aikenda and Gardu, which they shed amidst the general wailing (and probably also out of anger and frustration) dry up quickly. Someone else has died, not one of them (or at least these first bad tidings have not affected them personally) and I see the momentary relief, which they feel... Several women along with Shalombe and Laesho meet around the coffee pot a little later. I join them and record the women's conversation. The women don't want to talk about the raid and yet do, are drawn to it again and again, till one woman says, "Stop, there is no point in talking until we know facts." Ginonda picks this up and explains to me the danger of uncontrolled speaking. It is this kind of data that I am looking for and that's why I keep the tape recorder going continuously (Lydall/Strecker 1979a: 275).

Here I present only a short part of this conversation, full of anxiety and held in a liminal period between relief and grief, between news of life and news of death. Or rather, like an invisible poison the news is already there, but nobody wants to face up to it. Like Baldambe's sister Maiza, everyone tries to persuade herself and others that "people's talk might still be false". But, like in classic tragedy, there is one person who will not relent and will see to it that everything will be revealed. This is Orgo's wife, with whose lines case four begins:

Orgo's wife: (with the same depressed voice she has been using, trying to get her message through) "Down at the water hole somebody brought bad news. Something true or?" (pause)

Bargi: "At which water hole?"

Org: "Two of our men Wuino and Lolima who went quickly this morning to ask the news. They said that they had heard that this homestead, the Lorbamurra homestead, recently had begun a funeral rite. Did Gaito go too?"

Maiza: "Has he moved across to Moana?"

Gardu: "Leaving aside all you have said, what do you mean by Moana, Moana?"

Bar: "Now, if we say: 'Has he moved to Moana?' it's we who are asking."

Laesho: "*Bel*, he has moved over there."

Org: "It is said a shot was heard from the heart of Moana. That's why we are worried."

Mai: "He! *Barjo* has talked, people's talk might still be false!"

Org: "It might still be false, I don't know. The talk of that homestead reached ours in any case. It was the men Lolima and Wuino who brought it."

Lae: "From where?"

Org: "Didn't they return after they had asked at Kula's homestead?"

Lae: "This homestead!"

Org: "They went over there and returned. (pause) Down there the boy Rebo Barto's son..."

Lae: "Rebo, our father's sister's son? Yes?"

Org: "All by himself – all by himself, from now on he walks by himself."

Bar: "Also he? (stops talk, afflicted) – Isn't he the husband of a girl of ours, the daughter of Adama?"

Org: "It is said down there that this boy has died. His people have not yet returned, though."

Bar: "Did this boy own a gun?"

Org: "That does not matter, even if they have no gun they go."

Lae: "He had no gun."

Bar: "I didn't mean that. I mean that the warriors with the guns go ahead and are the ones who endanger their lives."

Mai: "It is not like this, it is the shot which misses the person nearby that hits and kills the one who stands far away."

Org: "They had recently begun to discuss the funeral rite for the brother and had said the rite should be quickly performed as the dead man died on a raid. They left it at that. Now the girl, my father's daughter—he was her genitor—Gaito's older brother Barre's wife, she almost died when they talked of performing a funeral and then didn't."

Bar: "So does it concern this one or what, when they say that someone has died?"

Org: "The oracle revealed that her sickness was caused by not performing the rite. It is said that for four days she was sick with pains in her belly and only then gave birth..."

Bar: "And now a shot has been heard in Moana?"

Org: "They say it was no shot."

Mai: "No shot."

Org: "No shot, no shot."

Bar: "*Hm*?"

Org: "Down there Kormorra's son's brother Gaito, the other that young one, Rebo."

Bar: "Who of Kormorra's son's brothers?"

Org: "Gaito."

Bar: (with a voice as if the news were neutral) "*Eh*!"

Org: "It's Kormorra's son."

Bar: (now darkening her voice) "*Eh*!"

Lae: (slowly, reflecting) "This — this — is it true? Let it be false."

Org: "*Ai!* This place of his, has there ever before been false news about it?"

Lae: "It is rumour, I have heard it. Is it true? Is it false?"

Org: "What do you think you will hear when you listen to the news a second time?"

Lae: "What was said in madness may well be false."

Org: "It may well be..."

Note how Orgo's wife begins by telling what she has heard and only saying that someone brought bad news: "Down at the water hole somebody brought bad news. Something true?" Note also that she raises the question whether the bad news are really true. All this shows her rhetorical skill of dissociating herself from the news, of keeping herself safe and away from the aura of doom. If she were to tell bad news bluntly, this would associate her with the bad news and might imply that her *barjo* was weak and insufficient.

Also, one can see her sense of drama, for she knows that everyone is on tenterhooks and that all will want to hear more even though they pretend not to, like Bargi (Ginonda) who answers Orgo's wife's revelation with the seemingly irrelevant question, "at which water hole?", as if the water hole rather than the content of the news mattered. Ignoring the question of the water hole, Orgo's wife goes on to say that two men, Wuino and Lolima, had heard that this homestead, the Lorbamurra homestead, recently had begun a funeral rite. And again she adds a tantalising question whether Gaito had joined the raid.

Anyone familiar with Hamar culture will understand this seemingly wayward and evasive comment as indicating that Gaito has died, or at least that it is rather probable that he will be among the dead, for according to Hamar lore, no one should go to war if he has begun a funeral rite or if it is time for him to perform any important ritual which has to do with the dead. If you so blatantly neglect the dead, they will kill you, and your going to war becomes a suicide mission.

Once again, Orgo's wife's question does not receive any direct answer. Now it is Maiza who answers with another seemingly irrelevant question: Has Gaito moved to Moana? Gardu and Bargi repeat the question, and when Laesho confirms that Gaito had recently changed his residence to Moana, and when Orgo's wife says that "a shot was heard from the heart of Moana", everyone gets very agitated and fears that Gaito has died. Maiza exclaims: "*He*! *Barjo* has talked, people's talk might still be false", and Orgo's wife dryly answers: "It might still be false, I don't know." Then follows a lull and a short pause in the conversation until Orgo's wife comes up with the news of a second death. This time she does not hide the news, but nevertheless she tells it indirectly: "Down there the boy Rebo Barto's son... All by himself – all by himself, from now on he walks by himself." This euphemism for death is understood by everyone and Bargi exclaims: "Also he?" and stops talk, afflicted. Little later, Orgo's wife indirectly comes back to Gaito's fate by talking of all the misfortune that came upon Gaito's older brother's wife when they talked of performing a funeral and then didn't. This leads Bargi to ask anew whether a shot has been heard in Moana and Orgo's wife and Maiza answer that it was a very loud shot, and with this the news of Gaito's death seem finally broken. Stubbornly, Laesho tries to question its truth and hopes that it may be false while Orgo's wife answers with the sarcastic question of whether from such a place as his (from the grave) there have ever been false news before.

As the conversation continued, the women begin with great rhetorical skill to accuse the spokesmen of leading their men to die in foreign lands, and their own men of letting themselves be incited to go to war:

> Org: "Oh my ancestor Maldo! (she sighs) They kill you, they bring you into foreign people's land and then leave you there. Oh mother who gave birth!

Bar: (dryly) Now you will rest, tomorrow and the day after tomorrow, but the next day you will trample again. Before, when Barto's son died, we thought that from then on people would break with it then and put their guns away."

Then they point to the fear and distress of the women who will suffer most if their husbands and lovers lose their lives in the war:

Org: "The people over in Ande have almost died of fear. 'It is over there,' they say, 'it is over there!' 'Where did the gun sound?' 'People say it is a homestead with several sons.' '*Uii*! (beats her breast) — we are lost!'"

Bar: "So they run to Alma's homestead."

Org: "*Yi*! Wasn't his mistress just told to return home?"

Bar: "What is it that made the mistress so angry? ... "

Gar: "People don't show compassion for you. If your husband has died and then your lover also dies, they don't feel sorry for you."

Org: "When you are hurt by his death, they don't show you any compassion."

Bar: "That is your crookedness."

Mai: "Here it is."

Gar: "People don't recognise your crying."

But as the talk gets too excited, the women remind each other that they should not talk so loud and chaotically, and say that the 'father of the homestead' would be angry if he heard such muddled talk:

Bar: "Women, stop this alarm."

Mai & others: "Stop it, stop this muddled talk."

Mai: "If you talk so loud and chaotically the father of the homestead will be angry when he hears it on his return."

Gad: "Yes, he will scold us."

Playfully, Bargi (Ginonda) evokes a funny picture or rather episode, where she turns herself into a mouse and escapes the wrath of the 'father of the homestead' when he returns:

Bar: (points to the wall of the house) "For me there is a small hole over there."

Gar: (laughs) "*Hahaha*."

Bar: (cheerfully) "I will escape through that hole. Otherwise I will use the big hole above Theoimba's head, there where the gourds are."

Gar: (laughing) "Ah!"

Bar: "Without touching anything I'll jump up there. Am I not prevented from escaping through the door? Like a mouse I'll run across the platform and climb down the outside of the house. There I am—down at the Pere River I rest."

But when I turn to her and ask why she is afraid, Bargi changes her attitude and in a serious manner and with a settled and informing voice says:

"If the country becomes as it is now, there must be no gossip. You drink your water quietly, *kulb-kulb-kulb*, having swept the gateway of your homestead for good luck. If you talk this and that it will madden and destroy you. It is bad. *Hm*. As the news comes in like gusts of wind, some of those who are said to have died will return to their country alive. Have you heard what we said just now? Gaito hasn't come and this man of Kadja, Rebo, has not returned. The talk leapt up on us just so, and that is all bad. That's why we say: 'Leave the talk, drink your water quietly, and put your *barjo* into your heart.' Woman gave birth; Man caused birth. You can't gather children together and put them back into your belly, the man can't put them back into his penis. Having been born they all went proudly and those who met their death met it, those who met something good, met it. Why should we cut up our talk like the meat which you cut into strips to dry it? Stop it, keep quiet, so that the father of the homestead keeps quiet too when he arrives... If people talk uncontrollably it will bring misfortune... Everything is with the milky way, with *barjo*."

(All quotes in the above section are from Strecker 1979a: 156-166).

How the men were provoked to go to war

In the morning of 24 January 1974, Baldambe and I went to visit Anombe, Baldambe's brother-in-law, who had taken part in the raid on Arbore (also referred to as Ulde or Marle). We found him, his wife and his friend Goiti drinking coffee. More cowhides were spread out and when the guests had settled down, Anombe gave a long account of the raid. Here I present especially those passages concerned with the way in which the spokesmen provoked the Hamar and drove them into war:

Baldambe: "You had a wound."

Anombe: "I was exhausted."

Bal: "Exhausted."

Ano: "My foot had swollen."

Bal: "Swollen."

Ano: "In-law, people would see me, but they would not ask themselves: 'Is so-and-so's son well?' No one would ask me: 'How is your foot?' You used to know them, but now they don't know you anymore and pass you by. That is why I stopped asking questions. Do you hear?"

Bal: "*Hm.*"

Ano: "What should I ask? They went looking for it, they returned after looking for it, what was there for me to ask? (at times Anombe speaks in an angry tone) I didn't ask how many of Assile had died – still my ears would hear and I would count. 'So-and-so's son has died, so-and-so's son has died,' I had already heard when we were returning through the reeds. When I got thirsty on the way I asked Shaela's mother's son..."

Bal: "The spokesman..."

Ano: "Spokesman."

Bal: "*Hm.*"

Ano: "Do you think that any of the spokesmen stayed behind?"

Bal: "Leave it, they are the ones who talk for you."

Ano: "They talk for us and send the people to that death! (imitates the spokesman's speech) 'Man! Those who run away are like the empty seeds of sorghum. The bulls of Kadja have not arrived here!' (speaks almost to himself:) I wonder where his fearlessness is! He told me: 'Aike, Kula's younger brother, has not returned. I heard of Gaito's death shortly after it happened. He was killed in the attack, already in the attack, he never turned around, Lorbamurra's son'. 'Yes'. 'He entered the reeds and sat down there bending his head on his knees. He was shot in the stomach'.

Bal: "Bad is the spokesman who adorns the people!"

Ano: "Adorns."

Bal: "Who sends them into the whips..."

Ano: "Sends them saying. 'True men have not come, those who run away are shit'. Not a single Hamar stayed behind... I heard that Baldambe's son Robe stopped his men from going."

Goiti: "They crossed to the other side and then he stopped them."

Ano: "Provoking them..."

Goi: "Provoking them! He would not have gone across, hadn't the men of Mirsha provoked him first by calling him and his men thin and haggard. In his speech preceding the raid Robe had said he would not run into the sharp spears and the traps which the others had prepared for us there. His provoking talk confused the warriors and they looked quietly at him as Assile got up and said: 'But we have prepared the raid well. We have brought many guns. All of us have come, truly and proudly. Why do you make us weaker than we are? Call for our good luck in the raid as we have done.' They said this again and again and Robe kept quiet, but in the end not many of his men joined the raid. He himself and his sons went, though..."

Bal: "... Tell me what was said at the meeting when you gathered for the raid. Assile had called you and you came."

Ano: (imitating the spokesmen) "I have called you."

Goi: "I truly have called you."

Ano: "I truly have called you. Today none of them will survive. He is a woman. I will pick him, he is soft like the *mulaza* plant."

Goi: "His gun won't fire."

Ano: "His gun won't fire. Man I have everything well prepared. Man, I have truly killed him. Go over there and kill him. Just fetch him, while he is weak like *mulaza*. I have poured water into his gun."

Goi: "Man, never before have I liked it as much as this time!"

Ano: "Man, never before have I liked it as much as this time!"

Goi: "Even old limping men will kill today."

Ano: "Please, what did he, the son of, I don't know his name, say? 'You, spokesmen of the other provinces, don't talk. Man, it's only I who will speak from now on. Man, only I will bless.' This is what he said..."

Bal: "What did the spokesmen of our side say after the other side had spoken like this? I had met Lomeromoi and Oitamba's son on their way."

Ano: "What Lomeromoi said I didn't hear. This is what Oitamba's son said. He spoke at the end of the speeches and provoked the men: 'I am the last to speak, now you will not talk anymore.' He provoked, provoked. Hadn't he taken his spear?"

Bal: "Taken."

Ano: "Provoking, provoking us: 'Today I have gone on my way after having prepared all the rituals well. I have gone on the way with babies, I have gone on my way with the blind. *Hm*. Now you, whom I have brought up, rise and sing the war song. If anyone asks you who you are, say 'I am the son of so-and-so'. Upon this your hunting-friend at first did not get up, he kept on sitting and only pointed his gun towards the enemy. Only slowly he got up and said: 'My father's name is Kala, I am the son of he who was called Kala'. 'Now let your hunting-friend get up!' But no one would rise..."

Ethnographer: "Did you men of Dambaiti talk here together before you left for the raid?"

Bal: "The word came from Assile to Lodjera together with a string with knots. They gave it to Arbala Kala and Aike Lomeromoi and then the word reached the whole area over here."

Goi: "All the way up to Banna."

Bal: "The string with knots reached even Banna? *Hm.* 'He who has consulted the sandal oracle is Djagi Bacho. He threw the sandals by himself after he had dreamt that he should do so.' Wasn't it like this?"

Goi/ Ano: "Yes, so it was."

Bal: "Some of it was his dream, some his sandals: 'This day, this day, if you now go down to the river and no rain falls immediately then I have not consulted my sandals, then I have not dreamt'. Wasn't it like this?"

Goi/ Ano: "Yes."

Bal: "'Man, if you don't get up in this month and finish him, then it's your end, then all the country will belong to him'. The one who said this was the son of Bacho and the one brought the news was Nyetigul's son Darsha. (sighs) Let it get lost."

                                        (Strecker 1979a: 182-190).

Note how when Baldambe and I visited Anombe to hear from him what had happened on the raid, he first told us how he hurt his foot as the raiders were crossing the swamps in the Woito Valley on their way to Arbore and how he reprimanded himself saying to himself: "You have come looking for it, so don't complain."

But although Anombe told himself not to complain, we find him nevertheless lamenting about his wounded foot, the lack of compassion shown by others towards him, and about the ill fate of the raid as a whole: On first sight, Anombe's lamentation seems to be a very personal affair. He has suffered, therefore he laments. But there is more to this, for, as I have often noticed, lamentation is a deeply ingrained feature of Hamar rhetoric culture. In fact, a few days before the Hamar raid on

Arbore I had been in Kara at the Lower Omo where I had heard a similar kind of lamentation, which I recorded as follows:

> Lokaribuk asks his wife to bring us honey wine and sorghum food. We feast and then Lokaribuk embarks on a long lamentation deploring the state of war, the continual state of anxiety and un-certainty and the imminence of fighting between the Hamar and Arbore, Hamar and Galeba, Kara and Bume etc. Choke answers him in the same lamenting tone. I get the impression that this lamentation stems from two sources. First, a true social concern for the well-being of everybody, but secondly... an attempt to absolve oneself of responsibility for what is happening, and yet to retain a recognisable claim on the control of public affairs (Lydall and Strecker 1979a: 254).

In our conversation with Anombe and his friend Goiti one also finds a good example of the Hamar practice of repeating or echoing what one's interlocutor has said. This can be a way of showing interest and compassion as when Baldambe echoes Anombe: "I was exhausted." "Exhausted." "My foot had swollen." "Swollen." Such echoing can also be a 'tuning in' with one another and in this way can clarify, amplify and extend each other's thoughts and expressions, like in the following instances:

> Ano: (imitating the spokesmen) 'I have called you.'
> Goiti: 'I truly have called you.'
> Ano: 'I truly have called you. Today none of them will survive.'
> Goi: 'His gun won't fire.'
> Ano: 'His gun won't fire. Man, I have everything well prepared.'

Furthermore, the practice of echoing and closely attuned turn-taking is a form of rhetorical bonding which may lead to a kind of complicity and exclusiveness of the interlocutors to the detriment of a third party as in the following case which I witnessed in Hamar:

> This morning I observe what I was often painfully aware of in England, namely that a close and intensive dialogue can be used to

exclude a third party. Last night a travelling Amhara trader arrived in Dambaiti, hoping to get Baldambe to pay back an old debt. It is obvious during the morning conversation by the coffee pot that Baldambe does not want to talk to the trader and he embarks upon a violent and serious conversation with Wadu. Wadu 'echoes' more than usual and Baldambe complains and laments... When the trader tries to get a word in, Wadu tells him to keep quiet because their talk is so very serious. Baldambe is clearly in a weak position since he is the debtor. But he plays this down by creating an atmosphere in which something else, of which obviously only he and Wadu know, is infinitely more important than this small, momentary debt. It needs at least two people to play such a game and both partners have to know each other's style of speaking well so that they can understand the implicit meanings of what is said and what is not said, of allusions, of metaphors and so on. Thus, tight dialogue in which a third party has no place has a double effect: it makes the aspirant participant aware of his impotence whilst at the same time it creates and enhances a feeling of omnipotence in the speakers (Lydall and Strecker 1979a: 207-08).

It seems that Anombe and his friend Goiti who both feel victims of the Hamar spokesmen who lured them into war, try to regain confidence and heal their humiliated selves by engaging in such a tight dialogue at the expense of an (absent) third party. That is, they vent their anger about the spokesmen by imitating their speeches, which now, after the Hamar have been defeated, sound utterly ironic. The irony is enhanced by the fact that the spokesmen themselves used irony as well as hyperbole as their weapons, and Anombe and Goiti can exploit this to create a double twist of irony enhanced by a kind of 'backfiring' of the initial hyperbole. It is Goiti who first provides the ironic punch lines while Anombe picks them up, repeats and at times develops them:

> Baldambe: Tell me what was said at the meeting when you gathered for their raid. Assile had called you, and you came.

Anombe: (imitating the spokesmen) 'I have called you.'

Goiti: 'I truly have called you.'

Anombe: 'I truly have called you. Today none of them will survive. He is a woman. I will pick him, he is soft like the *mulaza* plant.'

Goi: 'His gun won't fire.'

Ano: 'Man, I have everything well prepared. Man, I have truly killed him. Go over there and kill him. Just fetch him, while he is weak as *mulaza*. I have poured water into his gun.'

Goi: 'Man, never before have I liked it as much as this time!'

Ano: 'Man, never before have I liked it as much as this time!'

Goi: 'Even old limping men will kill today.'"

As we can see, Anombe's and Goiti's account reveals much of the rhetoric which the spokesmen employed in order to get the Hamar to join the war. They made much use of simile and metaphor, which combine well with hyperbole like in the following examples, each of them a paragon of warmongering:

"The bulls of Kadja have not arrived."
"True men have not come. Those who run away are shit."
"I have gone on the way with babies,
I have gone on my way with the blind."
"Man, those who run away are like empty seeds of sorghum."

There were also other forms of rhetoric, which the spokesmen used to impose their will on the Hamar. One is the classic form of bluffing, of asserting that one is totally in control of one's plans, of usurping the role of he who knows everything better. Thus, when a man called Robe tried to stop his men saying they should not "run into the sharp spears and traps which the others had prepared", another spokesman got up and said:

"But we have prepared the raid well. We have brought many guns. All of us have come, truly and proudly. Why do you make us weaker than we are? Call for our good luck in the raid as we have done."

This is an example of the kind of intimidation used by those who are trying to usurp power over others: If someone is not for them, they argue, he must be against them, if Rebo was not blessing, he must be cursing them (and therefore deserves to be cursed in turn). Interestingly, the spokesmen openly indulge and compete for the right to speak which has been delegated to them by their communities. This comes out clearly when Anombe quotes two spokesmen as saying the following:

> "You, spokesmen of the other provinces, don't talk. Man, it's only I who will speak from now on. Man, only I will bless."
>
> "I am the last to speak, now you will not talk anymore."

Behind this strong, boasting stance lies the mystical power attributed to the word in Hamar culture. Leadership is based on the good luck, the good fortune (*barjo*) which the voice of a leader brings, as Baldambe has explained:

> "The spokesman grows up like the *kuntsale* grass, he emerges from among his age mates, he is the one who knows how to talk, his heart is strong. So-and-so is a spokesman, let him become a spokesman." (Lydall and Strecker 1979b: 125)

If in this way someone appears to have a natural talent for speaking, he is given a spear by the elders and is made an *ayo*, a spokesman. But if subsequently his word does not bring good fortune, it will be said:

> "His word is bad, his command is bad. Stop him" (Lydall and Strecker 1979b: 109).

In terms of rhetoric, the office of the Hamar spokesman is thus based on metonymy, for the word of the spokesman is always understood as the manifest effect of a hidden cause, that is his *barjo*. 'His word is bad' means 'his *barjo* is bad', and 'his word is good' means 'his *barjo* is good'. Expressed differently, the office of the spokesman exploits the 'unsaid' behind the 'said' and conjures the idea of unlimited power, a power which does not only control one's own people, but also others and even the universe itself, like when Djagi Bacho called the Hamar to attack the Arbore saying: "This day, this day, if you now go down to the river and no rain falls immediately, then I have not consulted my sandals, then I have not dreamt." The phrase 'go down to the river' must here be understood as a euphemism meaning 'attack the Arbore', and 'if no rain falls immediately' insinuates that no rain will fall if the men do not listen to Djagi Bacho's call to go to war.

Conclusion

As we have seen, Hamar rhetoric in the context of war is a domain where the interdependence of rhetoric and culture becomes visible, and where one can show in detail how a particular cultural pattern—war—is generated and sustained in rhetoric. From the analyses presented in the paper, four major themes have emerged. They were combined and intertwined with other themes and accompanied by countless "imponderabilia of life" as Malinowski used to put it. Therefore, I mention the themes here again and try to bring them more clearly into focus.

Rhetoric of safety:

In the first case, we 'heard' a blessing, a calling forth of the good fortune and well-being of those who had gone to war. The belief that people's good fortune can be created and upheld by man himself is enshrined in the Hamar notion of '*barjo*' (good fortune). If people would not believe in the good luck they have received from the elders, they might not so easily be tempted to fight. Also, if the parents were not convinced that they can ensure their sons' safety, they might not so easily let them go to war.

Rhetoric of divination:

The second case showed men examining the early morning sky and arguing about what it said about the war and the fate of the fighters. Here we could detect a rhetorical process by which hopes and fears were projected into the sky. The human folly of going to war was invested with some kind of mystical destiny, even necessity, and by the same token all and everyone engaged in the (unnecessary!) fighting was offered an escape from responsibility. It was not freewill that was responsible but the sky, which all along had known what the fate of people was to be.

Rhetoric of lament and deception:

In case three and four we found telling instances of lamentation where both men and women similarly tried to absolve themselves from guilt, and hoped to dissociate themselves from the suffering which war invariably brings upon people. Lamentation was their rhetorical device, which helped them to erase the disturbing traces of their implication. There were also examples of people using their rhetorical skills to hide the bad news of death and to insinuate that the news might still turn out to be wrong.

Rhetoric of provocation:

The forth case provided abundant proof of the thesis that it is rhetoric which drives people to go to war – rhetoric which knows how to excite; rhetoric which knows how to bluff and blind; rhetoric which knows how to promise, how to intimidate and frighten, and, above all, rhetoric which knows how to provoke men into action. We got to know how the Hamar spokesmen managed to provoke the men, and we heard that if their provocation had not been so successful, the Hamar would have turned back and would have refrained from going to war.

By way of conclusion let me emphasise that even though it takes on culture specific features, Hamar rhetoric in the context of war has probably much in common with the rhetoric preceding, accompanying and following other people's wars at other times and in other places of this world. If I have looked closely at Hamar rhetoric, it is to better understand our own, as well as other people's predicaments.

PART III: RHETORICAL ARTICULATION OF KNOWLEDGE AND BELIEF

The *genius loci* of Hamar

THEORY
A phenomenology of the *genius loci*

The present paper is inspired by the work of Christian Norberg-Schulz who has brought back the ancient notion of the *genius loci* or 'spirit of place' into architecture. In his earlier works *Intentions in Architecture* (1963) and *Existence, Space and Architecture* (1971) Norberg-Schulz had already thought and written about experiential and psychic notions such as 'existential foothold' and 'existential space', but it was not until 1979 that he began to make use of the notion *genius loci*. As I will try to show below, this concept is not only relevant for architecture but for ethnography and anthropological theory as well. But first let me recapitulate the ideas outlined in *Genius loci: Towards a phenomenology of architecture* (Italian original 1979; English translation 1980).

People strive to create meaningful existential spaces where they can get a foothold, where they can dwell. Norberg-Schulz has taken the concept of 'dwelling' from Heidegger's essay "Building Dwelling Thinking" (1951) and has related it to the concept of *genius loci* as follows: "Man dwells when he can orientate himself within and identify himself with an environment, or, in short, when he experiences the environment as meaningful. Dwelling therefore implies something more than 'shelter'. It implies that the spaces where life occurs are 'places', in the true sense of the word. A place is a space that has character. Since ancient times the *genius loci*, or 'spirit of place' has been recognized as the concrete reality man has to face and come to terms with in his daily life" (Norberg-Schulz 1980: 5).

Places are qualitative totalities where events 'take place', where the different components relate to each other in a meaningful "Gestalt", and where the whole is experienced as more than its constituent parts: "A place is therefore a qualitative, 'total' phenomenon, which we cannot reduce to any of its properties, such as spatial relationships, without losing its concrete nature out of sight" (Op. Cit.: 8).

From here follows an interesting turn towards anthropology and a break with functionalism and international style in architecture: "'Taking place' is usually understood in a quantitative, 'functional' sense, with implications such as spatial distribution and dimensioning. But are not 'functions' inter-human and similar everywhere? Evidently not. 'Similar' functions, even the most basic ones such as sleeping and eating, take place in very different ways, and demand places with different properties, in accordance with different cultural traditions and different environmental conditions. The functional approach therefore left out the place as a concrete 'here' having its particular identity" (Op. Cit.: 8).

The 'here' where people 'dwell' goes beyond the house and comprises the whole world that they inhabit. Again Norberg-Schulz turns to Heidegger who has defined 'dwelling' as: "The way in which you are and I am, the way in which we humans 'are' on earth, is dwelling... the world is the house where the mortals dwell". To this Norberg-Schulz adds: "In other words, when man is capable of dwelling the world becomes an 'inside'. In general, nature forms an extended comprehensive totality, a 'place', which according to local circumstances has a particular identity" (Op. Cit.: 10).

This identity is meant by the *genius loci* or, less evocatively, by the notion of 'character'. All places have character, that is distinctive features, for example, 'festive', 'solemn', 'protective' for buildings or 'barren', 'fertile', 'threatening' etc. for land-scapes. Character also emerges from modes of construction or, as anthropologists would say, from modes of production and consumption, which in turn may change in time (Op. Cit.: 14).

People perceive the characteristics of their environment as a kind of 'environmental image', which provides them with an orientation and a sense of security. Following Lynch (1960), Norberg-Schulz therefore argues that "all cultures have developed systems of orientation,... spatial structures which facilitate the development of a good environmental image" (Op. Cit.: 19). To a large extent orientation is based on or derived from given natural features, and "In primitive societies we find that even the smallest environmental details are known and meaningful" (Op. Cit.: 20).

Thus, orientation and identification establish a kind of friendship, or, if not friendship then at least a meaningful relationship between people and the world they inhabit: "Nordic man has to be friend with fog, ice and cold winds; he has to enjoy the creaking sound of snow under the feet when he walks around, he has to experience the poetical value of being immersed in fog... The Arab, instead, has to be a friend of the infinitely extended sandy desert and the burning sun. This does not mean that his settlements should not protect him against the natural 'forces'; a desert settlement in fact primarily aims at the exclusion of sand and sun and therefore complements the natural situation. But it implies that the environment is experienced as 'meaningful'" (Op. Cit.: 21).

Genius loci and anthropological theory

Browsing through the rich and growing anthropological literature on architecture, landscape, place, space, locality, 'nature', ecology, geomancy, identity and belonging I could not find a single reference to the concept of *genius loci*. Some texts come close to it however, like for example Fumagalli's

Landscapes of Fear which examines how in the Middle Ages "nature was regarded as a reflection of humanity, as people recognised themselves in a landscape" (Fumagalli 1994: 1); or Tilley's *A Phenomenology of Landscape* which, like Norberg-Schulz builds on Heidegger and explores the proposition that "subjectivity and objectivity connect in a dialectic producing a 'place' for Being in which the topography and physiography of the land and thought remain distinct but play into each other as an 'intelligible landscape', a spatialization of Being" (Tilley 1994: 14). Also, other anthropological studies would merit mentioning, like the essays collected in Nadia Lovell's 'Locality and Belonging' (1998), but none of them has come closer to the topic of *genius loci* than the chapters by Caroline Humphrey and Alfred Gell in Hirsch and O'Hanlon (eds.) *The Anthropology of Landscape* (1995).

In the chapter "Chiefly and Shamanist Landscapes" Humphrey has painted an intriguing picture where "the Mongolian landscape seethes with entities which are attributed with anything from a hazy idea of energy to clearly visualized and named spirits" (Humphrey 1995: 141), and where nomadic life generates a kind of mystical relationship between people and their environment which closely resembles what Norberg-Schulz has called the *genius loci*.

Mongolian social power and hierarchy are embodied in the 'chiefly landscape' by a metaphorical "mapping of parts of the body on to the land" in such a way that "land-entities are seen as 'wholes', or 'bodies', centred on mountains" which may have a nape, spine, vertebra, cheeks, cheek bones, nose, mouth, forehead, brows, shoulders, ribs and even a liver (Op. Cit.: 144). While the surface features of mountains are characteristic of the 'chiefly landscape', the 'shamanic landscape' pertains to "the earth as a whole, with its subterranean depths" (Op. Cit.: 149), and while the former centres its ritual activities on the tops of mountains the latter chooses the cave as place for its cults, the cave as entrance into the interior of the earth, as point of departure of the 'ways' and 'paths' on which the shaman will travel.

Alfred Gell's chapter on "The Language of the Forest: Landscape and Phonological Iconism in Umeda" is especially interesting because it shows that the 'spirit' of a place emerges from an interaction of the environment and the human sensorium in such a way, that not only seeing but also other senses like hearing and smelling have a role to play. In Umeda, which lies in the dense jungle of New Guinea, "one sees the hamlet one happens to be in, not the 'village' as a whole. Looking out, one sees the tops of nearby trees, but not the gardens, paths, streams, hunting tracts, sago stands, and so on which really constitute the 'the bush'; these are hidden below... There is nothing to bind all this together, no privileged 'domain-viewing' point, like the view from the keep of the castle. But bound together it is, though, but in a quite different way. Lacking a visual landscape what the Umeda have instead, I would say, is a 'landscape of articulation', a landscape which is accessible, primordially, in the acoustic modality" (Gell 1995: 239-240).

No doubt, this 'acoustic modality' characterizes the *genius loci* of Umeda, and one could imagine how it manifests itself in general ideas and particular metaphors, like in the Mongolian case, except that the ideas and metaphors would not be based on vision but on hearing. However, Gell goes further than this and suggests that the prevalence of hearing (rather than seeing) in Umeda has asserted itself even on the most basic level of language, that is in phonology, and has led to the production of what he calls 'phonological iconism'.

He theorizes that, "there may be, indeed, an intimate re-lationship between the cultural factors shaping the phonology of certain natural languages, and the particularities of the land-scape setting within which the speakers of these languages live" (Op. Cit.: 232). Thus, phonological iconism flourishes in a world of heightened auditory perceptiveness like that of the

Umeda. It "corresponds to certain forest habitats and lifestyles, which privilege audition and olfaction and which de-
emphasize vision, especially long range vision" (Op. Cit.: 235).
Refusing to accept the Saussurean theory of the arbitrariness of
linguistic signs, he then goes on to say that while in English
"there is no basis for linking the concept 'mountain' to the
specific speech sounds which have to be enunciated in order to
say the word 'mountain'", among the Umeda things are
otherwise, for in Umeda "the word for 'mountain'... should be
understood precisely as 'the sound that a mountain makes', or
more precisely, 'the shape in articulatory/acoustic space' made
by a mountain" (Op. Cit.: 232).

To bring out fully this extraordinary example of a *genius loci*
embedded and expressed in phonological iconism let me quote
Gell again at length:

> I said, at the outset, that there was no culturally obvious way in
> which 'mountain' in English could be phonologically motivated.
> English mountains are silent and immobile, and it is hard to image
> that there could be any one vocal 'gesture' which would commun-
> icate the essence of mountainhood better than any other. In
> Umeda, things are otherwise, though it requires a cultural inter-
> pretation to bring this out. The Umeda word for mountain is 'sis'.
> Umeda 'mountains' are really ridges, with sharp tops, and they
> define the boundaries of territories, particularly to the north and
> west, where the major enemies of the Umeda reside. The sibilant
> 's' is uniformly associated with (a) male power and (b) with
> sharp, narrow things like pointed sticks... Male power comes from
> the coconut 'sa', and the ancestors 'sa-tod' (village/male/central).
> Sharp things like bamboo knives are 'sai', 'sa' plus the con-
> stricted, 'narrow' vowel 'i'. 'Sis', a symmetrical arrangement of
> sibilants ... is very appropriate for an Umeda 'mountain', that is,
> a narrow ridge, associated with masculine pursuits, danger, etc. As
> a ridge it is opposed to 'kebe' a flat-topped knoll of the kind
> Umeda hamlets are built on, which combines the hardness-

implying 'k' sound with 'ebe' (bilabial) meaning 'fat' (prosperous) (Op. Cit.: 242).

As I have said, these are the examples I have found in current anthropology which come closest to the concept of *genius loci* and the kind of research it implies. But there are also older texts in anthropology, which, although in a more general way, are of interest to *genius loci* theory. Here I can only briefly draw attention to three of them that is to texts from Malinowski, Benedict and Vico.

The question of 'existential foothold', which is central to *genius loci* theory has always been prominent in ethnography and anthropology. In fact, it has motivated many a fieldworker like for example Malinowski who in his introduction to the *Argonauts of the Western Pacific* wrote that the ethnographer's dearest goals were "to grasp the native's point of view, his relation to life" and "study what concerns him most ultimately" (Malinowski 1922: 25). These 'points of view', 'relations to life' and 'concerns' are aspects of the 'existential foothold' which people have in their respective cultural habitats, and it would be interesting to re-read Malinowski's ethnographies on the 'kula ring' and the coral gardens and their magic in terms of *genius loci* theory. This would be especially promising as Malinowski was not only concerned with people as agents (people holding the world) but also as patients (people held by the world), for he wanted to know "the hold which life has" on people, how their social institutions, values and aims, codes of law and morality etc. structure their expectations (Op. Cit.: 25). Here we are back to the two basic elements of *genius loci* theory: identification and orientation as basic human needs and dispositions.

The idea that each culture has its own 'spirit' has only been implicit in some anthropological theories, like for example in Ruth Benedict's theory of the 'patterns' of culture. Although Ruth Benedict did not use the term, she was concerned with the 'genius' of culture, as Franz Boas made explicit already in his introduction to the first edition of *Patterns of Culture* (Benedict 1934). She envisaged culture as an artistic structure, a building where experience takes place, be it excessive (Dionysian), measured (Apollonian) or any other kind (Benedict 1989: 79). Taking her primary model from architecture she explained the emerging character of culture as follows:

> Gothic architecture, beginning in what was hardly more than a preference for altitude and light, became, by the operation of some canon of taste that developed within this technique, the unique and homogeneous art of the thirteenth century. It discarded elements that were incongruous, modified others to its purposes, and invented others that accorded with its taste... When we describe the process historically, we inevitably use animistic forms of expression as if there were choice and purpose in the growth of this art-form. But this is due to the difficulty in our language-forms. There was no conscious choice, and no purpose. What was at first no more than a slight bias in local forms and techniques expressed itself more and more forcibly, integrated itself in more and more definite standards, and eventuated in Gothic art. What has happened in the great art styles happens also in cultures as a whole (Benedict 1989: 48).

As this text shows, there is a close affinity between Norberg-Schulz and Benedict. Both have a similar 'Gestalt' in mind, a comprehensive, emerging and synergetic totality in which people are both agents and patients and where the whole is experienced as mysterious or 'unspeakable' (see below).

Finally, let us remember Giambattista Vico, the founding father of cultural anthropology, who more than 250 years ago conjured the creative and poetic disposition, which enables people to gain an existential foothold and dwell in meaningful existential spaces. No one has ever surpassed the vivid imaginations of his *New Science* (Vico 1744; 1961) where he has provided us with an insight into the analogical thinking that is the basis of poetics, culture, and, I would say, the *genius loci*. I quote here from paragraph 540 in the chapter on "Poetic Economy":

> And, in other metaphors both beautiful and necessary, they [the ancient Greeks, I.S.] imagined the earth in the aspect of a great dragon, covered with scales and spines (the thorns and briers), bearing wings (for the lands belonged to the heroes), always awake and vigilant (thickly grown in every direction)... Under another aspect they imagined the earth as hydra... which, when any of its heads were cut off, always grew others in their place. It was the three alternating colours: black (the burned-over land), green (the leaf), and gold (the ripe grain). These are the three colours of the serpent's skin, which, when it grows old, is sloughed off for a fresh one. Finally, under the aspect of its fierceness in resisting cultivation, the earth was also imagined as a most powerful beast, the nemean lion (whence later the name lion was given to the most powerful of the animals), which philologists hold to have been a monstrous serpent. All the beasts vomit forth fire, which is the fire set to the forests by Hercules (Vico 1961: 146).

If one compares this with the Mongolian 'metaphorical mapping' of body and terrain, chiefs and mountains, shamans and subterranean depths etc. as described so well by Caroline Humphrey (see above) one immediately recognizes how relevant Vico still is today for an understanding of the role of tropes in the creation of a *genius loci*.

There is no room here to explore the relationship between anthropology and *genius loci* theory any further, but I hope that my short survey has at least indicated the way in which this theory resonates with some of the central ideas and concerns in past and present anthropology.

Genius loci and the unspeakable

It was Stephen Tyler who brought into current anthropology a new awareness of the unsaid and unspeakable in language and culture. In *The Said and the Unsaid* he proposed "a new linguistics which teaches us to appreciate language as indirect discourse and to use it effectively that speakers and hearers negotiate, amend, and reaffirm by communicating with one another" (Tyler 1978: 147), and language becomes a means by which we 'nudge' each other into recognizing our respective intentions (Op. Cit.: 176).

In a formidable instance of lucid criticism, Tyler has drawn attention to the way in which a refusal to acknowledge this incomplete, provisional and inferential nature of discourse leads to obstruction and paralysis rather than to better understanding: "Literalness in all its forms is reprehensible, but it is most odious in conversation, for its effect is obstructionist and is usually so intended. There is a certain 'looseness' about all of our conversational rules and our rules of social life generally, so that anyone who follows the rules literally, destroys the normative character of interaction and induces social paralysis. To ask for mathematical exactitude in our everyday rules and use of rules is to ask for disaster, the very destruction of the form sought rather than its fulfilment. Rigid rule-following is, of course, a highly effective method for obstructing interaction and discourse" (Op. Cit.: 396).

What Tyler has pointed out here has important implications not only for our every-day conversations but also for scientific discourse in general, and for the role we might be willing to allow notions like *genius loci* to play in ethnography and anthropology. Nothing would be easier than to put Norberg-Schulz down, asking him what he literally means by *genius loci* and to define precisely, possibly even in mathematical terms, the 'spirit' of a particular place. Yet this would be nothing but the 'odious' tactic pointed up by Tyler above. The communicative intentions of Norberg-Schulz would be obstructed and his potentially fruitful ideas would be lost.

If, however, one accepts Norberg-Schulz's use of the notion of *genius loci* as a 'creative accommodation of words and things' and a way of 'nudging' us to recognize certain intentions, then the notion of *genius loci* might still have an important role to play. Remember that Norberg-Schulz introduced it in order to address the fact that people often experience places as comprehensive totalities where various elements interact with one another and create a 'Gestalt', an 'atmosphere', a 'sense' or 'spirit' which cannot be reduced to any of its properties. But, paraphrasing Tyler, we now could add, that although a *genius loci* cannot be reduced to any of its properties it can be nevertheless evoked by them.

In *The Unspeakable* Tyler has outlined this creative role of evocation, its power to conjure "a fantasy whole abducted from fragments" and to make "available through absence what can be conceived but not presented" (Tyler 1987: 199, 202). In order to understand his theory of evocation let us listen here to Tyler at some length. First, as he criticizes naturalistic realism:

> The whole point of 'evoking' rather than 'representing' is that it frees ethnography from mimesis and that inappropriate mode of scientific rhetoric which entails 'objects', 'facts', 'descriptions', 'inductions', 'generalizations', 'verification', 'experiment', 'truth' and like concepts which, except as empty invocations, have no parallels either in the experience of ethnographic field work or in the writing of ethnographies. The urge to conform to the canons of scientific rhetoric has made the easy realism of natural history the dominant mode of ethnographic prose, but it has been an illusory realism, promoting, on one hand, the absurdity of 'describing' nonentities like 'culture' or 'society' as if they were fully observable, though somewhat ungainly, bugs, and on the other, the equally ridiculous behaviourist pretence of 'describing' repetitive patterns of action in isolation from the discourse that actors use in constituting and situating their action, and all the simple-minded surety that the observer's grounding discourse was itself an objective form sufficient to the task of describing acts (Tyler 1987: 207).

Then, as he reminds us of the fragmentary nature of field work:

> Life in the field is itself fragmentary, not at all organized around familiar ethnological categories like kinship, economy, and

religion, and except for unusual informants like Ogotemmeli, the natives seem to lack communicable visions of a shared, integrated whole; nor do particular experiences present themselves, even to the most hardened sociologist, as conveniently labelled synecdoches, microcosms, or allegories of wholes, whether cultural or theoretical. At best, we make do with a collection of indexical anecdotes or telling particulars with which to portend that larger unity beyond explicit textualization (Op. Cit.: 208).

And finally, as he develops his view of an emergent ethnography based on evocation, which "accomplishes a cognitive utopia not of the author's subjectivity nor of the reader's, but of the author-text-reader, an emergent mind which has no individual locus, being instead an infinity of possible loci. Here then is a new holism, one that is emergent rather than given, and one that emerges through the reflexivity of text-author-reader and which privileges no member of this trinity as the exclusive locus or means of the whole" (Op. Cit.: 209).

Genius loci and cultural comparison

I think that from the theoretical perspectives considered above it follows that *genius loci* theory may provide a fruitful approach to the study of cultural diversity in general and regional variation of culture in southern Ethiopia in particular. Surely, it would be interesting to compare the *genius loci* of Hamar (characterized by its dry impenetrable mountains, see below) with the *genius loci* of Aari (characterized by even higher mountains than those of Hamar and an abundance of rain and lush vegetation) and that of Arbore (at the fringe of the salty plains of Chew Bahir where the sun is so hot that most social life begins only with the relief of night) and of Dassanech(in the ever changing, promising and threatening river delta of the Lower Omo), and so on.

In his essay on "The Language of the Forest" to which I have already referred above, Gell has proclaimed that, "cultural theories ought to be anchored in the specifics of physical localities, technologies, lifestyles, rather than seeking to appeal to absolutes and essences" (Gell 1995: 252). This echoes Tyler's critique of the simple-minded surety of the observer's discourse (see above), and it encourages us, I think, to first pay due attention to the "comprehensive totality of places" as Norberg-Schulz has called it, and explore their characteristics and the 'existential foothold' which they provide for the people who live in them. Once this has been achieved, or perhaps in the very process of achieving this, all the many comparative interests which are so dear to our anthropological hearts (comparison of kinship categories, political structures, religious beliefs and the like) as well as questions of cultural contact and change will also find plenty of opportunity to get satisfied.

Baldambe Explains as source for the *genius loci* of Hamar

In 1979 Jean Lydall and I published *The Hamar of Southern Ethiopia, Vol. II: Baldambe Explains*. The plan for the book emerged already in the field when we began to appreciate the great expressive power of our host, friend and ethnographic mentor, Baldambe ('Father of the Brown Cow'). On September 18th 1971 I noted in my diary:

> In the evening, as Baldambe and I talk and I record his narratives, the project of our first possible Hamar book takes shape in my head: Baldambe describing his people, his family, his father and himself. There is so much poetry and expression in his descriptions. These and rhythm of his speech should be reproduced in a book: the fast passages and interludes, the accelerations, the lingering of his voice. What a job it would be to translate such tapes! But if we were able to manage the translation without losing the quality of the actual speech, than something beautiful could result (Lydall and Strecker 1979b: VI).

I need not recall the labour and vicissitudes under which *Baldambe Explains* eventually came about. They have been told in our *Work Journal* (Lydall and Strecker 1979a) and in the introduction to *Baldambe Explains* (Lydall and Strecker 1979b), but what I want to mention here is that I invited Baldambe with the following words to provide an account of life in Hamar:

> We have seen how you Hamar live and what you do. For many months we talked with you about Hamar customs. Yet our eyes don't see and our ears don't hear. We feel as if we have been handling separate pieces of wood, poles and beams. You know how the poles and beams fit together. Please take them and reconstruct for us the house to which they belong (Lydall/Strecker 1979b: x).

Note how close this imagery is to Heidegger's notion of the 'world as the house where the mortals dwell' which Norberg-Schulz took up in order to develop his theory of orientation and identification as basic necessities of human life and therefore also for architecture. What I did without knowing was to invite Baldambe to tell us how the Hamar dwell, how, in Heidegger's words, the Hamar "'are' on earth". No wonder then that he provided us with a formidable evocation of the *genius loci* of Hamar. This *genius loci* is a rhetorical construction, saturated with history, meaningful places, dramatic events, a host of 'dramatis personae' and countless dialogues, proverbs, songs, blessings and curses.

In what follows I will give a number of examples which show how Baldambe 'nudges' us into understanding the *genius loci* of Hamar, how he evokes its 'unspeakable' totality by means that come close to the 'future ethnography' divined by Stephen Tyler, that is by "a text of the physical, the spoken, and the performed, an evocation of quotidian experience, a palpable reality that uses everyday speech to suggest what is ineffable, not through abstraction, but by means of the concrete. It will be a text to read not with the eyes alone, but with the ears in order to hear 'the voices of the pages'..." (Tyler 1987: 213).

ETHNOGRAPHY
Rooks in the mountains

One passage of *Baldambe Explains* which Jean Lydall and I have given the title "In the Fields" begins as follows:

> Hamar country is dry, its people are rooks, they are tough. Living between the rocks, and drying up, they dig fields and make beehives. That's Hamar. The *maz* used to strum the lyre together with the elders:

> "Our father's land,
> *Bitta*, Banki Maro's land,
> When rain will fail is not told.
> Our father's land has no enemy,
> Only the wombo tree is our enemy."

> So the lyre used to be strummed '*kurr, kurr, kurr!*' The sorghum may get lost, but the Borana don't climb up the mountains. The Korre will kill men at Sambala, they kill down at Kaeske. The Male kill men in the open plains. They kill men at Sabin Turrin. They kill men at Bapho. They kill men over at Dimeka. No one climbs into the mountains. No one climbs into the mountains to kill. In the mountains, however, there is s tree called *wombo* which has a trunk which reaches high up. When the fruits ripen at the top, when one's stomach is grabbed with hunger, then one climbs up the ripe tree. Having climbed up one eats, eats, eats, eats, eats, eats, until one is swollen with food, and one's arms and legs are shortened. The way down is lost. So one sits in the branches and sleeps, and as one sleeps one falls—*wurrp*! *dosh*! one is dead. 'Our father's land, you have no enemies, only the *wombo* tree is your enemy. (Lydall and Strecker 1979b: 157-158)

Firstly, I like to draw attention to the laconic way in which Baldambe sums up the existence of Hamar. Such short, even abrupt statements, which nevertheless are full of tropes like in this case metaphor, irony and hyperbole are typical for Hamar. They are part of the 'dryness' of the country and the 'toughness' of its inhabitants (people and goats alike). The Hamar proudly play on this and mockingly and ironically say that they dry up between the rocks. But even though they are only skin and bones they work hard, digging fields and making beehives. Metaphorically they refer to themselves as 'rooks'. This image condenses a whole lot of attributes: Hamar nest like rooks inaccessibly high between the rocks; they never seem to need water like the rooks; they look thin, craggy and black like rooks perched on a tree; they are strong and playful like rooks whirling around in the turbulent air above the mountain tops; and, above all, like the rooks they have sharp eyes and are ever ready to rush down from high up and pick up from the ground what has been left unguarded (i.e., the goats, cattle and sheep of the surrounding neighbours in the lowlands).

The dry, laconic summary is counterposed with a lush, allegorical episode using a song and its exegesis. The initiates (*maz*) strum the lyre and sing that, after all, Hamar country is not too bad, because even though it may be terribly dry at times, no one fears that the rain will ever fail completely. So the Hamar in their mountains are safe, safe from hunger and from enemies. But no, they are not, because there is this deadly *wombo* tree, which makes one swell with food, and one's arms and legs shortened so that one falls and dies. Here all the laughter comes in which is so typical of Hamar, laughter about oneself and others, laughter that expresses what cannot be said and answers the many polarities and contradictions of existence.

Once Baldambe has provided an image of the old secure 'existential foothold' of the Hamar with its associated 'orientation' (note the deictic framework of time, place and action) and 'identification' (note how the Hamar identify with their 'tough' situation), he goes on to contrast it with the present-day situation. Here a lamentation begins which is typical for Hamar and its *genius loci*. Things are experienced as getting worse rather than better:

Our father's land, Sabo's land, Elto's land, Banki Maro's land,
Kotsa's land. In Garsho's land, rain never used to fail. Our *bitta*
never told of its failure. Our grandfathers did not tell, our
forefathers did not tell. There was rain. Nowadays the months
when you fail are many. In the month of *kilekila* you left us dry, in
the month of *dalba* you left us dry, in the two months of *mingi* you
left us dry, in the two months of *shulal* you left us dry. Altogether
that's seven months when you left us dry. Then in *barre* you made
us crazy and drove men to Aari, and drove men to Ulde. *barre* means
being crazy. Men getting crazy are lost (Op. Cit.: 158).

Note how in order to emphasize the initially secure grounding
of Hamar life; first the ritual leaders of several generations are
invoked. Implicit in this is the understanding that it was the
ability of the forefathers to bless successfully which brought
good fortune (*barjo*) to the country and that the ritual leaders of
today are no good. After this, Baldambe gives a dismal picture
where all the months are named when the rain is failing Hamar
today. The climax of disorientation is the 'mad' month where
people despair, get crazy and are lost. But having conjured this
devastation, Baldambe immediately swings back into a hopeful
mood. In fact he retracts from his lamentation and then goes on
to speak about the seasons and months of Hamar:

It was not told that you would pass by our fatherland. You will
come. So in the month of *surr* it rains a little. Down at the borders
there are rains, *kurr, kurr, kurr*! It rains just for the gazelle, just for
the oryx, just for the gerenuk, just for the zebra, just for the buffalo,
it rains just for the warthog, the father of the tusk bracelet.

"Let us plant! When will you fall? Come to plant our sorghum!
Plant it!" Saying which, the rain comes and plants the sorghum
into the ground. The wet season. Then when it has rained in that
month there comes the month of *puta* when the sorghum flowers.
When *puta* finishes there comes *zako*. Then the country is held by
cloud, the blanketing cloud and the black clouds which bring no
rain, and the clouds which drizzle. It is simply cold everywhere.
There is no cloth, so having put on skin capes, everyone sits at the

fire and shivers. *zako* means hugging the fire thus, that's the month of *zako*. The clouds are all clouds, the sun is not seen. The rain drip, drip, dripping brings only sickness. Hugging, hugging, hugging the fire your thighs get cooked and blotched like the spotted leopard. While you hug the fire the baboons eat the field clean. The pigeons eat the sorghum clean. That's *zako*. After *zako* come two months of *alati* when the country dries, the plants turn yellow, some ripen, and the grass dies off; *kai*, and *naj'* and *gorrin* are the first plants to lose their leaves. One month of *alati* is *karna-agai* when the sorghum down in the lowlands is ripe, up in the mountains it has yet to ripen. In the next month, *agai-phana*, the sorghum is ripe in the mountains. Then again come the months of no rain, *shulal, mingi, dalba, kilekila* and *barre*. These are the Hamar months." (Op. Cit.: 158-159)

While the short account of the various months is meant to show the change of the seasons, the longer, especially evocative descriptions of *barre* and *zako* characterize the two climatic poles of the year: heat and dryness associated with social dispersion, and cold and wetness associated with social im-mobility. In both these extreme situations people become some-what crazy, get themselves lost or loose their possessions. Again one can hear Baldambe laugh, as he conjures the picture of people getting blotched like the spotted leopard while the baboons eat their fields clean.

A fire in the mountains

In his talk, Baldambe first establishes the identity of Hamar through an account of its mythical origins:

Long ago, in the time of the ancestors, the Hamar had two *bitta* (ritual leaders). One was Banki Maro, one was Elto. The first ancestor of Banki Maro came from Aari and settled in Hamar in the mountains. He, the *bitta*, made fire, and seeing this fire people came, many from Aari, others from Male, others from Tsamai, others from Konso, others from Kara, others from Bume and others from Ale which lies beyond Konso. Many came from Ale. The *bitta* was the first to make fire in Hamar and said:

"I am the *bitta*, the owner of the land am I, the first to take hold of the land. Now may you become my subjects, may you become my dependents, may you become the ones I command" (Op. Cit.: 2).

This mythical scene combines topological features (the mountains) and archetypical activities (making fire) in order to back up and strengthen the usurpation of power by the *bitta*. The mountains and his visibility evoke height, control and centrality. He is both the 'first' in time and the 'first' in the social order. People are attracted to him, and Hamar becomes a place where people meet coming from all directions. They do not only come from different territories but belong also to different clans:

Now all the Hamar, Hamar, Hamar, Hamar, Hamar, Hamar, Hamar, Hamar, Hamar, Hamar arrived, Ba, Lawan, Gasi… Gasi came the Tsamai way, Lawan the Birale way, Misha the Tsamai way, Rach the Tsamai way, Bucha the Konso way. Many came from the Male, Aari and Konso ways, one Babatu, one Gasi, one Worla, one Ba. They all came from where the sun rises. The clans that came from where the sun goes down, from Bume and Kara, were only four (Op. Cit.: 3-4).

However, the fire not only evokes social visibility and centrality but also creative power. An active, imaginative and creative person is called '*edi nu*' (person fire). Fire also signals a new beginning. Just like after death the fires of a settlement are extinguished and newly kindled in conjunction with blessings, and just like every year after the harvest all fires are put out only to be kindled anew, the *bitta's* fire in the mountains means a new beginning of human habitation in Hamar.

Customs appropriate for the place

As the 'first' to arrive in Hamar, the *bitta* was the one who knew which rules and customs would be appropriate for the place. Baldambe has vividly recalled the people's original appeals and the help and advice which the *bitta* gave them on matters like collecting and sharing livestock, bride price, divorce, initiation and so on. To a large extent, the *genius loci* of Hamar is reflected in these exchanges between the people and their *bitta*. Baldambe begins with the question of how to share livestock equally among all the Hamar so that no one will remain poor:

Banki Maro said:

"Let these people be mine. Your *bitta* am I. Herd cattle for me, herd goats for me."

"*Bitta!*"

"*Woi!*"

"We don't have any cattle, only a few clans have cattle, only a few men have some. What shall we do?"

"You have no cows?"

"We have no cows."

"You have no goats?"

"Only one or two men have goats. Most of us are poor."

"If you are poor collect loan cattle and cultivate your fields so that you can bring sorghum to those who own cattle. Herding these cows, drink their milk…"

So then the people began to collect cattle. One man bought cows for goats, one went raiding and returned driving cattle, others came carrying goats. The people said to each other:

"The poor should not go down to the waterhole with nothing. The *bitta* told us that those who have cattle should share some of them, calling those to whom they give cattle *bel*."

"Whose cattle are these?"

"These are the cattle of so-and-so."

"And yours?"

"I have a cow from a *bel*, an arrow from which I drink."

A cow from a *bel* is called 'arrow' because one takes a blood letting arrow to draw blood from the jugular vein of the cow, and mixing four cups of blood with one cup of fresh milk, one feeds the children." (Op. Cit.: 4-5)

Then Baldambe goes on to tell how the question of marriage payment was raised once the people had collected some but not very many cattle:

When cattle had been collected in this way the elders called upon the *bitta*:

"*Bitta*!'

"*Woi*!'

"The people are all poor, they have no cows, they have no goats. It would be bad if one had to give much to get married. Tell us what to do."

"Do you ask me as the *bitta*?"

"We have asked you."

"*Eh-eh*. My country has mountains only. Over there Irgil Bala, here Mama Dunta and up there Bala Kuntume. Give twenty-eight goats plus one male goat and one female goat."

"Good. What about the cattle?"

The *bitta* said:

"Both rich and poor should give the same: eighteen head of cattle, plus one 'stone cow' and one 'cloth bull', which makes twenty altogether." (Op. Cit.: 5-6).

Note that the people use a hyperbole exaggerating their poverty. They have, in fact, collected cattle. This is why the question of bride wealth has arisen. The *bitta* accepts their plea for a low bride price justifying it using a similar form of exaggeration. That is, he says that Hamar 'only' has mountains, implying that the whole country is poor.

In order to fully understand the sentence 'Over there Irgil Bala, here Mama Dunta and up there Bala Kuntume"one has to know that Mama Dunta, the mountain where the *bitta* dwelt and spoke to the elders, lies almost in the centre of Hamar territory. Far to the South, marking the southern border of

Hamar, rises the high mountain called Irgil Bala, and to the North, bordering Tsamai territory, rises the even higher mountain called Bala Kunteme. Furthermore, the main vertical posts of a house (which, like Irgil and Kuntume, have a fork at the top) are also called *bala*. This likens Hamar country to a house and echoes Heidegger's view of the world as 'the house where the mortals dwell' (quoted already twice above).

Having settled the matter of marriage payment, the question arises whether marriage should be permanent or whether there could be also divorce:

"Some men are bad and troublesome, always beating their wives and then abandoning them. *Bitta*, tell us the rituals to do."

The *bitta* replied:

"A man of Gulet should become a 'butter man'. When the country is dry and there is no butter, cow dung and the dung of sheep shall become butter. Give gifts to the 'butter man'."

So they gave beads, iron rings and feathers, and the *bitta* put them on the 'butter man'. A cattle gateway was erected for him and they handed him a big right-handed food bowl:

"Here is the bowl, if a *maz* (initiate) comes to you rub him with butter. Before this, the girl should take the head-dress of the *maz* and throw it into a *giri* tree and the *maz* should lap milk from a cow's udder saying: 'From now on I will never again lap milk from a cow's udder.' Then they should come to the 'butter man' and put four sorghum rolls in his bowl. Let the girl bite the sorghum first and you, the *maz*, bite second. Next, butter shall be put on the hands of the girl and the boy and they shall rub each other's hands. After this the girl shall take the belt (made from dik-dik skin) from the waist of the boy and he shall take the string-skirt from the girl and they shall put them into the bowl. Finally the boy shall take the string-skirt and the girl the belt and they shall return home. From now on for good or bad they will never leave each other. There will be no divorce, it is forbidden. Whether they bear children or not they will always remain together until the grave."

"Who brought for this custom?"

"It was the *bitta*."

"Which *bitta*?"

"It was Garsho."

"Which *bitta*?"

"It was Ulawa." "*Eh!*" (Op. Cit.: 6-7)

How to get a foothold in the place

Put in *genius loci* terminology, the *bitta* also advised people how to 'get a foothold' in Hamar. Or rather one should say he told them to take sorghum and cultivate it:

> Dig fields. When you have done that, here is the sorghum. *Barjo* (luck, fortune, creation) has given us sorghum. Sorghum is man's grass. As cows eat grass so shall man eat sorghum. *Barjo* gave us the meat and milk of cattle and goats long ago, saying: Drink the milk of cattle and goats and eat their meat. Cattle and goats shall chew leaves from the bushes and cattle shall graze grass. Put fences around your homesteads so that hyenas, jackals and hunting dogs cannot enter. The one who enters is man. You have hands. Dig fields and when the sorghum is ripe bring some to the cattle owners, your *bel* (bond-friend), bring some to the goat owners, your goat *bel* (Op. Cit.: 7).

He also tells them to keep bees. First he instructs them how to make beehives and then, in order to encourage them, he explains how the bees will come from trees in the surroundings of Hamar and how he will bless them and keep away sickness:

> Make beehives taking the bark of the *donkala*-tree and binding the *arra*-grass around it with the *kale*-creeper and smearing the inside with cow dung. Place the beehives well in the forks of trees. The bees will come to you from Aari country. Up in the Aari mountains is a dark tree where there are bees. From there the bees will come. Down in Galeba country by the river and the lake grows the *shapi*-tree from which bees will come. From the *shapi*-tree of Ulde bees will come. From inside the *dongo*, the big dark tree, which grows

down in Kara, the bees will come. When the bees have come the
honey will ripen. When it is ripe, bring honey to the *bitta* so that
he may call forth the *barjo* of your cattle and the *barjo* of your
goats and that he may get rid of sickness for you (Op. Cit.: 7-8).

A protected place

Once one has gained a foothold in a place and has found
means of subsistence, there arises the need for protection,
especially against diseases and enemies. Baldambe relates how
first the people came to consult the *bitta* and how subsequently
the *bitta* on his own accord added a further form of protection:

"Eh, bitta!"

"Woi!"

"Sickness has come to the cattle, sickness has come to the
children. What would be good to do?"

"Isn't there a man of Ba?"

"There is."

"This man should go down to every waterhole and anoint
everything with the fat from the sheep's tail."

So the man from Ba went all round the country, anointing the
grass, the water, the earth and the hearts of children.

"The Bume are our enemies, the Galeba are our enemies, the Korre
are our enemies, the Borana are our enemies, we are surrounded by
them. *Bitta*, tell us what to do."

"Is there not Misha?"

"There is Misha."

"A man from Misha should take two dry flower stalks of the
wolkanti cactus and going to the border of the country there he
should hit them together: '*dak-dak-dak-dak-dak-dak-dak-ka-da-dak!*'
Then he should break them and throw them towards the countries
of Borana and Korre. Then he should take a sheep skin and flip it
towards the enemy county..."

Further the *bitta* said:

"Our country has borders. Ulde and Galeba and Bume and Aari and Kara and Banna and Tsamai, all are at our borders, aren't they? A bull of mine should go around-round-round-round-round-round the country. As he goes round, whenever the bull urinates, collect the urine in a gourd, whenever he defecates, collect the dung. The bull should follow the course of the Kaeska. He should not cross into Baldo but go to Bala, down to Maen, over Golla and up to Kadja, Dongalta, and Tsagamar. Going round these he should go up to Wareta, Edis, Segerenbaino, then down to Seleabaino and finally along Selleabaino up to the home of the *bitta*."

"Has the bull encircled the country?"

"He has gone around the country."

"The sorghum will ripen, the cows will be rich with milk, the honey will be plentiful."

This is the Hamar custom according to the word of the *bitta*. (Op. Cit.: 10-12).

A blessed place

Blessings resound in Hamar country. In fact, according to Hamar philosophy they create it. The Hamar say *apho barjo ne*, the word is *barjo*: creation, power of life, fate, fortune, luck. This is why on innumerable occasions they get together for a *barjo aela* where they jointly call forth *barjo*

Every elder (*donza*) has the power to lead a *barjo aela*, that is chant the invocation while others repeat his last words in a chorus, but on public occasions the lead is taken, according to circumstances, either by an *ayo* (political spokesman), or a *kogo* (man ritually responsible for a particular grazing area), or a *gudili* (man responsible for a settlement and its cultivation area), or a *bitta* (man ritually responsible for one of the two halves of Hamar territory). The *barjo aela* turns the world into what it should be. Without calling forth *barjo* the world could not be well, could not even exist. The rains would fail, the grass would wither, the cattle would die, people would perish. Only by repeatedly and insistently calling forth the desired state of being can people and their habitat exist. This ontology goes well, of course, with Heidegger's Norberg-Schulz's philosophy of 'being'.

Let us listen to Baldambe and other voices from Hamar, which he recalls as they evoke the setting and the performance of a major *barjo aela* which both mirrors and creates the *genius loci* of Hamar.

The *bitta* has decided that it is time to bless the country again. So he sends empty gourds to the low-lying, distant grazing areas where the gourds are filled. They then are brought to the permanent settlements in the Hamar mountains, where they are blessed and then sent on to the *bitta*. He receives the milk, calls forth *barjo*, puts cleansing plants into the empty milk containers and sends them back from where they have come:

"Let the milk containers come! Where are the herds?"

"The herds are down at Roto."

"Where are the herds?"

"The herds are down at Golla."

"Where are the herds?"

"The herds are down at Worsat."

"Where are the herds?"

"The herds are down at Mello."

"May these get milked to fill the gourds." [...]

 "The *bitta's* gourds have arrived!"

"From where have they come?"

"They have come from Kena."

"From where come the *bitta's* gourds?"

"They come from Lala."

"Whose gourds are they?"

"They are Elto's (name of a *bitta*)."

"Whose gourds are they?"

"They are the gourds of Sabo's son."

"What has happened?"

"The distant cattle's gourds are being milked."

Then in the evening, when they come from the distant cattle land, the people are called:

"*Hai-hai-hai-hai*, '*kambalo*' (people), everyone listen!"

"Children listen! Women listen! Elders listen! The *bitta's* gourd has come. Command a child, don't rest, tomorrow the gourd must go. Those who cry that they have no milk should hang up the empty gourd. Milk all the four teats of the cow, don't milk teats that are spoiled, don't milk cows whose calves have died, don't milk cows of people who have killed Hamar. Milk cows that are well. It is the *bitta's* milk container."

Then... down in Kizo, in Dunkan, in Omalle, in Saunabaino all the herds of each lineage are milked. Then all the gourds are brought to the *boakas*. People gather at the homesteads of the *gudili*. There the gourd of the *bitta* is filled. The elders consume what milk is left. The *bitta's* gourd is carried to settlements like Lodjera, like Wonyarki, like Medalla, like Atana, like Dunia, like Turmi, like Dambaiti. When it comes:

"Has the gourd come?"

"It has come."

"Collect the goats."

A young female goat is collected from Rach and a male goat is collected from Ba Balambala. Both goats are brought with the gourd to the *bitta*.

"May the master come forth from the house, may he come out. The gourd has come. Sweep the gateway."

The *bitta's* wife puts on her headdress, her goatskin cape and her cowry-shell belt, and sweeps the entrance to the cattle kraal. After this the *bitta* comes and stands by the gateway:

"Come, all you elders."

Now an uninitiated boy of the Binnas moiety (moiety to which the *bitta* belong), Worla, Ba or Warran, gives the milk container up to the *bitta*; married men don't give it. The *bitta* removes the *baraza* leaves, which close the gourd and holding the mouth of the gourd he begins to chant and the elders answer in refrain:

"*Eh-eh*! The herds are carrying sickness!

May the sickness go beyond

Labur (distant mountain in the West)," . . . "may it go,"

"May the sickness go beyond

Topo (distant mountains in the West)," . . . "may it go,"

"Cattle owners you have enemies down there, the Korre.

May the Korre who looks at your cattle die," . . . "die,"

"May his eyes fail," . . . "fail,"

"May his heart get speared," . . . "speared,"

"May they disperse like doves," . . . "disperse,"

"May they get up like birds and leave," . . . "leave,"

"May you put on his sandals," . . . "put on,"

"May we cut his heart," . . . "cut,"

"May his skin shiver as from cold water," . . . "shiver,"

"May his bones be bound up," . . . "bound up,"

"May his eyes get lost," . . . "get lost,"

"Sickness, sickness, *wollall* (away)," . . . "*wollall,*"

"Sickness *wollall*," . . . "*wollall,*"

"*Eh-eh!*"

"My herds, which are at Mello, in the open grass lands,

May my herds come lowing," . . . "come,"

"May my herds come lowing," . . . "come,"

"Grazing the grass may they come," . . . "come,"

"Having eaten may the calves come," . . . "come,"

"Leading their kids may the goats come," . . . "come,"

"Well may they come," . . . "come."

"There are boys among the herds, killing the

black ostrich, with its plume, may they come," . . . "come,"

"Dressing themselves with feathers, may

they come," . . . "come,"

"Killing the lion may they come," . . . "come,"

"Killing the elephant may they come," . . . "come,"

"Killing the rhino may they come," . . . "come,"

"Killing the leopard may they come," . . . "come." [...]

Like this the *bitta* calls *barjo*, the cattle *barjo*. Then the goats are given to him, and the milk container is given to him. He, the *bitta*, does not drink the milk but puts it into the sour-milk pot. Then he goes into the bush and pulls up four *karko* plants and four *gali* plants. He puts all eight plants into the milk container: "Go!"

These are the cleansing plants of Hamar, the *karko* and the *gali*, which are taken to every cattle kraal throughout the *bitta's* country. From *gudili* to *gudili* to *gudili* Kadja (a territorial segment) is completed. From *gudili* to *gudili* to *gudili* Marla is completed. From *gudili* to *gudili* to *gudili* Arkala is completed. From *gudili* to *gudili* to *gudili* and Dambaiti is finished. From *gudili* to *gudili* and Lodgera is finished. From *gudili* to *gudili* to *gudili* and Dunia is finished. From *gudili* to *gudili* to *gudili* and Omalle is completed. From *gudili* to *gudili* to *gudili*, from fire-man (*kogo* ritually responsible for grazing areas, see above) to fire-man and Dunka is completed. Fire-men only all the way to Kizo.

In this way the milk container is brought down crossing one settlement after another and at each place it crosses the *karko* and *gali* plants are taken out and new ones put back. This is the milk container of Elto, it comes from Kadja, from Simbale and Gulaba. The milk container of Banki Maro comes from Altera, from Macho, from Galepha, from Assile, from Wungabaino, from Mirsha, from Angude." (Lydall and Strecker 1979b: 12-16)

By way of conclusion

As I have said above, all of *Baldambe Explains* could be read as an evocation of the *genius loci* of Hamar. The six examples from his text I have presented could well be multiplied and my

analyses extended, but I think that for the purpose of this
paper the examples are sufficient. The purpose, as outlined in
the theoretical part, was to show how *genius loci* theory may be
helpful for the study of regional variations of culture, and to
emphasize, as Alfred Gell has done, that cultural comparison
and the analysis of contact phenomena should be anchored in
the specifics of localities.

What Baldambe evoked was a *genius loci* of the past, a *genius
loci* which he and his parents and grandparents remembered,
recreated and passed on to subsequent generations. He neither
thought that the *genius* of Hamar country would last
unchanged, nor did he believe that it would ever vanish. Getting
distraught about the present and the future he would lament as
follows:

> These were the customs of our ancestors. Nowadays they are
> neglected. When enemies come the people don't call *barjo* because
> they have become feeble. Now the country is exhausted. The
> sorghum burns up and doesn't ripen. Diseases don't leave the
> cattle, which die. The pox of the goats does not leave and so they
> die. In olden days there was no pox. There was no rinderpest
> among the cattle. There was no pneumonia. In olden days when
> the elders called *barjo*, when the man of Ba went and put sheep's
> fat into the grass and the waterhole, when the man of Bucha shot
> pebbles at the enemy, when the man of Worla brought fat to the
> homestead, then the milk of the cows was abundant! That's how
> it was in olden times (Lydall and Strecker 1979b: 18-19).

But then a goat would sneeze and Baldambe would laugh
and say, "have you heard what the goat has told? It told us,
'it's not true what you are saying, people are really not feeble,
the country is not exhausted, and the diseases will leave
eventually'" (see also Strecker 1979a and 1988a).

I wrote the main part of this paper a year ago (2001), and
now, as "Regional Variation of Culture" is going into print, I
have come across further anthropological studies of landscape,
place and space, and even soundscape and ethnoscape which

all have a close affinity to *genius loci* theory. Perhaps the most intriguing monograph about the genius loci of a single culture is James Weiner's *The Empty Place: Poetry, Space and Being Among the Foi of Papua New Guinea* (1991) which like the work of Christian Norberg-Schulz explores the implications of Heidegger's thoughts about dwelling, being and language. According to Weiner, the Foi create and recreate the (unspeakable) spirit of their locality and of their life discursively. Poetically they "preserve the sense of life's encompassing flow" and in their songs "construct a map" of the hills, streams, gardens and forests among which they live. Note how close this is to Baldambe's account where the *genius loci* of Hamar emerges from and is contained in conversations, songs, blessings, curses, admonitions, lamentations and the like.

The fact that the spirit of a place is partly created discursively or, as I would say, rhetorically, also comes out very strongly in "Place and Voice in Anthroplogical Theory" edited by Arjun Appadurai (1988), in *Senses of Place* edited by Steven Feld and Keith Basso (1996), and *The Poetic Power of Place: Comparative Perspectives on Austronesian Ideas of Locality* edited by James Fox (1997). The latter is particularly relevant and may act as an exemplar for our future comparative studies of localities in Southern Ethiopia.

Narrowly defined, the studies presented in *The Poetic Power of Place* are about 'topogeny', the "recitation of an ordered sequence of place names", but as the title says already, the contributions to the book are above all about the rhetorical energy which goes into topogenies and, more generally, into the creation of localities. In ways reminiscent of Vico's account of the metaphoric nature of culture, Austronesian topogenies are metaphorically grounded using *topoi* which are "variously referred to as 'nodes', 'points', or 'junctures' – using the metaphor of the growth of a plant or tree – or 'gates', 'halting places', or 'meeting points' – using the metaphor of a journey" (Fox 1997: 13).

The *topoi* offer the "possibility for an elaboration of knowledge" and in this way resemble the mnemonic devices of classic Western rhetoric. Fox draws attention to Aristotle's famous explanation of the relationship between spatial and mental orientation (*topoi* and memory) and adds that *topoi* are not only means for cognition but also serve as sources and targets of emotion. In other words, topogenies constitute or represent a particular form of 'persuasive style' (Bailey 1983) which involves both reason and passion and in this way is able to create a strong 'sense of place', a feeling of belonging and of individual and cultural identity. Here we are, it seems, right in the midst of genius loci theory, which says that people strive to create meaningful existential spaces, and in doing so create a 'spirit of place', which cannot be fully described but only evoked rhetorically.

Rhetorics of local knowledge

Introduction

The Hamar live in the mountains and steep valleys, on the high plateaus and low-lying plains north of Lake Turkana (formerly Lake Rudolf) and Lake Chew Bahir (formerly Lake Stefanie). This region is part of the East African Rift Valley which is not only geologically very varied but also has different habitats where—until now—natural species survive that have elsewhere been extinguished (leopards, baboons, dick-dick antelope, ostriches and others). Furthermore, the various ecological niches have also provided the opportunity for ancient forms of culture to persist.

Some of the groups of present day southern Ethiopia have a cultural repertoire that includes the lyre, the head rest, the hooked and forked stick (called in Hamar respectively *goala*, *borkoto* and *woko*), which are at least eight thousand years old and belong to the archaic cultural strata that preceded the civilisations of ancient Egypt and Ethiopia.

The way of life in these "Altvölker" (as A.E. Jensen titled them and thereby antagonised many 'progressive' anthropologist) can help us sense and understand some elements of early human existence. Or, put differently, current ethnographic work in southern Ethiopia—be it with the Hamar or their neighbours the Arbore, Dassanech, Nyangatom, Kara, Mursi, Bodi, Aari, Maale, Tsamai, Konso, Karmit, Borana or others—widens our *interpretative horizon* by helping us to discover what life might have been like before the rise of North-East Africa's "high cultures", and, perhaps more importantly, how with the use of only a minimum of material objects life can still be satisfying and provide each member of society with a strong sense of pride and self-esteem.

When, together with my wife Jean Lydall and our one-year-old son Theodore, I arrived in Hamar more than thirty years ago, I sometimes had the feeling as if I had 'dropped out of history'. Here is what I wrote in my diary when, for the first time ever, I spent a night at a Hamar cattle camp:

> 18.6.1970: We walk off together and arrive in the camp as night falls. There is a full moon and as the cattle, bathed in its light, arrive, I am struck by the lightness of their colouration: yellow, grey, a grey that is almost blue, light red, white and their movement is so relaxed and careful. We sit or lie on cowhides and the men, all of them young, talk and talk. They use their hands a lot, speak almost with their whole bodies. I wish I could understand what they are saying. Later, when it is almost midnight, we are served milk and blood mixed in huge calabashes. When I taste the smoke with which the calabashes have been cleaned, as I drink the milk and blood mixture and look across the Omo plain which is coloured red by fires burning on the steppes below, I have the feeling that I have dropped out of history (Lydall and Strecker 1979a: 15-17).

Local knowledge always has a historic dimension, and as we conduct our ethnographic researches, we do not only encounter knowledge that is characteristic of specific places but also of particular times. We should never forget this, although the central topic of the present essay is quite different, concerning as it does the rhetorics of local knowledge among the Hamar.

To begin with, let me provide an excerpt from a text provided by Baldambe (Father of the Dark Brown Cow) who for many years—until his death in 1995—was our friend, host and mentor in Hamar. He often mentions particular places, months, fruit, animals, sicknesses and so on that can not fully be understood by a reader unacquainted with Hamar, but this does not matter, for here the details are only meant to provide a first impression of the richness of Hamar local knowledge:

"This rainy season what will it be like? Will the rain fall a lot for us?"

Now there are a few big men who looking at the stars in the sky can tell how things will be. For six months of the year the sun moves down to the left. When it has reached its hole it sits there. As it sits there the people check its position against the profile of the mountains.

"*Nanato!*"

"*Yo!*"

"This year the sun has gone towards abundance. The stars this year will give water. The male star and the female star are sitting together. This year the elders won't get up. All the sorghum will ripen. For five months the rain will fall. First in *barre* when the sorghum, whether planted or not, will grow, then *surr* and *duka* and *puta* and *zako*."

This is what the stars say.

"Cut the bush well, in the mountains cut a lot, the homesteads down in the lowlands should cut a lot. This year the months when it will rain are six! The whole land will ripen. A hind leg will be produced."

This is when the stars come together, then the big rains and the small rains will meet, there will be no dry season in between.

"This year the stars will not give water. The male star has gone off to Korre. It has gone off to the left. It has gone off to Borana land. Last year when the star went to Aari she ripened the sorghum. This year store your seed well. This year the star has gone to Borana, gone to Korre. The male and female stars do not sit together. This year the sorghum will not ripen. This year only the red sorghum and tobacco and eleusine will ripen."

When the star goes to Borana and to Korre, there will be war, there will be sickness. The cattle sickness, rinderpest, the goats' sickness, pox, and the goats' sickness called *shokolo*. The country will be exhausted. *Barre* is dry season, *surr* is dry season, *duka* is dry season, only in *puta* will it rain. Should it rain in the month of *puta*, then the sorghum, which people plant in the plains where the sun urinates will burn. It will ripen only in the mountain gullies where the flood runs. Fast sorghum will ripen. Slow growing sorghum will not ripen. The fast sorghum with only two joints in the stem will ripen. You should not plant in riverbeds of the lowlands. Up in the mountains you should plant eleusine and red sorghum and tobacco. You should plant in between the stones where the *katsa* grass has been dug out, where the *sati* bush has been dug out and the *shaunbula* bush has been cut down, where the *golal* tree has been cut down and the *baraza* has been cut down. When rain falls in the month of *puta* then what is planted in *zako* will ripen so long as it rains a little in the month of *karna-agai*. That's the rainy season which becomes a drought. It happens when the female star goes towards Labur and the sun does not reach its home in the months of *barre* and *kile kila*. When the male star goes to Korre and faces Saber, then all the rivers in Hamar die. Shaukara dies, Wungabaino dies, Mishano dies, Angudebaino dies, Kadjabaino and Kalobaino die, Barto dies, Atino dies, Gulaba and Bakolte die, Kaeske alone does not die. Down there Omalle dies, Kizo dies, Saunabaino dies. Irbangude does not die, Letano does not die, that is up at Dimeka at the Kaeske where everyone moves to and gathers. The Kaeske is like a flowing river. At the rivers the people gather. Then it is said that the land has spilt its people.

When both the female and the male stars look towards Aari land, when they look up to Bala, when they rise from the hole where *wancho* rises and sit there together, then this year there will be water, the *mate* ritual will be performed, a hind leg will be produced, the sorghum will ripen even at Galapha, Turmi, Saunabain, Galama, and over at Leata. Up at Dimeka the bush will be cut. The bush that has been cut and left to dry will not burn. The big rains and the small rains will meet each other. This year the grasses at Dimeka will be too wet to burn. This year will be abundant. That's how it is. (Lydall and Strecker 1979b: 159-161)

Mental alertness and intelligence

Although the theme of this essay is local knowledge, I like to begin with a (slightly abbreviated) conversation where, not knowledge as such, but intelligence as expression of a general competence to live, is emphasized and applauded. As I have often heard, to be intelligent (*paxala*, literally 'bright') is the pre-requisite for all knowledge and the ability to cope with the vicissitudes of life in Hamar.

In the morning of the 20th of January 1974 I sat with my friends Baldambe and Choke in one of the houses of Dambaiti (see Lydall and Strecker 1979a), and while Ginonda (Bargi) was serving coffee, a conversation developed about Ginonda's young son Lomoluk and his intelligent actions:

Baldambe: Isn't Hamar something good? Look at this goat, which once got lost... Our herding boys said, just so:

"The fox has eaten it."

At that time the sorghum was ripe.

"Gino, look for the goat."

"I have searched for it aaall over the country."

Recently an age-mate of Lomoluk said:

"Lomoluk."

"*Woi.*"

"Look at this goat, it has the ear-cut of your goats, the goats of Berinas' homestead. Take it, it has already been a long while with us."

Now the goat has grown up. When it got lost it was small and thin, now it has become big and fat. See, this is Africa, Hamar.

Bargi: "One of your goats which went astray is among ours."

"Please let me see it."

Bal: Said Lomoluk?

Bar: Lomoluk. "Where is it?"

"When did it get lost?"

"It got lost a long time ago."

"It came to us a long time ago after it had been licking salt."

"Our goat which got lost was white with grey spots on the neck."

Choke: Said Lomoluk?

Bar: Gino lost it after the goats had been licking salt.

Cho: Yes, so it was.

Bar: "Please let me see it!" When Lomoluk arrived over there:

"*Uh*! Ours, it's him! Mother, mother, ours, it's him!"

Cho: He took it then.

Bar: Then Laesho's son was over there. Lomoluk said to him: "I am going with my cattle. That one is ours. Please let it go with your goats today." Then when Lomoluk returned in the evening with the lost goat I said to myself: "Look here, my small son has grown up, he as returned from the bush with the goat that was lost." *Hahahaha* (laughs happily, proudly) He gave the goat to Laesho's son to herd during the day while he was looking after the cattle.

Bal: Look here, my friend, see the intelligence of our Hamar children, of Africa's children.

Bar: Those who are stupid would not have recognised the goat and would have said "I don't know", would arrive and say "I don't know." (Strecker 1979a: 37-38).

Little Lomoluk was praised here for his mental alertness and intelligent decisions, which are demanded of a herding boy. This competence develops gradually as the child grows up. "Look here, my little son has grown up", says Ginonda after Lomoluk has proved himself so well, finding and returning the goat, which was said to be lost.

Enculturation and transmission of knowledge

In anthropological jargon we would say: The competence of Lomoluk is a result of his enculturation. His competence shows that he has become a Hamar. This competence concerns not only specific kinds and contents of knowledge but also intelligence and an ability to perceive and comprehend that develop and are enhanced in culturally specific ways. During the first days of fieldwork, when they have not yet been 'enculturated' and therefore are still like children, ethnographers are very impressed by this local knowledge that is so hard for them to grasp. Here are two passages from my diary, which illustrate something of this:

> 30.5.1970: Today I join two young boys, Aike and Kolle, to learn the art of herding goats and sheep. I get a taste of the slowness and casualness of herding. The boys are following rather than leading the herds and when they rest, the boys sleep or do some quiet work like braiding each others' hair. After five hours of "concrete poetry", I am exhausted and return.

> 8.6.1970: Early in the morning inside the kraals we do some exercise in the colour classification of goats and sheep. Then Jean goes into the fields while I follow a herd of cattle. At a waterhole in the company of some young men I try to name the different colour patterns of the animals but my old dilemma persists: I know the names, but cannot distinguish between the patterns and colours. What I call white, a Hamar may call grey, and what I call grey, a Hamar may call brown or yellow, and what I see as stripes, the Hamar see as blots. We obviously "see" differently. A young man chases the herds into the bush and I follow them for an hour and watch them graze. They walk in one direction only and obviously know where they are going, but I don't (Lydall and Strecker 1979a: 12-13).

Typically, knowledge is cultivated during morning or evening conversations around the coffee pot. I have already described this situation in several other publications because it is constitutive for Hamar every-day life. Here is one example where the focus lies on the transmission of knowledge:

> A Hamar elder comes to my mind as he sits opposite a number of younger men drinking coffee in one of the houses of Dambaiti. A coffee bowl stands on the ground in front of him and he leans across the steaming bowl towards the other men; stretching one arm out in a gesture that seems to take hold of each one of them, he emphatically calls out, *"Kansé, kate kansé!"* (Listen, listen well!). Then he speaks and the audience listens. The elder may speak for half an hour, for an hour, or even longer, and as he speaks and

tells his good story he frequently comes back to the same points, uses similar images and generally covers the same ground, going over it again and again from many different angles as his speech unfolds. In this way he not only informs his listeners but actually influences and moulds their views. Or, to put it differently, the repetitiveness and other redundancies act as a tool of persuasion and instil in the listeners not only details and singular occurrences but also, and more importantly, underlying cultural generalities and structures. Furthermore, the repetitiveness leads, so to speak, to addiction, in that the listeners begin to feel that they have still heard too little, that the speaker has in fact missed certain implications of what he has said, implications, which are also true and follow immediately from the premises that made him speak so long in the first place. When the coffee is finished, the youths go down to the dry riverbed and as they wait for the cattle to come to the water-holes, they sit in the shade of a tree and begin to talk again about what was said at the coffee pot (Strecker 1988a: 194-195).

Similar conversations occur in the shade of trees near the waterholes, where during the heat of the day, the herdsmen rest and, in the presence of the ever curious ethnographer, repeat and comment on what the elders have said and then follow their own interests and trains of thought.

A very important place for acquisition and transmission of special knowledge is the cattle or goat enclosure where—surrounded by goats, sheep and cattle—people can converse at length without risk of getting disturbed. Here is an example where, yet again, the knowledge of Hamar herding boys transpires:

When the sun has gone down I sit in the cattle kraal and watch Tsasi milking the cows and Lomoluk and Wollekibu driving the goats into their enclosure. Gino sits down next to me and so do Tsasi and Djobire. We talk about herding and I realise how knowledgeable the boys are. Moreover they talk clearly and freely to me, they don't talk in the muffled manner in which they usually answer questions of older people and in which they tend to express their rejection of authority. This is what Gino has to say about goats: When a young kid loses its mother, it is made to drink from another goat. The herding boy calls the motherless kid by a specific call and soon the kid learns that the call means that it will be led to its foster mother. Sometimes a boy finds several foster mothers for a motherless kid. Just now we have three such kids in our kraal. I ask about male goats and Gino says sadly that the strongest and biggest is dead, slain by a "killer", a male goat whose horns easily wound and kill an opponent in a fight. One day the strong goat and the "killer" goat started fighting with one another. Gino spent all day drawing them apart but in the end, the dangerous one wounded the strong one; one horn went straight through his neck. Gino treated the wound with the leaves of a tree and for several days it looked as if the goat was getting better, but then one day, in the evening, the goat did not return from the bush and was eaten by the hyenas. Did it not return because it was too sick or because it was too proud (*poramo*)? Male goats will turn against you when they are angry, but this is always a bluff, they never really attack. Cattle, however, do attack and may even kill you. Shalombe was attacked by a bull which hurled him into the air and opened an immense gash in his thigh. Bali who was present when Shalombe was attacked took a spear and killed the bull instantly. The ferocity of cattle is also a great asset, for they can defend themselves and their calves against the hyenas. Oxen are especially good as guards, for when the hyenas approach they roar and storm towards them and drive them away. One night, a hyena entered the cattle kraal of Dambaiti and was dragging away a calf when a young ox saw the hyena off even before the men arrived. When the ox had successfully rescued the calf, both the men and the ox inspected the prey of the hyena; the men with their eyes, the ox with his eyes and his nose (Lydall and Strecker 1979a: 119-121).

Drama and the loss of firm ground

Clearly, this conversation reveals a strong sense of drama and delight in entertainment. The ethnographer asks a single question, and immediately the stories begin, one after another, and all explanations are enriched with exciting examples, like Gino's beloved he-goat who was too proud to continue to waste away in the homestead, and the ox, which saved the calf from the teeth of the hyena.

At the same time, however, the ethnographer begins to detect elements that run against the grain of his, or her, studied 'reason'. He-goats are and remain he-goats, and if someone says they are proud (*poramo*), this can only be meant in a figurative, not in a literal sense of the word. But can we really be sure? Could Gino not be more right than we? Could it be, for example, that rather than the animal being given human attributions here, human behaviour is likened to animal behaviour? The he-goat would then be the paragon of *poramo*, of pride that won't be bent. Gino, the Hamar, is expected to walk through life with his head high like his favourite goat, and without fear he should turn against anyone who challenges him.

All domains of Hamar life are characterized by such transitions where people's thoughts seem at first well founded but then, gradually, loose their firm ground, and where, as Paul Grice (1975) would say, conversational maxims are flouted, and the listener is left to complete the hard work of interpretation on his own. I will illustrate this at length in what follows below.

Reading tracks

As we can well imagine, the reading of tracks is part of Hamar every-day life. Anyone who does not know how to read tracks will not find the stock that are lost in the bush, will not find game when hunting, will not detect the scouts before the enemy launches his attack. In other words, without discovering the track you will have no success. So what would be more natural—in anticipation of what is to come—than take to physical possession of a track and claim that its maker is now yours? Like my friend Baldambe who wanted to acquire a second wife: He went to a diviner who advised him to pick up the girl's footprint and bring the dust to his homestead. Soon afterwards the girl arrived at his homestead, "like a calf that had lost its way." I was surprised and confused when I heard this—while Baldambe laughed when he told it.

Listening and interpreting sounds

Without a careful, open ear no one can live competently in Hamar. People always need to listen, especially at night. They listen and hope not to hear the provocative, triumphant howling of hyenas hunting some animal of his herd that went astray in the bush. This seems very reasonable to us. But a Hamar also listens because he wishes not to hear the barking of a jackal at the gateway of his homestead, for this would tell of misfortune bound to arrive at the homestead.

One listens to the sounds of the animals in the enclosures. When they are quiet one feels comforted, but when they are restless and noisy, this means that they are still hungry and want to be lead to new pastures. The animals 'tell' that they are suffering, and that things can't go on like this. This sounds plausible, and we nod in agreement when our Hamar friends explain this to us.

But we shake our heads about the following: Goats, it is said, also listen to our conversations and comment on what we say. So it may happen that while we sit at night by the side of a goat enclosure and engage in conversation, one of us makes an assertion like for example, "Tomorrow we won't have rain." If at the same moment a goat produces one of its characteristic loud sneezes, one of the group will unfailingly be quick to retort, "No, my friend, haven't you heard the goat. There will be rain tomorrow after all."

We also find it at least a bit surprising when people say that livestock and children know in advance when sickness will enter the homestead. This observation may in fact be true and can be put empirically to the test, but statements like the following seem rather strange and hard to agree to:

> 18.9.1971: Baldambe tells me that he was bothered one night when Theo was crying badly. Why was he crying? He was not ill. He sensed that there was illness coming in his family. "You see, now Jean has fallen sick." Theo was like the cattle and goats who also sense sickness: "When the cattle walk straight home, the bells ringing strongly and regularly, that's a good sign, but if the herds don't want to enter the gateway, when they have to be driven in by repeated hitting, that's a bad sign, then there will be illness." (Lydall and Strecker 1979a: 52-53).

It is even more irritating when someone asserts that he not only knows the hidden meanings of certain sounds, but can hear what will happen in the future. Here is one passage from my notebooks that has already served as a key example in other texts concerned with knowledge, power and the puzzles of meaning:

> *Gemarro's fist of knowledge*: I sit with Gemarro in front of his house and we are talking. I think I hear far away a truck making its way through the bush and ask Gemarro whether he too hears it. He does not answer but blows the warm air from his mouth into his hand, then turns the palm into a closed fist and moves it to his right ear where he then slightly opens it again. Through the cylindrical hole he listens intensely and after a while turns around to me with his typical fox-like smile: "Brother-in-law, my ear is bad, it hears only the truth, it hears whether someone is going to live or die." No further explanation follows, and also no further comment on what he is hearing just now. As so often before, I feel let down. Knowledge is so personal and hazardous, so political and antithetical that no systematic line opens itself for inquiry.

There are some basic axioms concerning the prophetical properties of the planets, the clouds, etc., but the evaluation of the cosmos is a matter of individual psychology and is motivated, as I have said above, by political antithesis: if a political opponent uses the stars to support his point you yourself use them to support your point. When Gemarro shows me his fist, which increases the power of his ear, this acts like a test by which he finds out how far he has influence over me, how far I would accept his bid for greater power. Baldambe, rather like Gemarro, is also constantly operating with such individually usurped super-knowledge. Whenever it seems possible in an argument, he forces his specific points on what he thinks is significant in the sky on to the listeners. He does this, of course, not modestly but by means of outright assertions. And yet there is no end to plausible interpretations of the sky, not only because the combinations of the known stars and other phenomena are innumerable but also because all objective phenomena are thought to have a subjective motivation. So Baldambe can say: "There will be rain in this month because the sun will only go to rest in her hole (which she reaches on 21st December) if rain has cooled and softened it. The sun will only reach her hole when rain has fallen." So the sun is not an objective measure of climate and season if the personal knowledge of a Hamar wants it not to be so. At another moment, however, it is, and Baldambe will say that no one should plant before the sun has reached its "hole". You can be sure that when he says this he has some political reason for it, the motive to establish a social hierarchy in which he ranks at the top and is accepted as a decision-maker. All this works because everybody agrees that there is knowledge to be gained in the sky (and elsewhere) for him who is capable of catching it. The general discussions of the seasons, the weather, disease, hunger, war, etc., in terms of what the sky says, which I have witnessed so often, are like psycho-social experiments in the assessment and also in the exercise of personal power within the group, and it is interesting to note that some of those who keep quiet (offer no affirmation or rival interpretations) in one composition of the group are leading interpreters in other situations when the group is composed differently. Part of all is the constant abuse of knowledge of others. Either it is useful to you, and you steal it from the others, pretending the interpretation derives from yourself, or you dismiss it as false. Leaders especially like to slander one another in this way. Thus Gemarro, shortly after he has told me about the power of his fist, says that Wuancho, who like himself is a traditional spokesman of our area, is a goat and does not know anything." (Strecker 1988a: 197-198)

The weather and the stars have already played a role in "Gemarro's Fist of Knowledge", but I will deal with the discourse about these topics at length below because they play a central role in Hamar rhetorics of knowledge.

Observing and predicting the weather

All of us know the weather as a topic of conversation where the mind quickly moves from the evident and assured to what is more uncertain and hidden. One begins by saying, "what a beautiful morning", or "what ugly weather", and then continues, "but I don't think it will last," or "just wait, and you will see the sky clear up." Then one may offer further views and arguments that are grounded in traditional knowledge that is not easy to substantiate and often is expressed in proverbs such as "Red sky at night, shepherd's delight", "Red sky in the morning, sailor's warning", and the like.

Rain falls very unevenly in Hamar. It 'stands' on, as the saying goes, only one of a cow's horns, because there won't be enough for the other. Rain builds up (*woissa*) in grey columns under the gigantic white, and often also black, cumulus clouds, but it does not 'stand' on two or more legs, but simply on one.

In order to observe the course of the rains, the Hamar like to live on mountain ridges from where they can see far and wide, and can follow the drama of approaching rains that all too often veer off at the very last moment, bypassing them and leaving their homestead and surrounding pastures as dry and parched as before. From here they also follow the 'tracks of the rain' and deduce where in the future their herds will find grass and water. This, I am sure, everyone will find reasonable. We also can tune in with the hopes and fears that the Hamar show on such occasions, yet here we enter spheres were we gradually loose the firm ground provided by what we call 'knowledge'.

But hopes and fears are part of our lives. They are 'object-ively' necessary for us to master our lives. But what measure of hope and fear is appropriate in any given situation? As there is no easy answer, it quickly happens that one fear follows on another. A floodgate of fear opens, as it were, like I recorded in my diary:

8.7.1973: During the evening as we sit in front of Ginonda's house drinking coffee and talking, grey clouds collect all over Hamar and it begins to rain, heavy rain everywhere. This is good for the fields, there will be a harvest after all ... But Baldambe and old Zinu, who are sitting with us, are quick to point out the negative aspect of the rains: While it rains, the people hide in their houses and the crops become easy prey for the monkeys. Moreover, if it rains continuously for a long period, the heads of the sorghum plants will turn bad and will only be usable for beer. The rains are most dangerous for the cattle and the goats. If a day starts bright and without a sign of rain, the herds are driven far away, so that should heavy rains suddenly begin to fall, they will not be able to return home because of the roaring floods which quickly fill the dry river beds. Blocked by the floods, they will have to stay over night in the bush and thus become an easy prey for the hyenas. Their owner is not able to reach them to protect them, because he himself is cut off from them by the floods. Furthermore, he is unable to hear their bells because of the roaring of the floods and the drumming of the rain. In this connection, Baldambe complains about the contemporary settlement pattern. In the olden days, the homesteads stayed put on the same ridge for many years. In this way, the cattle would always find their way home. Today, people live dispersed in the bush and are continually changing their place of residence. So the cattle never really get used to a place and consequently don't find their way home under difficult circumstances. Yet another danger of the rains is that they soften the thorn fences of the cattle camps, making it easy for the hyenas to enter. After each prolonged rain down at Kizo, they lose a couple of goats or sheep. This is why the Hamar don't like long-lasting, slow rains, although they acknowledge their value for the fields. What they really like are the thunderstorms in which heavy clouds burst over a limited area for a limited period of time (Lydall/ Strecker 1979a: 151-152).

As can be expected, it is the aged who are prone to voice worries, for they know from many years of experience how some things that first seem beneficial later turn out to be detrimental. Zinu's and Baldambe's commentaries were also partly directed at the Ethnographer who had suggested that a grey sky with soft, continuous Atlantic rains would be exactly what the Hamar needed. But fertile as it may be, continuous rain hold many dangers: the baboons devastate the fields; the ripening crops begin to mould; the herds and herding boys do not find their way home; hyenas find it easy to pass through the thorn fences that have turned soft and soggy, and so on.

The limited, erratic, unpredictable rainfall in Hamar entails not only physical but also social dangers as my notes show:

29.12.1973: ... There have recently been some clouds and a few localised showers of rain have fallen, accompanied by thunder and lightning. The rain, or rather the possibility of rain, was enough to make Alma hurry and set fire to his field even though Ginonda's field, which borders his, has not yet been completely cut. Ginonda pointed this out to him, but Alma went ahead with burning his field. And then the fire did not burn well. Baldambe attributes this to the fact that Alma did not consult the sandal oracle, which would have determined the right day to burn the field. So, the sandal oracle always comes in when there are important decisions to make. Perhaps its function is mainly to obstruct rash decision-making. It seems to me like an institutionalized pause for reflection before action. Usually therefore this reflection involves not only the actor but other people as well. This latent conflict relating to the fields makes me reflect on the comparative strength of the office of "priest" (*gudili*), even today when other offices, such as the *parko* for example, have become less significant. The "priest's" function consists mainly of blessing the fields and ensuring the rains and the growth of the crops. But he also blesses the people. Why do they need his blessing? Not only because of their individual sufferings and illnesses, but also because of these latent conflicts perhaps. The fields bring together people who otherwise live apart and their mutually conflicting interests give rise to quarrels and anger at times, as for example, in the definition of borders, the timing of the burning of freshly cut bush, the stealing of crops, the timing of letting the herds into the fields to eat the dry sorghum stalks and so on (Lydall and Strecker 1979a: 224-225).

This discourse is conducted in a 'rational' mode that we find compatible with our 'scientific' thinking. Alma should not yet have burnt his field. He should have known that it was still too early. But the argument begins to assume 'irrational' dimensions when Alma's mistake lies not in the wrong timing of his field but in his neglect of the sandal oracle. He should have consulted a diviner. This kind of 'displacement' tends to occur when existential worries increase, feelings of helplessness rise and people search for guides of action that are incompatible with our scientific understanding of knowledge.

What the stars tell

Obviously, the heavenly bodies rule our life, most of all the sun, and as the sun rules over nature it also rules over society. It does this in manifold ways, depending on local and cultural circumstances, and in Hamar, for example, one can often hear calls like, "*nanato, dabaté, aino utidine*"(children get up, the sun has already risen); "*nanato, kulla wushaté, aino oididine*" (children, water the goats, the sun is getting hot), and so on.

Not just the day, but the whole year is governed by the sun. Everything is in one way or other influenced by the sun, and our scientific sentiment does not object to this observation.

Our 'rational', 'scientific' thought also agrees that in principal all other heavenly bodies, the moon, the planets, fix stars, and distant constellations may influence life on earth, even though these influences may be hard to measure and detect. Therefore, if the Hamar say that the stars influence the weather and herewith also human life, this is fully acceptable to us, rational. But then the Hamar go on and attribute the stars with meanings and influences that offend our 'rationality'. Here are a number of examples that relate thematically and bring out the main points before I finally embark on an interpretation. To facilitate orientation, I give each example a title:

(1) Rain and the protective male star:

It is afternoon. A bank of rain clouds which "stood" over Simbale and emptied itself there, found its way to Dambaiti and scattered a few drops here. The moist ground sparkles, the birds call and there is a beautiful afternoon light. To the south, towards Assile and Galapha, the sky is black and heavy thunder grumbles continuously… Kairambe calls to me in between the thunder, "Tomorrow they will be planting their fields in Assile and Galapha!" He adds that such early rain is particularly good for the southern regions because if the main rains come late, the fields in the south often dry up before the crops have time to ripen. Kairambe does not know whether he should go ahead with the burning of his field or not. There has been rain now in some parts of Hamar, but learned old Sago has said that there won't be much early rain since the male star has moved south of his wife's position "to protect her from the dangers of the south", from drought, hunger and war (Lydall/Strecker 1979a: 231-232).

(2) Stars sitting at a public meeting:

As evening comes I sit outside in front of the house on my cowhide. Soon the goats will come and later the cattle. Already even before it really gets dark, the moon and the male and female stars become visible. They have been "sitting in a semi-circle as in a public meeting" and that means trouble. They would not sit together like this if everything in the country were fine, for then there would be no reason to hold a meeting (Lydall/Strecker 1979a: 226).

(3) Conflicting interpretations:

At night we watch the new moon as we drink coffee. It stands right above the evening star and Baldambe says this means there will be trouble ahead. But when I ask old Kolmo what it means he insists on the contrary: there will be good luck (*barjo*) in the country (Lydall/Strecker 1979a: 142).

(4) Individualized celestial knowledge:

In the morning we have coffee in Aikenda's house. Baldambe is absent, but there are guests like Choke's friend Wualle Lokarimoi and Kula the "black". They say that the position of the stars indicates hard times ahead. While listening to the conversation, it strikes me that Hamar astronomical knowledge is mainly related to the period just before sunrise and just after sunset. It would appear that the position, which the stars occupy, then is decisive. The points at which the sun appears and disappears are also crucial because the "holes" where the sun "rests", predict the plenitude or scarcity of future rains. A second point is how *individualized* all astronomical knowledge is. Everyone has particular observations to make. Each man puts them forward with much force and mystique, yet no one attempts any systematic account of the various astral phenomena. For me, this reflects the social structure. Knowledge is generally individualized and specific (Lydall/Strecker 1979a: 227-228).

(5) Obsession with the sky:

This is truly the last day of the "mad" month. One thin, red sickle of a moon appeared just before sunrise and it vanished in the brightening sky a couple of minutes after it appeared. Yes, I have caught the Hamar obsession with the sky. I refer to the desire to extract something of personal significance from the signs of the sky. The sky speaks of death this morning. I don't look at the sky to understand it "objectively"... The Hamar taught me... that one has to decipher the sky in an individual and creative manner. One has to create categories of meaning as the interpretation develops. He who is most imaginative and sees the most striking correlations between the configurations of the sky and the events of the day will gain in stature and increase his power to control social affairs. Not only Baldambe and Wualle but also Choke and Banko have repeatedly referred to Berimba as someone who became a great leader because he could read the sky. People would keep their herds close to him because, observing the sky, he could predict what was going to happen (Lydall/Strecker 1979a: 270-71).

(6) Falling stars:

When night comes I sit in the goat kraal and watch the usual turmoil of goats, kids and children. Watching Ginonda I realise that she has become slim. Still she likes herding the goats. It feeds her with experiences that go beyond the small homestead and every evening when she returns she has new stories to tell which she picked up whilst herding and watering the goats. Under the clear, starry sky we drink coffee. I do some of the talking for a change and describe how light and sound travel. Then I get on to a theme which interests me very much: I say that customs are like language, arbitrary and beyond good or bad. Wadu likes the sweet part of it, the one that implies that Hamar customs should not be criticised. But the part which implies that no one's metaphysical constructs should be taken seriously, he finds sour and disagreeable. Baldambe insists that there is more than just talk to metaphysics, because the falling stars so obviously predict disaster. He argues that one day I myself will come to read the language of the stars and this will persuade me to acknowledge that there is a mysterious cause to all that is happening in the world around us (Lydall/Strecker 1979a: 211-212).

These examples speak, mostly, for themselves, including observations and remarks that, though not central, nevertheless pertain to the topic of local knowledge, like the lines about Ginonda who enjoyed the strenuous task of herding goats because it involved many events and adventures that provided ample material for interesting stories in the evening.

Example (1) combines the topics of weather and stars in a revealing way. We witness how carefully Kairambe observes the rainfall from a distance and intelligently reflects about the effects of an early onset of the rainy season. But should he burn his field already now and begin to plant tomorrow? He does not know and cannot say for certain whether the rains will last and be sufficient to allow the crops to grow. He has even consulted old Sago, diviner and storehouse of traditional knowledge, and was told that one could not trust the weather because the 'male' star (Jupiter) had moved 'below' (south) of the position of his wife, the 'female' star (Venus) who he is to protect against dangers coming from the South, against drought, hunger, and war.

In (1) we have an example of the modality and breadth of Kairambe's knowledge. One part of the world he sees with his own eyes and therefore knows something about it; another part (ecological developments in the South of the country) he deduces, basing his arguments on earlier first hand knowledge of the South; he is uncertain about some things (he knows that he can't know for certain whether there will be enough rain); and finally there is something he is unsure of (he does not know whether the diviner is right or not). Therefore we can say that Kairambe does not only behave rationally, he also shows considerable calm in a situation that seems in fact to be quite precarious.

Example (2) concerns an early evening when I sat in front of my house and observed the moon, Venus and Jupiter, remarking that the stars and the moon had for quite some time already been "sitting in a semi-circle as if they were holding a public meeting". This meant misfortune, for they would have no reason to hold such long deliberations, if everything was well in the country. The text is written in a plain and distancing style pretending as if stating some simple facts. But at the same time it is ironic, for I pretended that evening to have become a true Hamar *donza* (elder), who uses the constellation of heavenly bodies to interpret the present and forecast the future.

In (3) I note two different interpretations of one and the same phenomenon. The moon stands directly above Venus, and while Baldambe argues that this means misfortune, old Kolmo suggests that this constellation speaks of good luck. Here, as in (2), the simple style of presentation is deceptive and hides the ethnographer's shortcomings. Instead of asking my friends how both interpretations might in some way be right, I conceitedly tell myself that both must be wrong and accordingly learn nothing more about the matter.

Example (4) shows once more how important the coffee pot is in Hamar. Innumerable conversations develop around it in which local knowledge is transmitted and discussed, and figures of speech are cultivated. Three *anamo* (age-mates) converse with each other on this morning. None of them makes much use of plain style, for this would bore the others. Also, as they are equals they like to indulge in rivalry. Therefore, they make use of all their rhetorical skills and figures such as hyperbole, simile, metaphor, synecdoche, metonymy and irony. This means that an outsider finds it difficult to understand the exchanges, especially when the *anamo* converse about the sky and what it augurs for the future.

Also, here we witness again how no one really aims for consensus. The undeterminable provides the opportunity for discussions that allow a demonstration of mental and emotional alertness, brilliance, superiority, and ultimately a claim for social power.

In example (5) I too have been caught by an obsession with the sky and begin to detect the signs of death in the thin, red sickle of the dying moon and in the configuration of the stars. These were the days when the Hamar departed, thousands of them, to raid the Arbore with whom they had earlier been friends. Baldambe's sons and nephews and many of our friends are also among them. We are worried about them and project our fear into the sky. Already the day before I had observed how Baldambe and his friend Wualle had interpreted the sky:

> Just before sunrise the sky is extremely red over Arbore to the east. The fading red sickle of the "mad moon" also hangs low over Arbore. Baldambe and the two old men who stayed as guests over night move as black figures on the backdrop of the red sky. Baldambe holds Wualle's hands, then points to the clouds and interprets them for Wualle. I can't hear what he is saying; only when they turn around to dive into the house for coffee, do I hear Baldambe say, "If that which I have said is not true, I am not the son of Berinas." (Lydall/Strecker 1979a: 267-268).

Example (6) has at last the dialogical character without which, as I have said above, no good understanding of others and therefore also no good ethnography can develop. Again night has fallen, again we sit under the star lit sky, again we drink coffee, and again we are all interwoven in conversation. After I have tried to explain how, according to my under-standing, light and sound travel, I arrive at my favourite topic, cultural relativism. Old Wadu and also Baldambe enjoy when I say that no one should object to Hamar customs, but when I question the ultimate validity of their world-view, for example their idea that stars can 'tell' you something, they don't accept this and say that I have simply not stayed long enough yet in Hamar to be able to know. If I were to remain longer, the stars themselves would convince me that they speak of approaching misfortune.

In other words, at that time I was not yet fully in tune with Hamar traditions, and I lacked what Tedlock and Mannheim have called the 'collusion' between conversational partners who comply with each other and interpret events within a jointly shared frame of reference (1955: 13). Collusion is a prerequisite for tradition and shared local knowledge. In my early years of field-work I did not speak (and in fact never had heard) of collusion, but thought in terms of *recourse to historical authority* instead:

> At night while Bali speaks to us sitting on our cowhides, more and more young men join us and listen with quiet intensity... An audience materializes almost inaudibly, making the speaker feel that he is saying something, which they value highly. And then slowly the members of the audience sitting in darkness start to speak themselves. Their speeches are long and are listened to by the assembled company. They constantly invoke the "old", the "fathers", the "older brothers" and refer to the "precedents" of which I have talked above. There is a confidence and trust in the old and the established which has never seemed to me quite so marked before (although I realise now that it has always been there). I suddenly realise that here may lie one of the keys to understanding Hamar "conservatism" and (paradoxically?) its "anarchy". The cattle camps play a big part in the socialization of the young men. Here, to a large extent, they are free from the strict domination of the elders. Here they have to make their own decisions, and these decisions are made on the basis of precedents, by referring to what the great men of the past would have done in such-and-such a situation. By invoking a precedent the speaker almost becomes the historical person himself, so by invoking *historical authority* they reject the *present authority* of others. One might argue that Hamar anarchy is a result of the fact that everybody rejects a living person's decision if it is based on purely individual and contemporary judgment. Outright individual cleverness and power are taboo and no one may openly aspire to them. Instead one must make a precedent of an incident in the historic past which will be acknowledged by others as offering the appropriate answer to a specific problem in the present (Lydall/Strecker 1979a: 249-250).

Conclusion

Tedlock and Mannheim write in *The Dialogic Emergence of Culture*: "Ethnography, then, is a peculiar kind of dialogue and a peculiar zone of emergence, at once constitutive of and constituted by radical cultural difference" (1995:15). In this essay I have tried to put some of this program of dialogical ethnography into practice by fathoming the possibilities and limits of trans-cultural understanding. It appears that the greatest obstacles were the differing premises on which the Hamar and I would base our thoughts, words and deeds.

Baldambe and his friends argued that if I stayed long enough in Hamar I would change my premises. But now for more than thirty years I have come and gone without ever being able to change my deeply ingrained cultural premises, and I still feel that one cannot properly answer such basic threats as drought, hunger and war by turning to the stars and divining their meaning.

Here I refuse to follow my Hamar friends. But I also do the same at home in Western culture where I don't accept that someone thinks in one context rationally (scientifically), but prays in another context to "the Lord, our Father" and begs him for help. In fact, I feel much closer to my Hamar friends who detest every sort of social hierarchy and do not try to split their thought into 'science' and 'religion'. They have no god, devil, sin, shame, master or serf, and they don't really care for any of the inventions of 'high culture' and 'civilisation'. Instead they, or rather their forebears, have developed a world-view that unites culture and nature in a continuous process of creation. The whole cosmos, the heavenly bodies, the Earth and all that is on it contain that which gives them their ideal, harmonic form of being. This is *barjo* (good fortune, luck, well-being). Anything that has no *barjo* must die and vanish. The prototype of *barjo* is the star-studded sky, especially the Milky Way (*sabe*), master trope of infinity, plenitude, harmony and permanence. But also each blade of grass, each fly, each river, each mountain has its own *barjo*, and—of course—each human being. Old persons have especially strong *barjo* that is manifest in their old age, and it is the aged who have the task to call forth *barjo* over and over again in order to ensure the harmonic continuance of life.

According to Baldambe, the calling forth of *barjo* also affects the stars, for the *parko* (ritual expert) can call them to return to their proper positions:

> This is the ritual of the *parko*, the one who has a forked staff and looks after the country. The one who, if the stars forebode hard times, sits on the *boaka* with the elders and brings the stars back with his forked staff: "May the stars not go off course, bring them back with the forked staff. May the stars not go to the left, may they not go to Korre, nor to Borana. Bring them back, back towards Aari country, to the mountains." So the elders and the *parko* call together, and with *barjo* the stars come back for them (Lydall and Strecker 1979b: 19).

This, no doubt, is a proud attitude, even hubris. But not a bent, twisted, contradictory hubris, which on the one side practices science and on the other side proclaims that all drought, hunger and war derive from the benevolent hand of God.

Meanings and rhetoric of the *barjo aela*

The Hamar who are the southernmost group of Omotic speaking populations in Ethiopia have an institution they call the *barjo aela*. When a *barjo aela* is performed, men get together and chant. One of them, usually the oldest, leads, and the others repeat the last word of each phrase. Here is an example:

The rain shall fall,	fall (*hanshe*)
the children shall play,	play (*yege*)
the plants shall smell good,	smell good (*game*)
the rains shall lie in puddles,	lie (*kate*)
the rain shall turn into plants,	turn (*mate*)
the herds shall enter the homestead,	enter (*arde*)
the flood water shall flow upwards,	flow (*mirse*)
(it shall be like) butter,	butter (*bodi*)
rain,	rain (*dobi*)
well-being,	well-being (*nagaia*)
sickness shall go away,	go away (*yi'e*)
it shall fall like a dried up leaf,	fall (*pille*)
away,	away (*wollall*)
	(Strecker 1979b)

The verb *aela* resembles the English term 'call', for as in Hamar, in English one may say "go and call so-and-so", meaning "go and tell so-and-so to come". This calling may be done very politely as when one invites or requests someone to come, or more authoritatively as when one orders or commands another to come. Given this meaning of *aela* the question arises what is meant by *barjo*. Who or what is *barjo* that it can be called to come?

Barjo may be the spoken word

The Hamar say, "*apho barjo ne*" (the word is *barjo*) like in the following example: One evening Baldambe was sitting in his hut drinking coffee and blessing the homestead of Dambati. He said: "My father used to call *barjo*, my ancestors used to call *barjo*. I inherited the word from my father, I inherited the word from my ancestors. Let *barjo* herd my father's cattle, my father's goats, my father's children, well, well, well..." (Strecker 1979a: 4). Baldambe means here that the word, which he has inherited, the *barjo aela*, is itself *barjo*.

Barjo may be some kind of substance

Sometimes, when the Hamar speak of *barjo*, one gets the impression that they are speaking of something which is an aspect of substance, as in the following example where Baldambe tells of a thief who fearing that he will get killed by the elders, saves himself through marriage. Upon marriage, the wife's *barjo* enters a man, and to harm him would therefore mean to harm his wife also. So the elders do not kill the thief, saying: "Stop! Even if he is a thief the girl's *barjo* is joined to him as if he had eaten her..." (Lydall/Strecker 1979b: 156)

Yet again, at a moment of crisis within the small community of Dambaiti one woman reprimands the others saying: "Leave the talk, drink your water quietly, and put your *barjo* into your heart..." (Strecker 1979a: 166).

The statement that someone's *barjo* has vanished or finished when he has died, may be interpreted as referring to some kind of substance. People say "*barjo kissa makab*" (his *barjo* has finished) almost in the same way as we say: "His life has finished", where it remains open what precisely we mean by the word 'life'.

People may be *barjo*

I first noticed that people may be *barjo* when one day an old Hamar woman came to me and said: "*Inta edi gibi ne, inta barjo ne, tampon inne ima*" (I am a big [i.e. senior] person, I am *barjo*, give me some tobacco).

Big, important people like the ritual leaders of Hamar (the *bitta*) or one's mother's brothers may be referred to as *barjo edi* (*barjo* people), much as in the following example where the term *barjo* is extended to the modern Ethiopian government. One day my friend Lomotor told me what was said at a recent public meeting where the Hamar and Dassanech tried to make peace:

> "*Ya, 'mengist ainu' amata? Pogamo assa. Har aiaya? Ta mengist gon dalkab. Bairo mengist*" (*Ya*, 'who is the Government?' didn't you say this? That's your falseness. What have you achieved? Now the Government has spoken truly [i.e. has shown its power]. The Government is *barjo*) (Strecker 1979b: 5).

Animals may have *barjo*

Livestock partake of their owners' *barjo*. So Baldambe tells of a Hamar custom where milk gourds are sent to the ritual leader (*bitta*) so that he may bless the whole country with the milk, which has come to him from all over the country. But the milk from some cattle should not be brought to him. These cattle are those of the magically powerful clans of Misha and Ba Gumpo. The people of Misha and Ba Gumpo once fought with the *bitta*, wounded him and killed one of his family. Therefore they and their cattle are said to have no *barjo*, at least in relation to the *bitta* (Lydall/Strecker 1979b: 12).

Plants may be *barjo*

Certain plants may be spoken of as being *barjo* plants as in the following instruction about marriage: "Ask an elder whom you call 'father' to be your marriage go-between. Tell him to take a staff of *baraza* (Grewia mollis Juss.) which is a *barjo* tree, and to ask for a girl" (Lydall/Strecker 1979b:8). One of the *barjo* plants most central to Hamar culture is coffee. One evening Baldambe blessed his homestead like this: "This coffee which my friend Theoimba brought from Konso, let it speak well for my father's homestead, let it speak well, let it speak well (Strecker 1979a: 4). The coffee, being a *barjo* plant is here understood as being able to cause wellbeing. I have already pointed out how the 'word' may be *barjo*. The *barjo* of the spoken word is increased when accompanied by a mouthful of coffee, which is then sprayed from the lips... "*Psssss*".

In some rituals a number of whole coffee beans (most often four of them) are used. Thus Baldambe explains how coffee beans are put down by the *gudili* (ritual guardian of the fields) at the edge of the field in order to protect it against the baboons, ground squirrels and other animals: "Grandfather", says the *gudili* as he deposits the coffee beans, "stop the baboon, you are the *barjo* plant" (Lydall/Strecker 1979b: 165).

Things may be *barjo*

In certain rituals people have to sit on a cowhides which are *barjo*. "They prepare the *binyere* (a ritual necklace) in the cattle kraal sitting on a goat-cow hide which is *barjo*" (Op. Cit. 145). A goat-cow is a cow which has been purchased in exchange for goats, and the hide of a goat-cow is *barjo* only once the rituals of the goat-cow have been completed.

Places may be *barjo*

Baldambe describes how a young man, as part of his transition rites, is cleansed in a dry river bed which is *barjo*: "Then he runs off, over to a gully, a *barjo* gully... (where) the washer washes the *ukuli* (the initiate) with sand... he washes away all badness" (Op. Cit.: 81). A *barjo* gully is one within the sacred boundaries of Hamar, and one where the sand has not been disturbed by man or beast.

Water and grass may be *barjo*

People talk of healthy and beneficial water and grass as *barjo noko* (*barjo* water) and *barjo shudi* (*barjo* grass). The owner of an animal may give it to his age-mates or stock associates, relatives etc. saying that the animal is good for them to eat because it has consumed *barjo* water and *barjo* grass (Op. Cit.: 30).

Body parts may be *barjo*

In some contexts the vagina is referred to as *barjo goiti*, which means *barjo* path.

Barjo may be some kind of invisible subject or agent

In some cases people use the term *barjo* as if *barjo* was a kind of invisible and undefined subject or agent (without any indication of gender) that has the power to give, as in the following:

For a girl, *barjo* tells her about birth, her parents don't tell her (Op. Cit.: 70).

There is no one who says that the earth has a mother who gave birth to it. The one who put down the land is *barjo* (Op. Cit.: 163).

According to Baldambe in olden days the Hamar elders would sometimes forcefully take a girl and give her to their ritual leader (*bitta*) in marriage, saying:

"*Bitta*, here is the girl. Bring cattle to her father."

And the *bitta* would then answer:

"I won't refuse. Even though I am the *bitta* I will give what is the custom. *Barjo* gave that girl to her father, may she bear children for me" (Op. Cit.: 10).

Barjo is a state of wellbeing

The most general use of *barjo*, which also explains all the particular usages enumerated so far, is to indicate (and induce) a state of wellbeing, luck, good fortune. To give some examples: During his life, a mother's brother repeatedly calls *barjo* for his sister's sons. For this they thank and honour him at his funeral.

"The dead man", explains Baldambe, "used to call *barjo* for his sister's sons like this:

'May the Mursi not see you, may the lion not see you ... Instead may you kill a lion, may you kill a Mursi.' Thus he used to call forth *barjo*, you see. So now the sister's sons get up saying:

'Our mother's brother has died ... Yesterday an our behalf he called 'may your eyes be quite sharp'" (Op. Cit.: 52).

According to Baldambe the founding ancestor of Hamar instructed the people, saying:

"When the bees have come the honey will ripen. When it is ripe, bring honey to the *bitta* so that he may call forth the *barjo* of your cattle and the *barjo* of your goats, and that he may get rid of sickness for you" (Op. Cit.: 8).

One description of a *barjo aela* sums up the wellbeing that is invoked as follows:

"The *bitta* takes hold of the (goat's) foreleg and calls for sickness to depart, and calls forth the *barjo* of the cattle: 'May the grass smell sweet, may the water smell good, may the cow hides become good, may they smell good like *karko* (Ocimum canum L.), may they be soft like *gali* (Ipomoea spatulata Hall.) leaves'" (Op. Cit.: 133).

Only people who have well-being can call well-being:

When the honey wine is ready, the elders are called and enter the *bitta's* house, and holding a right-handed drinking bowl they call *barjo*. Some elders are feeble, feeble, feeble, only the bright, bright, bright ones take part. They call the cattle *barjo*, the goat *barjo*, the sorghum *barjo*: "May the sorghum ripen, may the cattle multiply, may the sickness go away" (Op. Cit.: 18).

To close with an example which involved my own *barjo* in Hamar. One day I noted in my diary:

I put the car under a tree last night. This morning Choke realised that one set of wheels had just passed between two extremely hard and jagged tree stumps which could have cut the tyres open

if I had driven over them. Choke points to the tread mark between the stumps, "you always ask what *barjo* means. This is
barjo" (Lydall and Strecker 1979a: 255).

The *barjo aela* as a rhetorical strategy

As we have seen, the term *barjo* (or the alternative term *bairo*)
has many aspects. There is no room here to fully explore the
concept of *barjo*. But let me indicate, by way of conclusion, how
the *barjo aela* may be explained as a rhetorical strategy. I
summarize my argument in eleven points:

1. Hamar culture is based on a diverse economy (some slash
    and burn cultivation, herds of goats, sheep and cattle, bee
    keeping, some hunting and gathering). The economy does
    not need large corporate groups but rather encourages
    individualism and a lot of spatial mobility. The goats on
    which people depend, especially in times of drought, allow
    a quick build-up of herds and don't need large social groups
    for long term planning and insurance against personal loss.
    Rather, the management of goats is better achieved by a
    multitude of small, largely independent units who in times
    of crisis lend each other support.
2. The basic agents in Hamar politics are the *donza* (married
    men) of a settlement area who act collectively and are
    likened to a certain grass (*zarsi*), which reticulates over the
    ground.
3. A *donza* may leave his neighbourhood freely and join
    another whenever he wants. In fact, economic reasons often
    make such movements necessary (see above).
4. According to the *donza*, they carry their *barjo* with them
    wherever they go. Whenever it seems necessary to exercise
    some specific control over the world the *donza* get together
    and call *barjo* (*barjo aela*).
5. Seniority is an important factor, which distinguishes
    between different *donza*. The greatest authority in a home-
    stead (*dele*) always lies with the oldest living brother

(*djalepha*) of the sibling group. When older and younger brothers are present at a *barjo aela* it is always the older one who performs the 'calling' while the younger ones, together with the other *donza* provide the echo.

6. In various ways the *donza* delegate the *barjo aela* to specific persons, for example to the *gudili* (guardian of the fields), *kogo* (guardian of the herds) and the *bitta* (guardian of Hamar country).

7. Hamar society has no centralized social structure. The two *bitta* (who may have had more actual power than they have today) can in no way be called 'king' or 'chief'. In the same way as there is no single centralized structure, there is also no 'God' to whom people would 'pray'.

8. If the term *barjo* sometimes seems to mean a substance which one shares, sometimes seems to refer to an immanent power to live, sometimes indicates simply a general state of well-being or the specific well-being which goes with a person, animal, plant or object etc., then this lack of distinction and the openness of the concept go very well with the absence of any single locus and mode of social power in Hamar.

9. Although Hamar social structure is not centralized there still exist some basic hierarchies. It is within these hierarchies that the concept of *barjo* and the practice of the *barjo aela* function.

10. Who tries to control whom in Hamar may be seen by who calls *barjo* for whom. It is the older, married men who call *barjo* for the young, the women, the livestock, bees, and by extension, the whole world around them. Women and children are not allowed to call *barjo*.

11. The *barjo aela* is a brilliant rhetorical strategy because it does two important things at once: it allows the men to exercise control over others while inhibiting the control of others over themselves.

Magic and the rhetorical will

Theoretical orientation

Arthur Schopenhauer was the first to point out that the primary source of insight, reasoning and knowledge is the human *will*. In response to Descartes and Kant, he wrote:

> Will is first and original; knowledge follows in second place as a tool belonging to the phenomenon of will. Therefore every person is what he is through his will, and his character is original, for willing is basis of his nature. Through the knowledge which comes later he learns in the course of experience *what* he is, *i.e.*, he gets to his character. Thus he *knows* himself in consequence of and in accordance with the nature of his will, instead of (as the old view would have it) *willing* in consequence of, and in accordance with knowing (Schopenhauer, 1995: 191-192).

This primacy of the *will*, which Schopenhauer has stressed so emphatically, underlies the basic human propensity for magic, characterised by Julian Huxley as follows:

> Magic, in the strict anthropological sense, is based on the belief that both nature and man can be brought under compulsion and controlled by psychological means through spells, incantations, prayer, sacrifice, and special personal or professional powers. Magic systems are logical, but not rational: they are based on the non-rational premises of primitive projective thinking and may continue to be believed in even where the rational-empirical approach has produced efficient new technological results: e.g. crop fertility rituals as necessary backing for Neolithic agricultural techniques.

> Magical belief-rituals survive and play a part even in the highest and most scientific cultures of today. They survive in our

superstitions, our Polycrates complexes, our compulsion neuroses, in our reliance on the sacred force of oaths and on religious as against civil ceremonies for baptism and marriage, in our hero-worship and our devotion to political and religious leaders, and in pilgrimage and petitionary prayer. And when we say that we are 'under the spell' of beauty or great music, or call a view of a work of art 'magical', we are acknowledging the existence of magic, in the extended sense of non-rational, emotional and often un-conscious formalizing or patterning forces, which are essential for all transcendent experience. Instead of rejecting these forces or pretending that they do not exist, we must explore them and ritualize them to best advantage (Huxley 1966: 264-265).

Magic in this extended sense abounds in human life. All and everything that we value highly may be said to have a magical quality. But although "unconscious formalizing or patterning forces" may underlie magic, 'spell-binding' is first and foremost subject to the rhetorical will.

Stanley Tambiah, has explicated this in his famous lecture on *The Magical Power of Words* where he argues that because the Trobriand Islanders know of the ever-present magical power of beauty they beautify themselves by magical means. Beginning with Roman Jacobson's distinction between metaphorical and metonymical forms of expression, he has shown how the beauty of magic, and also ritual, derives from a rhetorical use of metaphors and metonymies:

Both linguistic procedures, metaphorical through substitution permitting abstractions, and metonymic through building an organic whole through details, are accompanied in Trobriand magic by action. Objects and substances are used as agents and vehicles of transfer through contagious action. In these vehicles of transfer we find expressed Frazer's substitution (or similarity) and contiguity principles, imitative and contagious magic, but never in an exclusive manner. A close analysis of Trobriand ritual shows that it actively exploits the expressive properties of language, the sensory qualities of objects, and the instrumental properties of action simultaneously in a number of ways (Tambiah 1968: 190).

Michael Carrithers, has recently drawn attention to similar "vehicles of transfer", saying that in everyday life people tend to transfer their mental models of the animate onto to the inanimate world. This throws light on how the rhetorical will works and how it is prone to lead to magical practice:

> We are particularly good at imagining and understanding things, even material things, when we attribute intentions or, plans to them. This does not, of course, mean that we need really to believe that inanimate objects have minds. For example, a cabinet-maker l know talks of old wood as 'wanting to split' and a painter l know speaks of certain kinds of paint as 'wanting to lift' and even 'getting tired and wanting to let go'; yet they certainly do not believe that wood or paint are actually persons. Rather, we use a set of mind whose original focus was to make calculations 'where the evidence on which... calculations are based is ephemeral, ambiguous and liable to change' in order to do something relatively less difficult, and that is to manipulate the physical world. This suggestion is supported by recent psychological research that shows there to be an 'interactional bias' in human thinking. That is, we do indeed tend to reason as if the inanimate world were human—or animal-like, made in the image of thinking, planning, intending beings (Carrithers, 1992: 44-45).

Such leaning towards magic can even be found in the natural sciences, which do not just develop because people are rational, but because they have intuitions, fanciful ideas to which they often cling against all odds, against all sober reason. Michael Polanyi made this point when he wrote:

> We are often told that great scientific discoveries are marked by their fruitfulness; and this is true. But how can we recognize truth by its fruitfulness? Can we recognize that a statement is true by appreciating the wealth of its yet undiscovered consequences? This would of course be nonsensical, if we had to know explicitly what was yet undiscovered. But it makes sense if we admit that we can have a tacit foreknowledge of yet undiscovered things.

This is indeed the kind of foreknowledge the Copernicans must have meant to affirm when they passionately maintained, against heavy pressure, during one hundred and forty years before Newton proved the point, that the heliocentric theory was not merely a convenient way of computing the paths of planets, but was really true.

It appears, then, that to know that a statement is true is to know more than we can tell and that hence, when a discovery solves a problem, it is itself fraught with further intimations of an indeterminate range, and that furthermore, when we accept the discovery as true, we commit ourselves to a belief in all these as yet undisclosed, perhaps as yet unthinkable, consequences (Polanyi 1967: 21-23).

Keeping in mind the theoretical orientation provided by the work of Schopenhauer, Huxley, Tambiah, Carrithers and Polanyi, I now turn to some empirical examples from Hamar. They concern recurrent threats and situations of worry, which lead people to intensify the search for magical solutions. Typical threats come from the environment, the human body and from society.

My main source is—as so often before—*Baldambe Explains* (Lydall/Strecker 1979b).

The threat of drought

Then the rain, then the thunder, then the rainy season, then it comes. Whether it is the month of *barre* or *surr* or *duka: gugugugu-gugukukukuk*, it will beat down. After the first rain has fallen and ceased, the fields are not planted but left to drink, for the land had been very dry. When the next rain falls, the *gudili* gets up and announces:

"Tomorrow I will start the fields, tomorrow I will make fire."

And he goes to find the nest of the sparrow-weaver and some dry *baraza* sticks and pulls them over the cattle kraal gateway. Getting up early next day,

"Throw out the old ashes, kill the old fire."

And all the ashes are thrown out and the fires extinguished. The *gudili* and his *ukuli* twist the fire drill and when the fire begins to fall through the hole all the elders come and hold and twist the drill together. Twisting the stick they send away sickness and then call for rain...

Next everyone gathers in the field of the *gudili*. First of all, the *gudili* takes four coffee beans and going over to one side of the field he puts two beans down on account of the ground squirrel. He goes over to the other side and puts two more beans down on account of the ground squirrel, so that the ground squirrel might not come and pinch the seed.

"Grandfather, stop the baboons, you are the *barjo* plant.
Here, stop the squirrel, you are the *barjo* plant.
Stop the francolin, you are the *barjo* plant.
Stop the quail, you are the *barjo* plant."

Then the *gudili* goes and cuts a branch of *baraza* or *garogasha* and sharpens its end. Returning to the field he rubs this digging stick with butter, either sheep's fat or white butter. Then he digs four holes and plants red sorghum in them. Now the elders dig holes and the women plant the seed, and working together they plant the field of the *gudili*.

"It is enough, go to your own fields."

And the *gudili* gives a handful of seed to each elder. Taking the seed in their hands, the elders go to their fields. There each field owner does the same as the *gudili* did in his field. Each one puts down coffee beans to stop the squirrels and rubs a *baraza* digging stick with butter and digs several holes in which to plant the *gudili's* seed. Thus they initiate the planting (Lydall and Strecker1979b: 164-65).

Baldambe's text speaks largely for itself, but I will pick up some of his points to give them further emphasis. First of all we can see how the evident and mysterious dimensions of the world organically join together: Thunder and lightning come, and *gugugugugugkukukuk* the rain falls and enriches the earth.

But will the rain also fall later when it is needed for the crops to grow and ripen? This is not at all certain, and here lies a danger that needs to be countered by magic. A note from my diary (6.1.1974) helps to illustrate this:

> It is the afternoon. A bank of clouds which 'stood' over Simbale and emptied itself there, found its way to Dambaiti and scattered a few drops here. The moist ground sparkles, the birds call and there is a beautiful afternoon light. To the south, towards Assile and Galapha, the sky is black and heavy thunder grumbles continuously Kairambe calls me in between the thunder, "Tomorrow they will be planting their fields in Assile and Galapha!" He adds that such early rain is particularly good for the southern regions because if the rains come late, the fields in the south often dry up before the crops have time to ripen. Kairambe does not know whether he should go ahead with the burning of his field or not. There has been rain now in some parts of Hamar, but learned Sago has said that there won't be much early rain since the male star has moved south of his wife's position "to protect her from the dangers of the south", from drought, from hunger and from war (Lydall/Strecker 1979a: 231-32).

It is because there can be no doubt about the uncertainty of rain that recourse is taken to the mysterious means of magic. Drought, predictably unpredictable, is kept away magically, and in the very same context sickness is sent away. In the fields, once they have been planted, similar uncertainties reign that have to be countered with magical devices: the earth squirrel and baboons are kept at bay by giving them some beans of coffee, and in order to ensure a rich crop the digging sticks are anointed with sheep's fat or with butter.

The threat of disease

"Eh, bitta!"

"Woi!"

"Sickness has come to the cattle, sickness has come to the children. What would it be good to do?"

"Isn't there a man of Ba?"

"There is."

"This man should go down to every waterhole and anoint everything with the fat from the sheep's tail."

So the man from Ba went all around the country, anointing the grass, the water, the earth and the hearts of the children (Lydall/Strecker 1979b: 10).

The *bitta* was a mythical ancestor whom, as Baldambe explains, the Hamar would consult on all matters concerning the right way of life, and whose answers even today provide something like a charter of Hamar culture. This includes magical responses to the threat of disease. Representatives of certain clans such as Ba are magically powerful and can keep away sickness. They are also able to bless the grass, water, the earth and the hearts of children by anointing them with the fat of a sheep's tail.

The threat of men

"The Bume are our enemies, the Galeba are our enemies, the Korre are our enemies, the Borana are our enemies, we are surrounded by them. *Bitta*, tell us what to do."

"Is there not Misha?"

"There is Misha."

"A man from Misha should take two dry flower stalks of the *wolkati* cactus and going to the border of the country there he should hit them together: *dak-dak-dak-dak-dak-dak-ka-da-ka-dak!* Then he should break them and throw them towards the countries of Borana and Korre. Then he should take a sheep skin and flip it towards the enemy country. Also a man of Bucha should get up and go to the borders of Galeba and Bume where he should flick small pebbles, beat *wolkanti* flower stalks and flip a sheep skin towards the enemy. After they have done this, neither of these men should drink cow's milk nor eat meat. They should only eat honey. When they get home each one should take two pieces of charcoal and biting from them spit on to his heart. Only after this may they drink coffee and eat food" (Lydall and Strecker 1979b: 11).

It is the *bitta* who speaks here, and what he says is similar to what he said about disease. But this time the threat comes from clearly distinguishable, known enemies, and not persons of the clan Ba but of the clans Misha or Bucha are demanded. The persuasiveness of the magic which the *bitta* offers derives largely from the intelligent use of rhetorical figures such as metaphor, synecdoche and metonymy (see Tambiah's argument in *The Magical Power of Words* above) which allow multiple possibilities of interpretation and create the sense of mystery that is the hallmark of all magic.

The threats of nature and society do, of course, interact and therefore lead to forms of ritual and magic that pertain to both realms. Here is an example from *barrae*, the 'mad month' at the height of the dry season when people do not know from where to get enough food for their families and herds, and therefore are prone to loose their temper if not their mind:

> In Hamar the 'mad' month asserts itself... at a waterhole near Lodgera, where there is now very little water, two women got into a fight during which one hit the other with her digging stick so hard that she broke the other woman's arm. Her angry husband then took a piece of quartz and threw it into the waterhole. This act automatically causes the waterhole to dry up. The men of Lodgera retaliated by threatening to curse the man and his wounded wife. So he had to give in. He offered a goat to the men of Lodgera and the men then went to the waterhole with a small lamb, pulled out the quartz, killed the lamb and dropped the content of its stomach and its fat into the waterhole, thereby ensuring that the water would continue to flow (Lydall/Strecker 1979a: 231).

Today, more than a quarter of a century later, I wonder how matter-of-factly I then recorded the strange and fantastic events without any commentary, without ever voicing surprise. But this is what the ubiquity of magical thought and action leads to. In the end one simply takes for granted that the natural is mustered to control the social, and the social is mustered to control the natural. Both, nature and society are interwoven in a mysterious pattern of causality that each member of society interprets and magically influences in his or her own individual fashion.

The most important medium of magic in Hamar is *apho*, the mouth, the voice, the word, rhetoric. *Apho barjo ne*, the word is fortune, fate, creation, as in the *barjo aela*, the calling forth of good fortune, where the word is repeated again and again. On the recording *Music of the Hamar* there is an example of such an invocation or convocation of good fortune. This recording may serve as a final example of the rhetorical roots and the ubiquity of magic in Hamar:

> Meanwhile the coffee is ready and has been placed in steaming bowls (made from gourds) in front of the singers. Before they drink, the men all lift their bowls, fill their mouths with the liquid and spray it from their lips towards the earth, towards where the sun rises and towards where the sun sets. Murra also sprays it towards the fireplace and the coffee pot and then he begins to bless. He blesses the homestead, the people and herds within it, the fields, the pastures, nature. He calls for rain and sends away sickness. The men answer him and emphasize what he says by repeating it immediately. The words of Murra and the men never overlap as in the preceding songs, yet there is never a pause. The last and most important word of each of Murra's sentences is repeated and amplified by everyone at once. In this way there remains (in the philosophy of the Hamar) no room for doubt or negation, and thus the world will take on the shape which is conjured up by the magical power of Murra's and the men's voices:

The rain shall fall .... fall *(hanshe)*

The children shall play .... play *(yege)*

The plants shall smell good .... smell good *(game)*

The rain shall lie in puddles .... lie *(kate)*

The rain shall turn into plants .... turn *(mate)*

The herds shall enter the homestead .... enter *(arde)*

The flood water shall flow upwards .... flow *(mirse)*

It shall be like butter .... butter *(bodi)*

Rain .... rain *(dobi)*

Well-being .... well-being *(nagaia)*

Sickness shall go away .... go away *(yi'e)*

It shall fall like a dried up leaf .... fall *(pille)*

Away! .... away! *(wollall!)*

(Strecker 1979b).

Mantic and magical confidence:
The work of persuasion

Here I offer some notes on the rhetorical creation of mantic and magical confidence. Like in so many other publications, I quote more or less directly from my unpublished notebooks.

How to indicate the height of a child

Lomeromoi asked me the other day whether Theo had grown up during the time I had been away from Hamar. I answered "yes" and showed him with my hand how high he has grown now. Lomeromoi then corrected me and said that one does not indicate the height of a child by holding the palm of one's hand horizontally. The hand should be held in a vertical direction with the fingers pointing upwards. The implicit meaning of what Lomeromoi said was obvious: don't arrest the growth of a child with your gesture, let it grow continuously and express this by the movement of your hand.

There is a curious little note, which I wrote in brackets under this entry. It says that my friend Baldambe, a political rival of Lomeromoi, later commented that Lomeromoi had told me nonsense and that any gesture may be right to indicate the height of a child. But on the other side I remember vividly how one day I stretched out my index finger to point at a person. Baldambe stopped me and showed me how to bend my finger in such a way as not to harm the one at whom I am pointing. Similarly, a hunter should bend his finger if he points at an animal, otherwise it would run away before he could shoot it.

Thus Baldambe and Lomeromoi see things in much the same way, even though they may disagree in particular cases. For them a gesture may have two aspects at once, it may tell something and it may do something. As with the gesture that indicates the height of a child: the hand held horizontally arrests the stage of growth it indicates, and the hand held vertically continues or even enhances the growth it indicates.

Mouse and fly

I have killed a mouse in my trap, and thinking I am following the logic of Hamar customs, I am going to throw it 'away with the sun', that is towards the West, when Aikenda exclaims: "No, no! This is forbidden (*kais*), throw it towards the direction from where the sun rises".

Immediately I understand and ask: "Is then the mouse like the fly?" "Yes, it is. Just like the fly arrives with the milk, the mouse arrives with the sorghum. We kill it, but then we throw it towards where the sun rises and from where the rains come, asking it to return with more sorghum".

Later, Ginonda tells me that mice arrive even before the sorghum gets ripe and in this way forecast a good harvest: "This year many grey and white mice turned up. Usually they are busy in the bush, and when they all come to our houses and to the fields, we know that there will be a good crop.

On the one side, one can see here how Aikenda and Ginonda predict from the coming of the mice, an abundance of sorghum, and from the arrival of flies, an abundance of milk. On the other side, one can see how they think that one would cause the future absence of milk if one would senselessly kill the flies which swarm around the milk containers and sit on people's faces, or if one killed mice and threw them away towards the setting sun. To throw a mouse away towards the setting sun would, in Hamar terms, be a gesture which would have the effect that one never would see the mouse again, and as the presence of mice is closely associated with the presence of sorghum, the gesture would also cause the sorghum to disappear forever.

The tortoise

We drive through the rain towards the cattle camps. Choke discovers in the high grass two turtles mating. The male (small) one snarls in anger when I touch him. We watch them a while and then say that it is time to continue our journey. But before we leave, Choke rips off some grass, and putting the two turtles head to head he places the grass gently across them: "They are our cattle, let them eat grass". Then he explains further: "When we are returning to our home or the cattle camps and meet a tortoise on our way, we give her some grass and call her our cow. But when we are on our way to hunt game, then we kill the tortoise because otherwise the hunt would not be successful and we would return hungry".

Here the tortoise figures in the first instance as a domesticated animal (cow) and in the second instance as a wild animal (game). Its identity depends on the direction towards which a traveller is heading. If he is heading towards his cattle, then the tortoise is a cow, and by feeding it he ensures the well-being of his cattle. If he is going on a hunt, the tortoise is a wild animal, and by taking its life he begins, so he thinks, a sequence of successful killings. As the tortoise is easy to handle (i.e. either to feed or to kill), it always predicts and causes good luck when one meets it on the way, no matter where one is heading.

Black ants

Yesterday evening, when we were walking from Dambaiti to Kadja, Baldambe and I came across a large group of black ants who were carrying some white substances which I was not able to identify. I thought they were seeds of a grass called 'buska', but Baldambe said the black ants were carrying white ants which they had caught. Each ant was carrying something, and one could see the light spot in front of each ant very well. Baldambe pointed to the ants and said: "This is how the country will be rich now. People will be carrying goods". However, an hour later, when we were nearing the homestead of Baldambe's mother, another folk of black ants crossed our way and no little white points greeted us. The mouths of the ants were empty! Baldambe got angry, swore, and with his stick brushed the black ants aside.

Here we see the same mantic and magical confidence at work, which we have seen in the first three examples. The only difference is that Baldambe's gesture was not positive and hopeful but rather negative and despairing.

Stars

The Hamar say that the stars say everything and cause everything. They make no clear distinction between SAYING and CAUSING. The planets, especially Venus and Jupiter, go north and say that there will be rain and time of plenty, and when they go south they say that there will be drought and hard times ahead. Every conceivable good or evil is caused or foretold by the stars. For example, the pests which today threaten the fields are there BECAUSE the stars have said that there would be pests.

This note, which I wrote down in the field, summarizes the point, which I want to make here: there is a close nexus between 'telling' or foretelling and 'causing' something in Hamar. That which 'tells' (foretells) something may also be that which 'causes' something. But there is often an element of uncertainty whether an agent is a primary or derived cause, like in the following example.

The whirlwind

A whirlwind comes roaring towards Dambaiti. Men and women get out of their houses, and we see grass flying into the air down at Kalleinda's homestead. Everyone spits towards the whirlwind and makes gestures to move it away. Yet the whirlwind comes towards us, and passing between Ginonda's and Aikenda's house, it moves right through Lukusseinda's house whirling the grass off its roof through the air. After the whirlwind has gone, there is a moment of silence in Dambaiti. Then Ginonda calls her daughter Kuli, and a little later Kuli appears with a bowl full of water, which she spills on the path which the whirlwind took. "So that it goes away", says Ginonda: "*Ogoro kossa artamo*, this is the magic for the whirlwind". She adds: "We used to consult the sandal oracle, but we have given this up because there have been so many whirlwinds this dry season."

Baldambe remarks: "There are sick people in Lukusseinda's and Kalleinda's houses, Let us hope that the whirlwind took their sickness away". But Baldambe's old friend Bajjeimba, who is visiting us at the moment, murmurs: "There will be more serious sickness in those houses over there."

Three different interpretations were given here:

1) Ginonda spoke of some remote agent, which was sending the whirlwinds to Dambaiti. People tried to identify this agent by consulting sandal oracles (for a description of divination see below), but they were not successful and gave up in the end.

2) Baldambe looked at the whirlwind in a positive way and hoped that it would have a good effect. That is, he interpreted it as a primary cause, as an agent, which would take the sickness away.

3) Bajjeimba also interpreted the whirlwind as a primary cause, but he saw in it, like in all the whirlwinds, which preceded it, the cause for the sickness that had come to Dambaiti. The last vehement whirlwind caused and foretold further suffering of the people living in the houses which it hit.

Thunder, theft and lightning

It rains heavily, and thunder and lightning crash down on Dambaiti. We sit and drink coffee in Baldambe's house. An immensely frightening flash of lightning comes down near us and Jean asks jokingly whether men who have stolen girls are also in danger of getting killed by lightning. She is alluding to the fact that Baldambe has stolen his young wife into marriage, and to the following Hamar practice: when someone has been robbed, he or she may go to a specialist of the clan called Duma who can kill the thief by means of lightning. Everyone laughs and Baldambe says that he is in no danger. But his sister Maiza then tells the following story which is meant to prove that the threat of the Duma specialist works: Several years ago, her father, Berimba, was sitting together with two friends in his house while rain, thunder and lightning swept down on them. One flash of lightning after the other came down close to them, and it seemed as if the flashes were aiming at the house in which the men were sitting. So Berimba said that there was something wrong, and he ordered the fire to be put out.

Next morning, Berimba found his beautiful giraffe skin sandals which had been missing for some time in front of his house. One of the two men who had been with him during the night had previously stolen the sandals, but when the lightning came nearer and nearer, and when Berimba pointed out that the lightning meant that something was wrong, he felt threatened and returned the stolen sandals as soon as possible.

This is an example where the powers of nature are clearly harnessed to the will of humans. The flashes of lightning, which threatened the thief that night SAID something because they were sent by Berimba who had asked (or could have asked!) the specialist of the clan Duma to punish the thief.

In fact it was quite ironic that on the occasion the thief and Berimba were sitting next to each other, and that even though he himself did not know it at that time, Berimba was mustering the support of the lightning when he said that something was wrong and extinguished the fire as a precaution. The thief 'knew' of course the precise meaning of the threatening flashes of lightning, and his precaution was to return the stolen sandals at once.

As my fieldwork continued, I began to ponder more and more about Hamar mantic confidence and the relationship between the symbolical, predictive and magical mode of Hamar thinking. Where lie the differences between these three modes, and how do they interact? These are, of course, old anthropological questions, which go at least as far back as to Levy-Bruhl

(1911). But as the answers are very difficult and confusing, my notes from the field may be useful, or at least interesting.

I first give a short example in order to show the psychological element of self-persuasion which, I think, is inherent in all mantic and magical thinking, and then I provide a longer example which includes my reflections on the subject.

On the way

We are on the way to Kadja. Waya and Duka are going ahead of us. At one point Baldambe says: "The girls are now quietly calling the names of the children in the homestead to which we are going. They ask them, 'please lift my legs' (*ro issa dasa*). This makes them go faster and reach the distant home more easily."

I like this magic because it allows me to see how it must be psychologically effective. Of course, the distant children can't hear you calling; of course, they can't make you go faster. Only you yourself can lift your legs. You go faster by using this magic.

When I asked them, Waya and Duka did not know themselves how the magic really works. They did not spell out whether the children at the far away homestead really could hear them, and they did not explain how from a distance anyone could help you lift your legs. But even though, they insisted that the magic worked. As I wrote already in the notebook, it is easy to see how it may be psychologically effective to call your distant brothers and sisters for assistance. By this you persuade yourself that they are helping you and find that your legs move more swiftly.

As an aside, I like to mention that on the same day, Baldambe and I followed a Hamar practice, which had a similarly helpful effect:

Walking and talking

We were climbing up the steep path to Kadja last evening. Whenever I did the talking, Baldambe asked me to go ahead, for it is Hamar custom to have someone talk as you walk, and that the one who does the talking goes ahead. If the one in front has to listen to the one who follows, he does not hear well, may have to turn his head around, may loose the way, may stumble or get hurt by thorns. But there is even more to this sensible practice: The one who goes ahead pulls the one who follows. As the listener wants to hear what is being said, he (she) automatically keeps up with the speaker and forgets thereby the efforts he has to make when walking.

This example is similar to the previous one in that a traveller is helped in his effort to walk by someone who physically is at a distance from him. Almost 'magically' the traveller is pulled towards his destination. But there is a difference in the kind of persuasion that occurs. The listener who follows the speaker does not need to persuade himself of anything because the speaker does the persuasion. By telling this and that story, by giving an account of this and that event etc. the speaker draws the attention of the listener (and also himself!) away from his arduous physical activity and makes him almost forget that he is walking.

Now follow what I consider to be my most crucial notes on the relationship between mantic confidence, i.e. symbolic or metaphoric anticipation and magical action, which I have written in the field:

Kolmo's magic

We are sitting in Kairambe's house and Alma tells me how clever old Kolmo is. Kolmo cannot hear well anymore. In fact he is almost deaf. But, as Alma says, in his heart Kolmo 'knots up' thoughts and then goes on to put them into action. One often finds out only much later how clever his seemingly strange actions really are.

Here Alma's story begins: A long time ago, Kolmo came to his house when they were drinking coffee. After the coffee was finished, Kolmo asked Alma's wife Hailanda for some butter. In

Hamar culture it is quite unusual for a man to make such a request, and Alma and Hailanda were surprised. Nevertheless, Hailanda gave Kolmo the butter which he had demanded. As he tells the story, Alma imitates how Kolmo quickly grabbed the butter when it was given, and how he greedily rubbed it on his forehead, his legs and other parts of his body.

"Then", Alma says, "Kolmo departed", and laughingly he adds: "I never have asked him why he wanted the butter and why he rubbed it on himself". Again he laughs and repeats: "I never have asked him, I never have asked him".

Alma ends here, but my friend Woro spells out the essential part for me, the part which an outsider typically can not understand: "Kolmo acted very cleverly. At that time, Alma's homestead was rich with cattle, goats and sheep. Look how rich Kolmo has now become and how few heads of cattle are left in Alma's cattle enclosure".

So Alma's "I never have asked him" meant: "I did not need to ask him what his seemingly crazy action meant, for I slowly came to realize it. Kolmo rubbed himself with a part (or effect) of my herds, and in this way the wealth moved over to him. He robbed the animals very cleverly from me. His thought is deep, and his actions which may at first look odd later reveal themselves to be very meaningful, – and magical".

In my notebook I went on to generalize from the story of Kolmo's magic. I quote here only some of my attempts at understanding what was going on:

The story is very telling to me. Especially the fact that Kolmo is almost deaf and does not want to communicate with anyone is interesting. He does not speak to others but only to himself. Therefore the symbolism, which he uses in his action is centered on himself. He does not bother whether others understand him; he only wants to act effectively for himself.

His seemingly crazy actions have a magical aim and are the result of his analogical thinking. I envisage Kolmo as he contemplated several possible means by which to increase his wealth. There are the obvious ones used by everybody in the society, such as to drive your herds to the right pastures and wells, keep the enclosures clean, go raiding etc., and there are the less obvious ones such as to ask a diviner or, as in the case of Kolmo, rub yourself with the butter from the cow of a rich man.

I think that a kind of self-persuasion must have taken place before Kolmo acted in that 'strange', 'odd' or 'crazy' way which later turned out to be magical. He must have 'discovered' and persuaded himself that by taking a part of Alma's herd he eventually also could take over the whole.

Interestingly, no one knows whether Kolmo really ever intended to act magically when he rubbed himself with butter. But as Alma's laughter and Woro's comment shows, people are convinced that Kolmo acquired his wealth by means of magic, and they all share the same way of thinking. They believe that they can further their aims by acting analogically.

At the root of this lies the all-pervasive practice of thinking and speaking metaphorically. People know from experience that metaphor is a useful cognitive tool. And in my view it makes sense that in societies like Hamar analogical, or rather metonymical and synecdochecal thinking should abound. Where cause and effect, whole and part, etc., can not always be clearly distinguished, where many causal relationships in nature are still an open question, much analogical reasoning should be allowed.

But the problem is that analogies often have limits, which are difficult to check. Therefore, even though they lie at the heart of discovery and are essential for an extension of knowledge, they do have their pitfalls and can become an obstruction to objective knowledge.

Modern science is an enterprise where in an ideally egalitarian discourse slowly more and more untenable theories are ruled out and reasonably tenable theories are established.

No theory will ever have a claim to ultimate truth, but the ground for its tenability will be made transparent and would never be based on social authority.

In societies like Hamar where no institutionalized science exists, the use of analogy is always inextricably linked to social relations and differences in power. Here the socially powerful determine the meaning of metaphors and the extent to which analogical reasoning, and by extension also analogical action, that is magic, may be employed.

When I said that the Hamar have no institutionalized science, I did not mean that in practical everyday life validation does not go on. Of course it does! People argue soberly, as in this example:

"The goats got sick in the lowlands."
"Why?"
"Because they were stung by Tsetse flies."
"Nonsense, there aren't any Tsetse flies now."
"So it could have been the water... ."

But then someone, typically a socially powerful person, will come up with a statement like this:

"The goats got sick because we did not put 'gali' leaves and the fat of a sheep into the water before we let the animals drink. They will only get better when we perform these rituals". How does one answer this expression of mantic confidence, and how is one to validate or falsify such a statement? As there is no way to prove or disprove it, it becomes a matter of social influence whether people accept or reject the proposal to use 'gali' leaves and the fat of a sheep as a means to make the water healthy and thus ensure the well-being of the animals."

There are further entries in my notebooks, which speak of this mantic confidence and the problematic shift from scientific observation to uncontrolled analogical argumentation, as in the following case.

Cactus and sorghum

In the early evening, Baldambe and I take a walk in the surroundings of Dambaiti. Baldambe points to the towering flower of the 'wolkanti' cactus, touches the seeds of the flower and says: "This is sorghum". I first think he is saying that one can eat the 'wolkanti' seeds like sorghum. But this is not the case. Rather, the 'wolkanti' tells us how the next sorghum harvest will be. Baldambe speaks here of a specific observation. Hamar traditional knowledge says that when the 'wolkanti' flowers well, and when its fruits are rich, then the next sorghum harvest will accordingly also be rich. The observation sounds reasonable and would in principle allow an empirical validation.

But then Baldambe goes on to extend his predictions into realms where causal connections seem less plausible and validation less possible. For example, he says that just as the first flowers of the 'wolkanti' may be weak and the second strong, so the first growth of the sorghum will be expected to turn out weak while the second will be strong. And he says that the sickness which befalls the 'wolkanti' will later befall the sorghum.

I do not quite understand the other analogical extensions. Perhaps they are after all not as farfetched as they seem to me. The principle, I think, is clear: The Hamar allow all sorts of causation. Like modern science they deduce one event from another or infer one phenomenon from another. But as there is no scientific community and no institutionalized science, deductions and inferences may get more 'wild' and quickly get an element of usurpation of knowledge which makes use of uncontrolled analogy and metaphor.

In Hamar one finds both, a lot of reasonable 'scientific' practice and a lot of 'wild' reasoning. People seem to feel themselves integrated in a wider context in which they can influence things which we of the modern world would not dream of influencing, at least not with the magical means the Hamar use.

Yet the Hamar are also not hysterically given to beliefs in magic and sorcery. They speak occasionally of sorcery and have some remedies against it, and they believe in the spirits of the dead and sacrifice animals for them, but this does not overshadow their practical reasoning in everyday life.

*

With this I end this little excursions into Hamar mantic and magical confidence as it manifests itself in everyday life. This confidence—in our view more poetical than effective—is part and parcel of the 'undomesticated' or 'savage' mind (Levi-Strauss 1966, Goody 1977), which makes unbounded use of analogical thinking (metaphor) and analogical action (magic), and which anthropologists have the agonizingly good fortune to explore. We also find other, more institutionalized expressions of mantic confidence in Hamar (reading the entrails and throwing the sandals for example), but they are too grand and unwieldy to be included in this short essay.

What caused Baldambe's death?

Anthropology attracts us because we want to know, want to understand, want to extend our horizon, want to "grasp the native's point of view, his relation to life", as Malinowski put it long ago, and "study what concerns him most ultimately" (1922: 25). This endeavour includes an exploration of the limitations of knowing, the frailty of understanding, the insecure grasp we—actors and observers alike—have of our and other people's "relation to life".

When writing in the field I was often confronted with, or better enmeshed in, contexts governed by insecure knowledge, doubt and inaccessible truth. An example is the death of Baldambe (Father of the Dark Brown Cow) who was for many years host, mentor and friend of Jean Lydall, myself and our family in Hamar, southern Ethiopia. Not unlike Cohen, the protagonist of Geertz' essay on "Thick Description" (1973), Baldambe was ultimately defeated by what he himself used to call the *k'au* (thicket) and the *zani* (snares) of social relationships. He was tormented by the fact that he did not and could not fully know the circumstances that preceded and, as people later said, led to his death—and those who survived him, including me, find themselves in a similar position.

In March 1995, when he was brought to hospital, the doctors diagnosed "renal collapse" as the cause of Baldambe's death.

A cholera epidemic had swept through Hamar killing many people, including Baldambe's youngest child, a baby boy. He witnessed all the misery, and in his helpless and distraught state was infected himself and eventually succumbed to the disease. As I wrote in the obituary (Strecker 1998/ see "Prologue" above), Jean and I witnessed Baldambe's death and later were also present when he was buried in the Hamar mountains. Afterwards we flew back to Europe, but three months later I returned to Hamar where people seemed almost to have been waiting to tell me the deeper causes of Baldambe's death. I then made the following notes:

> 22.8.1995.
> What has caused Baldambe's death? Up in Kadja, after we had buried Baldambe, it was said that Baldambe had caused his own death by offending the spirits of the dead (*maeshi*). He had promised to perform the final funeral rites, the *duki* for his mother and older brothers, but then instead of going ahead with this he had let his sons perform their initiation rites, that is leap over the cattle and marry. So the *maeshi* got angry and caused him to die. Baldambe became more and more sick after each of the initiation rites, which were performed in Kadja, and in the end he died.

> But now, as I have returned to Hamar, I hear that Baldambe died because the elders of Baldo (the settlements of Lodjera, Wonyarki, Borea and the grazing areas of Kizo and Dunka) cursed him. Donumba, an elder of Baldambe's age told me the story first, and this morning it was confirmed by Tsasi (Baldambe's oldest son), Laesho, Woro, Birinde and other neighbours. Here is the story as it unfolded this morning during the conversation around the coffee pot:

> Long ago Berimba had made peace with the Bume, and when one Hamar broke the peace, Berimba had him thrown into the Omo river for the crocodiles to devour. This showed to all— Hamar and Bume alike—how serious he was in his attempt to establish lasting peace with the Bume. Later a big peace

ceremony followed at which Loteng, the Bume spokesman, brought a spear across the river and handed it to the Hamar. The Bume have never seriously attacked the Hamar ever since. But the Hamar have occasionally killed the Bume who came to Hamar. This happened particularly during the drought, which developed at the beginning and the middle of the Seventies as told in our *Work Journal*.

Woro says that the Bume were at first treated well when they came to Dambaiti in great numbers in 1973. A cow was slaughtered and four goats and so on, but when they went on to Bashada (a region adjacent to Hamar), they received little grain there and returned disappointed, saying, "the Bashada kill us with hunger".

As the drought continued, Bume kept coming across the Omo and harvested the *kirya* berries, which were ripe in the Omo plain. They also hunted game, both with rifles and with traps. One day an elder from Lodjera who was at the cattle camps said to the young Hamar herdsmen that they should kill the Bume because they ganged up with the Galeba (Dassanech, a group neighbouring Hamar in the south) who were acting as spies. So the Hamar went down to the plains where they found the Bume eating *kirya* berries. There was no agreement among the Hamar. Some wanted to kill the Bume, but Bali (Baldambe's brother) for example didn't agree to this So when the Hamar began to kill the unprepared and defenceless Bume, Bali saved one of them. He brought them to the elders at the cattle camps, and later the Bume—an elderly man—was escorted back to the river and returned to Bume land safely. Woro added that the Hamar elders then did not scold the spokesman who had encouraged the young men to kill the Bume. Rather they scolded the young men and said they should be beaten for breaking the peace.

Later, the killing of Longole happened. Together with half a dozen Bume he had come to the cattle camps at Kizo and had been treated there well. The Hamar gave him and his friends plenty of milk, and then when the guests were sleeping, full milk containers at their sides, the Hamar slaughtered them. The killing was done by Wualle, the friend of Choke's older brother, and by some of his relatives and friends.

This horrific betrayal was never forgotten by the Bume, and the sons of the slain grew up and swore revenge. This revenge came recently when they killed the sons of Kalle Gaia and of Walle Lokarimoi who both are renowned Hamar spokesmen and very close friends of Baldambe. It seems that the Bume wanted to kill sons of important leaders of the Hamar. They had said so before and found in the sons of Kalle Gaia and Walle Lokarimoi their target.

The two young men had gone to the Omo river to trade goat skins for bullets with the Bume. They both had rifles and plenty of bullets with them, and they were killed from behind as they sat together with their Bume host discussing their transaction. After the killing, the Bume pressured a man from Galeba who was staying at the river to tell the false story that men from Kara had done the killing. The man then told the police that two Kara whose names he mentioned were the killers and had taken the rifles with them.

Baldambe went to Galeba to talk to this man who told his story so convincingly that Baldambe thought it was true. Also the police believed him. So the Kara men were put into prison in Jinka (capital of South Omo administrative region). Convinced that the Kara had done the killing, and appalled by the fact that both the Kara and Hamar kept saying it had been the Bume who had done the killing, Baldambe suggested to the Bume to attack the Kara, and he began to sing songs in which he anticipated the revenge of the two boys who had been killed so treacherously.

When Baldambe then took the spear of Loteng from his home in Dambaiti and prepared to go with it to Bume, the Hamar elders at Lodjera whisked the spear away when Baldambe had entered a house there to drink coffee. They argued that the Bume were tricking Baldambe into bringing the spear across the river, and that they would take it away from him to use its magical power in their attack on the Hamar. Upon this, Baldambe returned to Dambaiti and from there went on to Kadja. Meanwhile, however, the Hamar elders at Lodjera cursed him for plotting war against the Kara and the Hamar. This curse, it is said, killed Baldambe.

27. 9. 1995.

The story of Baldambe's anger at the Hamar continues. Sago (Baldambe's son-in-law) told it last night as follows: From where do the Kara get their *pala*, their scarifications? They are friends with the Bume, the Galeba, the Mursi, the Banna, Bashada and Hamar. So every *pala* means a betrayal of friendship. Baldambe had witnessed throughout his life how the Kara would join with the Banna to attack the Mursi, join with the Mursi to attack the Banna and Bashada, join the Hamar to attack the Bume or Galeba, and so on. This is why Baldambe thought it very possible that it was the Kara who killed the sons of Walle Lokarimo and Kalle Gaia. Also, Baldambe had seen over the years how the Hamar did not respect the peace, which Berimba and Loteng had created. He detested the way in which the Hamar would kill helpless Bume who had come to their territory. Therefore, he objected to the idea which some Hamar pro-pagated, that is the idea that it was the Bume who had killed the boys. This was in his eyes one more way to insult the Bume who in Baldambe's eyes were honest and would not kill the Hamar in the treacherous way so typical for the Hamar. So when he heard the following story he was prepared to believe it—like Sago believed it last night when he told it:

A man from Galeba was living at Irsha, a development site at the west bank of the Omo. As the site was somewhat neutral territory, the man continued living there even when the relations between Bume and Galeba deteriorated. But then the Bume came and drove him away. He fled to Kara where he told two young men called Dagino and Muda where they could find and kill some Bume who would cross the river to hunt buffalo on the east bank of the Omo. But when Dagina and Muda arrived and were ready to ambush any Bume coming their way, the sons of Walle Lokarimoi and Kalle Gaia arrived. They talked and settled down together to eat some fresh sorghum that Dina and Kolle had brought from Bume. As they ate, the Kara shot the Hamar boys and then took their rifles and—hiding their footprints—went back to the river to follow it upstream.

The Galeba man was with them, and they gave him hundred dollars to keep quiet, or rather to tell the story to the police that it had been the Bume who had done the killing. The Galeba went up to Hamar and there told people that he had seen two dead men on the path from Bume and that he had no idea who had done the killing. The Hamar went to see and found the two dead boys. They then informed the police that the Galeba had seen the dead. The police then chased after him and found him in Arbore (a group neighbouring Hamar to the east). They brought him to Turmi (administrative town in Hamar) where they forced the 'truth' out of him that Dagino and Muda had done the killing.

So the two were arrested and put into prison in Jinka. As the case was heard, the judge asked for the witness, the Galeba who had accused the Kara, but he was never found again. Meanwhile the Kara paid bribes to the police and the judge, which led to a lenient treatment of the prisoners. They were allowed to move around in Jinka—and then one day they fled. It was they, says Sago, who did the killing, and the whole event was just one more example of the cunning of the Kara. The people who put the blame on the Bume, Sago says, just follow the old betrayal of Berimba's peace. This is why Baldambe got up, went to Lodjera and pretended he was going to return Loteng's spear to the Bume. He did not really mean to go there. Weren't his legs much too weak for such a venture anyway? But the Hamar took his words as if they said exactly what he meant. This is why they took his spear so that he could not give it to the Bume. Baldambe had meant to say: "You always betray the Bume. If you want to fight with them then let it be a honest and open fight. Let's return the spear to the Bume and see how they will come and teach you cowards a lesson.

Here my notes about the causes of Baldambe's death come to an end. But my thoughts move on in circles, and I wonder who was right, those who talked to me drinking coffee in Dambaiti, or Sago with whom I conversed at his home a month later. I simply cannot know what 'really' happened. But nor can they, for we are all confined to particular *deictic* fields, to singular contexts of time, place and action that allow no overarching, 'objective' knowledge. We can see and evaluate events only from our individual perspectives, and like the witnesses in Akira Kurosawa's film *Rashomon* we are bound to tell conflicting, contradictory, and open-ended stories.

BIBLIOGRAPHY

Abbink, Jon 1994. "'Tribal' Violence, Peacemaking and Ethnology: A Comment on Prof. I. Strecker's Paper on War and Peace in South Omo." In *Proceedings of the XIth International Conference of Ethiopian Studies*, Vol II, edited by Bahru Zewde, R. Pankhurst and Taddese Beyene. Addis Ababa: University, Institute of Ethiopian Studies. Pp. 1-7.

Abu-Lughod, Lila. 1986. *Veiled Sentiments: Honor and Poetry in a Bedouin Society*. Berkeley; Los Angeles; London: University of California Press.

Aebli, Hans. 1980/81. *Denken: das Ordnen des Tuns*. 2 vols. Stuttgart: Klett Cotta.

Appadurai, Arjun, ed. 1988. "Place and Voice in Anthropological Theory." In *Cultural Anthropology*, 3,1.

Bailey, Frederic G. 1983. *The Tactical Uses of Passion: An Essay on Power, Reason and Reality*. Ithaca; London: Cornell University Press.

——. 2009. "The Palaestral Mode of Rhetoric." In *Culture, Rhetoric and the Vicissitudes of Life*, edited by Michael Carrithers and Anna-Maria Brandstetter. New York · Oxford: Berghahn Books. Pp. 107-120

Bakhtin, Michael. 1985. *Problems of Dostoevsky's Poetics*. Minneapolis: University of Minnesota Press.

Bartels, Lambert. 1983. *Oromo Religion*. Berlin: Dietrich Reimer Verlag.

Baumann, Richard and J. Sherzer, eds. 1974. *Explorations in the Ethnography of Speaking*. Cambridge: Cambridge University Press.

Baxter, Paul. 1965. "Repetition in certain Borana ceremonies." In: *African Systems of Thought*, edited by Fortes, Meyer. London: International African Institute. Pp. 64-78.

Bender, John and David E. Wellbery. 1990. "Rhetoricality: On the Modernist Return of Rhetoric." In: *The Ends of Rhetoric: History, Theory, Practice*, edited by John Bender and David E. Wellbery. Stanford: Stanford University Press. Pp. 3-39.

Bender, M. Lionel, ed. 1976. *The Non-Semitic Languages of Ethiopia*. East Lansing: African Studies Center.

Benedict, Ruth. 1989 [¹1934]. *Patterns of Culture*. Boston: Hough Mifflin Company.

Berger, Peter. 1970. "The Obsolescence of Honor." In *Archive of European Sociology*. XI: 339-347.

Bitzer, Lloyd F. and Edwin Black, eds. 1971. *The Prospect of Rhetoric*. Englewood Cliffs, NJ: Prentice-Hall.

Bloch, Maurice, ed. 1975. *Political Language and Oratory in Traditional Society*. London: Academic Press.

Bourdieu, Pierre. 1979. "The sense of honour." In *Algeria 1960*. Cambridge: Cambridge University Press.

Brenneis, Donald L. and F.R. Myers, eds. 1984. *Words: Language and Politics in the Pacific*. New York: New York University Press.

Brown, Penelope and Stephen Levinson. 1978. "Universals in language usage: Politeness phenomena." In *Questions and Politeness. Strategies in Social Interaction*, edited by Esther Goody. Cambridge: Cambridge University Press. Pp. 56-324.

——; ——. 1987. *Politeness: Some Universals in Language Usage*. Cambridge: Cambridge University Press.

Burke, Kenneth 1969 [1950]. *A Rhetoric of Motives*. Berkeley: University of California Press.

Carrithers, Michael. 1992. *Why Humans Have Cultures*. Oxford: Oxford University Press.

Evans-Pritchard, Edward E. 1937. *Witchcraft, Oracles and Magic among the Azande*. Oxford: Oxford University Press.

Feld, Steven and Keith Basso, eds. 1996. *Senses of Place.* Santa Fé: School of American Research Press.

Fernandez, James W. 1986. *Persuasions and Performances: The Play of Tropes in Culture.* Bloomington: Indiana University Press.

——, ed. 1991. *Beyond Metaphor: The Theory of Tropes in Anthropology.* Stanford: Stanford University Press.

——. 2009. "Rhetoric in the moral order." In *Culture, Rhetoric and the Vicissitudes of Life*, edited by Michael Carrithers. New York · Oxford: Berghahn Books.

Fox, James, ed. 1997. *The Poetic Power of Place: Comparative Perspectives on Austronesian Ideas of Locality.* Canberra: Department of Anthropology.

Fukui, Katsuyoshi. 1979. "Cattle Colour Symbolism and Inter-Tribal Homicide among the Bodi." In *Warfare among East African Herders*, edited by Fukui, Katsuyoshi and D. Turton. Osaka: Senri Ethnological Studies, 3.

Fukui, Katsuyoshi and David Turton, eds. 1979. *Warfare among East African Herders.* Osaka: Senri Ethnological Studies, 3.

Fumagalli, Vito. 1994. *Landscapes of Fear: Perceptions of Nature and the City in the Middle Ages.* Cambridge: Polity Press.

Gardner, Robert. 1972. *Rivers of Sand.* [Film]. Cambridge, Massachusetts: Harvard Film Study Center.

Geertz, Clifford. 1973. "Thick Description: Toward an Interpretative Theory of Culture." In *The Interpretation of Cultures*, edited by C. Geertz. New York: Basic Books. Pp. 3-30.

Gell, Alfred. 1995. "The Language of the Forest: Landscape and Phonological Iconism in Umeda." In *The Anthropology of Landscape: Perspectives on Place and Space*, edited by Eric Hirsch and M. O'Hanlon. Oxford: Clarendon Press. Pp. 232-54.

Goethe, Johann Wolfgang von. 1828. *Werke, Zweyter Band.* Stuttgart · Tübingen: Cotta'sche Buchhandlung.

Grice, H. Paul. 1975. "Logic and conversation." In *Syntax and Semantics*, Vol. 3: *Speech Acts*, edited by P. Cohen and J.L. Morgan. London: Academic Press. Pp. 41-58.

Haberland, Eike. 1963. *Galla Süd-Aethiopiens*. Stuttgart: Kohl-hammer.

Hauschild, Thomas. 1982. *Der böse Blick: Ideengeschichtliche und sozialpsychologische Untersuchungen.* 2nd revised edition. Hamburg: Renner.

Heidegger, Martin. 1954. *Was heißt denken? Bauen, Wohnen, Denken, Das Ding, „...dichterisch wohnet der Mensch...."* Tübingen: Niemeyer.

Hertz, Robert. 1909. *Prééminence de la main droite.* Paris: Gaillard

Hirsch, Eric and Michael O'Hanlon, eds. 1995. *The Anthropology of Landscape: Perspectives on Place and Space.* Oxford: Clarendon Press.

Homer. *The Iliad.* Transl. Richard Lattimore. 1962. Chicago: University of Chicago Press. [English translation used by Jean Nienkamp]

Howell, Signe and Roy Willis, eds. 1989. *Societies at Peace: Anthropological Perspectives.* London · New York: Routledge.

Humphrey, Caroline. 1995. "Chiefly and Shamanist Landscapes in Mongolia." In *The Anthropology of Landscape. Perspectives on Place and Space*, edited by Eric Hirsch and M. O'Hanlon. Oxford: Clarendon Press. Pp. 135-62.

Huxley, Julian, ed. 1966. "A discussion on ritualization of behaviour in animals and man." In *Philosophical transactions of the Royal Society of London. Series B, Biological sciences*, no. 772, vol. 251. London Royal Society. Pp. 247-526.

Isocrates. 1928. *Isocrates in three volumes.* Cambridge, Mass.: Harvard University Press.

Jarratt, Susan C. 1991. *Rereading the Sophists: Classical Rhetoric Refigured.* Carbondale: University of Southern Illinois Press.

Kennedy, George A. 1998. *Comparative Rhetoric: An Historical and Cross-Cultural Introduction.* New York · Oxford: Oxford University Press.

Kövesces, Z. 1986. *Metaphors of Anger, Pride and Love.* Amsterdam, Philadelphia: John Benjamins Publishing Company.

Lakoff, George and Mark Johnson. 1980. *Metaphors We Live By*. Chicago: Chicago University Press.

Leach, Edmund. 1976. *Culture and Communication*. Cambridge: Cambridge University Press.

Lévi-Strauss, Claude. 1962. *Le totémisme aujourd'hui*. Paris: Presses Univ. de France.

———. 1976. *The Savage Mind*. London: Weidenfeld and Nicolson.

———. 1992. *A View from Afar*. Chicago: University of Chicago Press.

Lienhardt, Geoffrey. 1961. *Divinity and Experience: The Religion of the Dinka*. Oxford: Oxford University Press.

Lovell, Nadia, Ed. 1998. *Locality and Belonging*. London and New York: Routledge.

Lydall, Jean. 1994. "Beating around the bush." In *Vol. II of Proceedings of the Eleventh International Conference of Ethiopian Studies*, edited by Bahru Zewde, Richard Pankhurst and Taddese Beyene. Ethiopia: Institute of Ethiopian Studies, Addis Ababa University

Lydall, Jean and Ivo Strecker. 1979a. *The Hamar of Southern Ethiopia. Vol. I: Work Journal*. Hohenschäftlarn: Klaus Renner Verlag.

———; ———. 1979b. *The Hamar of Southern Ethiopia. Vol. II: Baldambe Explains*. Hohenschäftlarn: Klaus Renner Verlag.

McDermott, R.P. and Henry Tylbor. 1995. "On the Necessity of Collusion in Conversation." In *The Dialogic emergence of Culture*, edited by Dennis Tedlock and Bruce Mannheim. Urbana and Chicago: University of Illinois Press. Pp. 218-236.

Malinowski, Bronislaw. 1922. *Argonauts of the Western Pacific*. London: Routledge & Kegan Paul.

———. 1935/1978. *Coral Gardens and their Magic: A Study of the Methods of Tilling the Soil and of Agricultural Rites in the Trobriand Islands*. Bd. 1. London: Routledge & Kegan Paul.

Maquet, Jacques. 1961. *The Premise of Inequality in Ruanda: A Study of Political Relations in a Central African Kingdom*. London: Oxford University Press.

Middleton, John and D. Tait, eds. 1958. *Tribes without Rulers*. London: Routledge & Kegan Paul.

Middleton, John and E.H. Winter, eds. 1963. *Witchcraft and Sorcery in East Afrika*. London: Routledge & Kegan Paul.

Montague, Ashley, ed. 1978. *Learning Non-Aggression. The Experience of Non-Literate Societies*. New York: Oxford University Press.

Needham, Rodney, ed. 1973. *Left and Right: Essays on Dual Symbolic Classification*. Chicago: University of Chicago Press.

Nienkamp, Jean. 2001. *Internal Rhetorics: Toward a History and Theory of Self-Persuasion*. Carbondale: University of Southern Illinois Press.

Norberg-Schulz, Christian. 1980: *Genius Loci: Towards a Phenomenology of Architecture*. London: Academy Editions.

Paul, Anthony. 1992. *The Torture of the Mind:* Macbeth, *tragedy and chiasmus*. Amsterdam: Academisch Proefschrift.

Peristiany, John, ed. 1966. *Honor and Shame: The Values of Mediterranean Society*. Chicago: University of Chicago Press.

Plutarch. 1975. *Makers of Rome: Nine Lives by Plutarch*. Transl. and introduction by Scott-Kilvert. London: Penguin Books.

Polanyi, Michael. 1967. *The Tacit Dimension*. London: Routledge & Kegan Paul.

Richards, I.A. 1965. *The Philosophy of Rhetoric*. New York · Oxford: Oxford University Press.

Rose, Carol M. 1994. *Property and Persuasion: Essays on the History, Theory and Rhetoric of Ownership*. Boulder: Westview Press.

Sapir, David. 1977. "An Anatomy of Metaphor." In *The Social Use of Metaphor*, edited by J.C. Crocker and J.D. Sapir. Philadelphia: University of Pennsylvania Press. Pp. 3-32.

Schopenhauer, Arthur. 1995. *The World as Will and Idea: Abridged in One Volume*. Edited by Berman, David and translated by Jill Berman. London: Everyman.

Schulz-Weidner, W. 1959. „Die Shangama." In *Altvölker Süd-Äthiopiens*, edited by A.E. Jensen. Stuttgart: Kohlhammer. Pp. 107-161.

Sperber, Dan. 1975. *Rethinking Symbolism*. Cambridge: Cambridge University Press.

Sponsel and Gregor, eds. 1994. *The Anthropology of Peace and Nonviolence*. Boulder and London: Lynne Riener Publishers.

Strecker, Ivo. 1979a. *The Hamar of Southern Ethiopia. Vol. III: Conversations in Dambaiti*. Hohenschäftlarn: Klaus Renner Verlag.

———. 1979b. *Musik der Hamar / Music of the Hamar*. [Double LP + booklet]. Berlin: Museum für Völkerkunde Berlin-Dahlem.

———. 1979c. *Der Sprung über die Rinder*. [Film]. Göttingen: Institut für den wissenschaftlichen Film.

———. 1988a. *The Social Practice of Symbolization: An Anthropological Analysis*. London · Atlantic Highlands, NJ: Athlone Press.

———. 1988b. "Some Notes on the Uses of '*Barjo*' in Hamar." In *Cushitic-Omotic: Papers from the International Symposium on Cushitic and Omotic Languages. Cologne*, edited by Marianne Bechhaus-Gerst and F. Serzisko. Hamburg: Helmut Buske Verlag. Pp. 61-74.

———. 1990. "Political Discourse among the Hamar of Southern Ethiopia." In *Proceedings of the First National Conference of Ethiopian Studies, Addis Ababa, April 11-12, 1990*, edited by Richard Pankhurst, Ahmad Zekaria and Tadesse Beyene. Addis Ababa: Institute of Ethiopian Studies. Pp. 39-47.

———. 1993. "Cultural Variations in the Concept of Face." In *Multilingua* 12: 119-141.

———. 1994. "The Predicaments of War and Peace in South Omo." In *Proceedings of the XIth Conference of Ethiopian Studies*, Vol.II, edited by Bahru Zewde, R. Pankhurst and Taddese Beyene. Addis Ababa: University, Institute of Ethiopian Studies. Pp. 299-308.

———. 1998. "Our good Fortune brought us together! Obituary for Baldambe." In: *Paideuma* 44: 59-68.

———. 1999. "The Temptations of War and the Struggle for Peace among the Hamar of Southern Ethiopia." In *Dynamics of Violence: Processes of Escalation and De-Escalation in Violent*

Group Conflicts, edited by Georg Elwert, Stephan Feuchtwang and Dieter Neubert. [*Sociologus Sonderband*]. Pp. 219-252.

———. [forthcoming] *The Hamar of Southern Ethiopia IV. Berimba's Resistance*. Münster · Berlin: Lit Verlag.

Strecker, Ivo and Stephen Tyler, eds. 2009. *Culture and Rhetoric*. New York · Oxford: Berghahn Books.

Taddesse Berisso. 1994. "Warfare among the Guji-Oromo of Southern Ethiopia." In *Proceedings of the XIth Conference ofEthiopian Studies*, Vol. II, edited by Bahru Zewde, R. Pankhurst and Taddese Beyene. Addis Ababa: University, Institute of Ethiopian Studies. Pp. 309-323.

Tambiah, Stanley. 1968. "The magical Power of Words." In *Man* (n.s.) 3: 175-208.

Tedlock, Barbara, ed. 1987. *Dreaming: Anthropological and Psychological Interpretations*. Cambridge: Cambridge University Press.

Tedlock, Dennis and Bruce Mannheim, eds. 1995. *The Dialogic emergence of Culture*. Urbana and Chicago: University of Illinois Press.

Tilley, Christopher. 1994. *A Phenomenology of Landscape: Places, Paths and Monuments*. Oxford et al.: Berg.

Tornay, Serje. 1979. "Armed Conflicts in the Lower Omo Valley, 1970-1976: An Analysis from within Nyangatom Society." In *Warfare among East African Herders*, edited by Fukui Katsuyoshi and D. Turton. Osaka: Senri Ethnological Studies, 3.

Turner, Victor W. 1975. *Dramas, Fields and Metaphors*. Ithaca: Cornell University Press.

Tyler, Stephen. 1978. *The Said and the Unsaid: Mind Meaning and Culture*. New York; San Francisco; London: Academic Press.

———. 1987. *The Unspeakable: Discourse, Dialogue and Rhetoric in the Postmodern World*. Madison: University of Wisconsin Press.

Vickers, Brian. 1988. *In Defence of Rhetoric*. Oxford: Clarendon.

Vico, Giambattista. 1961. *The New Science of Giambattista Vico*. Transl. from the third edition (1744) by Th.G. Bergin and M.H. Fisch. New York: Anchor Books.

Weiner, James F. 1991. *The Empty Place: Poetry, Song and Being among the Foi of Papua New Guinea*. Bloomington: Indiana University Press.

Wikan, Unni. 1984. "Shame and Honor: a contestable pair." In: *Man*, (n.s.) 19: 635-652.

Woodburn, J. 1982. "Egalitarian Societies." In: *Man* (n.s.) 17: 431-451.

MAP: The Hamar and their neighbours

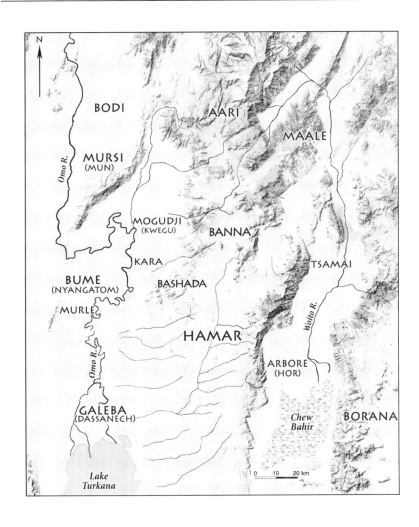

aela	call, call forth
anamo	age-mates
apho	mouth, language
arra	grass, *Hyparrhenia cf. filipandula*
asha	hide away, curse
assaue	personal negotiation, discussion
atap	tongue, slander, curse
ayo	spokesman
bakulo	hearth, 3 stones of fireplace
banzi	phallus, ritual symbol
baraza	bush, *Grewia mollis*
barjo	creative power, good fortune, well-being
barjo aela	calling forth *barjo*, blessing
barrae	mad month
bel	bond-friend
binyere	collar, married woman's necklace
biri	tree
bitta	'the first', ritual leader of Hamar
boaka	meeting ground, public place
bodi	fat, richness, fertility (used in blessing)
boko	staff with round head, ritual use
dele	homestead
djalepha	eldest brother of sibling group
djilo	war magician
dongo	tree, *Cordia ovalis*
donkala	tree, *Euphorbia abyssinica Gmel.*
donko	profound narrative
donsha	control oneself
donza	married man, elder
duki	burial, funeral, grave
dumai	big toe, shin
elkima	last will, inheritance
garo	calf, 'child' of initiate
giri	tree, *Scelorocarya birrea*
gisha	herd, look after,
goala	lyre, praise song
goshpa	praise, adorn
gudili	guardian of the fields

gurda	settlement, village	*morare*	favourite animal
hakati	playful talk	*mulaza*	plant with weak roots
indanas	members of own moiety	*muna*	sorghum roll
irima	insult, provoke	*nabi*	name
kale	creeper plant	*osh*	public meeting
kalma	oxen present at male intiation	*pala*	scarification
kara	noisy talk (*baida*)	*palli*	argument, quarrel
kelima	instruction, admonition	*parko*	ritual expert, forked staff
kemo dalk	marriage negotiation	*paxala*	bright, intelligent,
kiri	gateway	*pen gia*	tell the news
kogo	guardian of the fires	*poramo*	proud, provoking
kubai	sincere discussion	*raega*	war song
kubu	men married into same lineage	*sabe*	milky way, metaphor of *barjo*
kuntsale	fast growing grass	*shokolo*	hoof rot
kurkum	important discourse	*tsangaza*	members of marriageable moiety
maeshi	spirits of the dead	*tsinti*	territorial section
mate	yeast, ritual for brewing beer	*ukuli*	initiate, rite of male initiation
maz	initiate, neophyte	*wolkanti*	cactus, *Aloe sp.*
mermer	gossip	*wombo*	tree, *Ficus sp.*
michere	whipping wand	*woti*	forehead
misso	hunting friend	*wupha*	gossip
moara	diviner	*zani*	rope, snare
		zarsi	reticulating grass people of neighbourhood

INDEXES

Index of themes

Index of dramatis personae

Index of places and peoples

Index of authors

Mainzer Beiträge zur Afrika-Forschung

hrsg. von Thomas Bierschenk, Anna-Maria Brandstetter, Raimund Kastenholz, Carola Lentz und Ivo Strecker

Ivo Strecker; Jean Lydall (Eds.)

The Perils of Face

Essays on Cultural Contact, Respect and Self-Esteem in Southern Ethiopia

At the end of the 19th Century, southern Ethiopia was one of the last areas to experience the "Scramble for Africa", as Emperor Menelik II sent his armies south to conquer and incorporate this territory into his empire. For almost hundred years, the peoples of southern Ethiopia had to live under the highly centrali sed rule of the Emperor and later that of the Marxist Dergue regime, but this changed in 1991, when a new constitution was proclaimed and all barriers of class, gender, ethnic affiliation, religion and place of birth were officially abolished. But how can such a transformation to a new social order be achieved? What are its obstacles and what are its prospects? To answer this question it is indispensable to know how the culturally different peoples of Ethiopia remember their past, and what conceptions they entertain of each other. The present essays try to address this issue. In particular, they explore the dangers inherent in situations of cultural contact and examine how the powerful notions of pride, honor, name, and self-esteem come into play, as people struggle to maintain their identity, individually or as a group. The master trope for this kind of sensitivity and vulnerability in social and cultural interaction is "face". This is why the volume is entitled "The perils of face".

Bd. 10, 2006, 448 S., 29,90 €, br., ISBN 3-8258-6122-8

LIT Verlag Berlin – Münster – Wien – Zürich – London

Auslieferung Deutschland / Österreich / Schweiz: siehe Impressumsseite

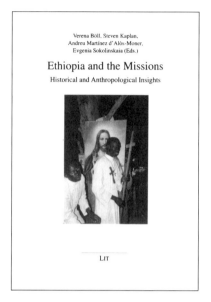

Rudolf Agstner
One week in Ethiopia, forever with God
Guidebook to the Foreigners' Cemeteries in Addis Ababa, Ethiopia
Tucked away at the outskirts of Ethiopia's capital Addis Ababa, a group of civilian and military cemeteries tells the story of the Armenian, Greek, Italian and other smaller communities in Addis Ababa during the 20th century and their contribution to the development of the country to the few visitors who know of their existence. The author was able to identify more than 3700 tombs in the Greek Orthodox, Armenian and Catholic cemeteries at Gulele, Addis Ababa. The Cimitero Militare Italiano and the Commonwealth War Graves Cemetery, situated side by side, are testimony to the history of Ethiopia between 1935 and 1941. The small Jewish cemetery is even less known than the Christian cemeteries at Gulele. Another small cemetery is located – off limits – in the British Embassy Compound. All these cemeteries are part of Ethiopia's history and a symbol for the hospitality the Ethiopian people offered to foreigners.
Bd. 25, 2009, 216 S., 19,90 €, br.,
ISBN 978-3-643-50091-5

Verena Böll; Steven Kaplan; Andreu Martínez d'Alòs-Moner; Evgenia Sokolinskaia (Eds.)
Ethiopia and the Missions
Historical and Anthropological Insights
Since the sixteenth century, Ethiopian Orthodox Christianity and the indigenous religions of Ethiopia have been confronted with, and influenced by, numerous Catholic and Protestant missions. This book offers historical, anthropological and personal analyses of these encounters. The discussion ranges from the Jesuit debate on circumcision to Oromo Bible translation, from Pentecostalism in Addis Ababa to conversion processes among the Nuer. Juxtaposing past and present, urban and rural, the book breaks new ground in both religious and African studies.
Bd. 25, 2006, 272 S., 29,90 €, br., ISBN 3-8258-7792-2

LIT Verlag Berlin – Münster – Wien – Zürich – London
Auslieferung Deutschland / Österreich / Schweiz: siehe Impressumsseite

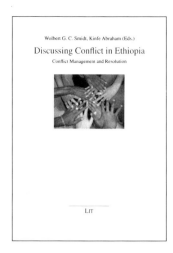

Wolbert G. C. Smidt; Kinfe Abraham (Eds.)
Discussing Conflict
Proceedings of the Ethio-German Conference
on Conflict Management and Resolution,
Addis Abada 11 to 12 November 2005
This volume contains the papers presented at the
Conference 'Ethiopian and German Contributions to Conflict Management and Resolution' of
November 2005, Addis Ababa. The aim of this conference was to bring researchers and those working
in the practical field of conflict resolution together,
before the background of renewed internal and international conflict. Research in conflict resolution
mechanisms is one of the most hopeful fields in
modern social sciences. Local conflicts can have
devastating effects on the state and even involve the
international level. In turn, international conflict
can also destabilize society and create new local
conflicts. However, local conflict resolution mechanisms could be of a great importance even within
the international scene. This volumes examines the
experiences in Ethiopia and the impact the acquired
knowledge could have for future conflict resolution
and management.
Bd. 32, 2007, 296 S., 29,90 €, br.,
ISBN 978-3-8258-9795-6

Eva-Maria Bruchhaus;
Monika M. Sommer (Eds.)
Hot Spot Horn of Africa Revisited
Approaches to Make Sense of Conflict
This volume contains papers that are related to academic peace studies and to the politics of peace.
The emphasis of the contributions is on the analysis
of current violent conflicts in and between states
and within societies, on all levels, local, regional
and international. *"This is an excellent volume, (...
)it can make an important contribution to deepe-
ning the knowledge of the complex conflict arenas
in the Horn of Africa."* Prof. Dr. Volker Matthies in
his foreword
Bd. 37, 2008, 304 S., 29,90 €, br.,
ISBN 978-3-8258-1314-7

LIT Verlag Berlin – Münster – Wien – Zürich – London
Auslieferung Deutschland / Österreich / Schweiz: siehe Impressumsseite

Heinrich Scholler
100 Jahre deutsch-äthiopische diplomatische Beziehungen – 100 Years of German-Ethiopian Diplomatic Relations
Von der traditionellen Monarchie zum modernen Staat
Unter Kaiser Menelik II. kam es im Frühjahr 1905 zur Entsendung einer deutschen Delegation und zum Abschluss eines Freundschafts- und Handelsvertrages. Menelik II. suchte Schutz gegen drohende Übergriffe europäischer Kolonialmächte. Durch die beiden Weltkriege wurden die diplomatischen Beziehungen unterbrochen, aber schon im Jahre 1954 kam Kaiser Haile Selassie I. nach Deutschland. In den 80er Jahren begann die Bundesrepublik sich von der alten Hallstein-Doktrien zu lösen und besonders Äthiopien, den Sitz der Afrikanischen Union, in ein neues System der Entwicklungspolitik zu integrieren. Die entstandenen politischen Schwierigkeiten konnten nach 1991 im Wesentlichen überwunden werden.
Under the reign of Menelik II. a German diplomatic mission under professor Friedrich Rosen was sent to Ethiopia and concluded a treaty of commerce and friendship. The emperor wanted to be more protected against the European colonial powers. Worldwar I & II interrupted the friendly and economic relations between the two countries. However already in 1954 emperor Haile Selassie I. paid an official visit to Germany. Starting with the 80ies Germany by and by got rid of the traditional Hallstein-Doktrin and tried to include Ethiopia, where the African Union had its headquarters, into the new political African policy. Political problems, which had developed under the Rule of Mengistu, were overcome after 1991.
Bd. 5, 2007, 40 S., 14,90 €, br., ISBN 978-3-8258-9720-8

Eva Brems; Christophe Van der Beken (Eds.)
Federalism and the Protection of Human Rights in Ethiopia
This book brings together articles by Western and Ethiopian jurists and political scientists that are all based on original and recent research. The link between federalism and human rights in Ethiopia is the central theme of the book and acts as the context against which the different articles must be situated. The book consists of two parts. The first part contains contributions that study aspects of Ethiopian federalism from a constitutional and public

international law perspective. The contributions of the second part aim to provide a better insight in a number of current human rights issues in Ethiopia such as the right to self-determination, land rights, press freedom and gender equality.
Bd. 8, 2008, 312 S., 29,90 €, br., ISBN 978-3-8258-1128-0

Abdulkader Saleh Mohammad (ed.)
The Customary Law of the Akele Guzai Muslims [the Saho]
Issued by the British Military Administration in 1943. Re-issued by the permission of the High Commissioner of the Eritrean National Police, Department of Criminal Research. Translated and edited by Abdulkader Saleh Mohammad
This book presents the first English translation of the Saho customary law in Eritrea, with an introduction discussing the historical and socio-cultural background of the Saho community and the role of traditional conflict mediation in contemporary Eritrea. The law has a strong communal character and rules both economic activities and social life. It was orally transmitted from generation to generation and printed in 1943, of which only one copy is known. It is based on local traditional and Islamic law and its principles are respected up to the present day. The volume is a significant contribution to the study of Eritrean customary law, which presents an important cultural heritage.
Bd. 9, 2009, 120 S., 19,90 €, br., ISBN 978-3-8258-1980-4

LIT Verlag Berlin – Münster – Wien – Zürich – London
Auslieferung Deutschland / Österreich / Schweiz: siehe Impressumsseite

Studien zur Orientalischen Kirchengeschichte
hrsg. von Martin Tamcke

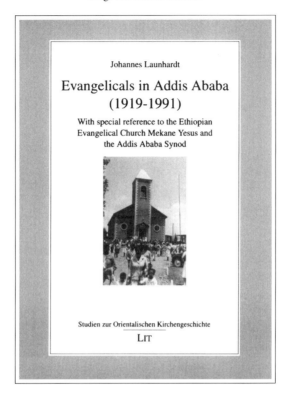

Johannes Launhardt
Evangelicals in Addis Ababa
(1919-1991)
With special reference to the Ethiopian
Evangelical Church Mekane Yesus and
the Addis Ababa Synod

Studien zur Orientalischen Kirchengeschichte

LIT

Johannes Launhardt
Evangelicals in Addis Ababa (1919 – 1991)
With special reference to the Ethiopian Evangelical Church Mekane Yesus and the Addis Ababa Synod
Orthodox reformers, Protestants from Eritrea and Wollega moving to the capital, and European missions asked by the Imperial Government to open educational and medical institutions in town, marked the beginning of Evangelical Christianity in Addis Ababa. After the Italian occupation church leaders of the capital worked for the unity of all Ethiopian Evangelicals and formed the Addis Ababa Synod. The author describes responses of the big churches to urban needs in the 1970's and lists activities and sufferings of Christians under the Marxist Derg Regime.
Bd. 31, 2005, 360 S., 24,90 €, br., ISBN 3-8258-7791-4

LIT Verlag Berlin – Münster – Wien – Zürich – London
Auslieferung Deutschland / Österreich / Schweiz: siehe Impressumsseite

Quellen und Beiträge zur Geschichte der Hermannsburger Mission und des Ev.-luth. Missionswerkes in Niedersachsen

Ernst Bauerochse
A Vision Finds Fulfillment
Hermannsburg Mission in Ethiopia
In 1853 A.D., it was the vision of Pastor Louis Harms of the Hermannsburg Mission that the Oromos should hear the Gospel. Therefore he sent a group of missionaries towards Ethiopia in order to reach them. The way was blocked at that time and also a second trial failed. Only 75 years later, in 1928 A.D., the vision of Louis Harms found fulfillment: four men from Hermannsburg could start Gospel work in Ethiopia. God used these missionaries and their successors to contribute to a movement which led to the Ethiopian Evangelical Church – Mekane Yesus. This book tells the story of their work up to the end of the Derg regime in 1991 and beyond. It is part of a History of the Hermannsburg Mission, prepared for its 150th anniversary in 1999. Ernst Bauerochse, the author, draws from written sources in the Hermannsburg archives and his own experience as a missionary in Ethiopia from 1954 to 1974. After the death of his first wife Brunhilde in 1979, he married Martha Wassmann. They live in retirement in Hermannsburg (Germany).
Bd. 15, 2008, 168 S., 29,90 €, br., ISBN 978-3-8258-9880-9

LIT Verlag Berlin – Münster – Wien – Zürich – London
Auslieferung Deutschland / Österreich / Schweiz: siehe Impressumsseite